SUBURBAN DREAMING

AN INTERDISCIPLINARY APPROACH TO AUSTRALIAN CITIES

Edited by Louise C. Johnson

Deakin University Press

Published by Deakin University Press, Deakin University,
Geelong, Victoria 3217
First published 1994
Reprinted 1996
© Louise C. Johnson 1994

Edited, designed and typeset by Deakin University
Course Development Centre
Printed by McPherson's Printing Group

National Library of Australia
Cataloguing-in-publication data

Suburban dreaming: an interdisciplinary approach to
Australian cities.

ISBN 0 949823 40 6.

1. Suburbs—Australia. 2. Suburbs—Australia—History.
3. Suburban life—Australia. 4. City and town life—Australia.
5. Australia—Social conditions—20th century.
6. Australia—Social life and customs—20th century.
I. Johnson, Louise, 1953–

307.740994

Cover image by John Wilkins

To Brian McLoughlin
Friend, colleague and student of the Australian city

Contents

IntRoduction | # Spinning the suburban dream
Louise C. Johnson

Australia is not only one of the most urbanised countries in the world, it is also one of the most suburbanised. The dreams and the realities for most are a house in the suburbs. This is a book which explores these desires and their landscapes. It does so by examining the ways in which the Australian city and its suburbs have evolved over two centuries and how they have been thought about by academics, writers and designers. This study draws on a range of disciplines—history, geography, planning, sociology, architecture and literary studies—and a variety of theoretical frameworks, ranging from the empirical to the postmodern. The aim is to canvass some key events in the settlement of this country and to explore these in an interdisciplinary way from a range of interpretative frameworks.

The focus on urban Australia—especially on the major capitals in the south-east of the continent—reflects the lived reality for the vast majority, but it is also a bounded starting point. Those who have written for this collection are primarily based in Melbourne and move within a settled, metropolitan, university culture which has traditionally favoured city over country, men over women and Anglo-Celts over other groups.

Concern with housing and the built form belies those without either—the homeless and the itinerant. In concentrating on the metropolitan experience, the role of the small city and the country town is not detailed, though the processes of settlement, suburbanisation, capital accumulation and socio-spatial division are as applicable to the hamlet as to the large city. Such a focus does, however, lead to a regional, racial and class bias. This bias assumes added significance when it is recognised that only 24 per cent of the Aboriginal and Torres Strait Islander population live in cities of more than 100 000 people (House of Representatives Standing Committee on Aboriginal and Torres Strait Islander Affairs 1992). In contrast, the vast majority of overseas-born people arrive and stay in the State capitals (National Population Council Migration Committee 1990). This basic demography and the politics surrounding racial, ethnic and gender inclusions and exclusions in the academy are reflected in the writers and their pieces for this collection.

Thus there is no Aboriginal contribution—though extensive efforts were made to secure one, and all writers were asked to address issues relevant to indigenous Australians in their essays. Also, with the exception of two writers—Guenter Lehmann and Mirjana Lozanovska—all of the writers are of Anglo-Celtic origin. The majority of contributors are men (57 per cent) and it is ironical, but not surprising, that it is only those contributions from women which explicitly consider this group in their discussions. Further consequences of such a sample of writers, different also in their disciplines, approaches and ideologies, are for the reader to divine. All, though, have a common concern—with urban Australia.

The ways in which this concern is displayed derive from the disciplinary orientations brought to the task—with the historians focused primarily on the nineteenth century and on changes over time, the architects, planners, sociologists and geographers far more concerned with the present, its theorisation and socio-spatial patterning—and by a number of common themes which inform this study of Australian cities. Common to many of the essays is an awareness of Australia's place in a changing global economy. From the earliest days of white history, that place within an expansionist and confident British Empire shaped the economy and sociology of Australian cities. The possible model provided by the British industrial city is explored by Roy Hay, while the historical location within the British Empire is considered by both Lionel Frost and Graeme Davison. More recent situations in a global economy ruled not by formal empires, but by multinational capital, are considered by Mike Berry and Louise Johnson. Despite this common context, the form, functions and character of each Australian city is unique. This arises, according to the architects and planners, Nick Beattie, Guenter Lehmann and Brian McLoughlin, primarily from the local negotiations of these larger socio-economic structures.

Global forces mediated and remade locally is a process deemed by many writers to shape the pattern of cities across the continent (considered in Part 1) and their internal morphology (the subject of Part 2). The way cities actually work is considered in relation to retailing by the cultural historian Peter Spearritt, while the form and meaning of housing are considered by Renate Howe, Margo Huxley, Lyn Richards and Mirjana Lozanovska. In such considerations, the social division of the city by class, gender and ethnicity is addressed from historical, feminist and postmodernist perspectives.

While not always explicit, concern for the various ways in which the city, suburbs and housing are represented—be it in academic discourse, government policy, or in literature—is present throughout. In particular, in the chapters on reading and deconstructing the migrant house (Lozanovska), on literary representations of the city (Devlin Glass) and on the gendered power dynamics present in the suburban home (Huxley), emphasis is on the politics surrounding the imagining of houses and suburbs. It is a self-conscious dreaming, one which keeps the themes of global structures, local agency and representation to the fore.

The study of such dreamings and realities begins with a historical precursor of the Australian town—the industrial city of Manchester, England. Migrating at a time of rapid economic change, those Europeans who initially came to Australia were escapees from the social and political excesses of British industrialism. In the first chapter, the historian Roy Hay examines Manchester as a possible model for the Australian city. Dating from Roman times and a thriving trade and manufacturing centre in the eighteenth century, Manchester retained for many years the small scale, compact but socially diverse character of the pre-industrial city. Onto this core were overlaid the many changes wrought by factory production. The consequences of rapid urban growth were subsequently etched on to its physical and social landscape as workers crowded into inner-city tenements and the wealthy escaped to the clean air of the elevated suburbs. In its history and economy Manchester was very different from contemporary Australian cities. However, in its social and spatial organisation and in the reforms to deal with rapid and unregulated industrial growth, Hay sees some precursors for those settlements which grew in the colonies.

The nature of those cities in the nineteenth century is examined in Chapter 2 by the economic historian Lionel Frost. He identifies Australia as one of a number of 'New World' countries settled by an expansionary Europe in the eighteenth century and details the way in which the demands of the British Empire—for raw materials, investment opportunities and foodstuffs—shaped the economic foundations of the Australian city. Driven by the world capitalist economy, the consequences for the original occupants of the continent were dire; as land was stolen, violence reigned unchecked and introduced diseases created havoc. Forced to the edges of cities and the pastoral frontier, Aborigines received no benefit from the wool economy or from the gold rushes which briefly supplanted it in the 1850s. The settlement pattern of the eastern colonies was changed by the influx of migrants and capital which the discovery of gold brought—with the ports declining in relative significance and inland, mining towns, growing rapidly. But the colonial capitals regained their pre-eminence as the century came to a close—buoyed by the commercial rural economy and the rebuilding, suburbanisation and gradual physical improvement of the cities themselves.

The concern evinced by Frost and a number of other historians for Australian cities in the European history of the continent is a relatively recent one (Glynn 1970; McCarty & Schedvin 1978; Berry 1983). Further, in their approach to urban history, many have adopted what the political economist, Mike Berry, describes as an 'empiricist methodology' with particular cities appearing as bundles of facts, all carefully documented and welded together by the historian's particular world view (Berry 1983, pp. 4–5).

In contrast with the resulting 'urban biography', Berry offers a theoretically explicit framework for interpreting the Australian city. Drawn from Karl Marx's analysis of capitalism, he places Australian urbanisation into a model of global capital mobility which creates both development and dependency as well as cycles of boom and bust. The movement of capital from 'colonial accumulation' to mercantile or trading activities and, thence, into industry transforms both the character of nineteenth-century cities and creates whole new ones. Subsequent centralisations of capital into larger, more powerful and diversified global entities and away from productive activities towards financial ones, are seen by Berry to typify our more recent urban history. His interpretation suggests that Australian cities emerge primarily from two elements—global capital accumulation and contraction, and local capital–labour relations; both of which are unevenly articulated between industries and sectors and across space.

This faith in one, overarching theoretical framework to explain the nature of Australian cities has been called into question by a diverse philosophical and design movement called *postmodernism*. In Chapter 4, the geographer Louise Johnson assesses the usefulness of this term for an understanding of contemporary Australian cities. The postmodern has been discussed as an architectural style, an era and a state of human existence increasingly characterised by uncertainty, media images and computer technology. While it is hard to test out all of these claims, Chapter 4 concludes that some elements of Australian urban life—such as the proposed Multifunction Polis and the growing social and spatial polarisation of Adelaide, Sydney and Melbourne—do resonate with elements of the postmodern condition.

Just how these cities are designed and experienced is taken up by two architects— Nick Beattie and Guenter Lehmann—in the following chapter. They ask the question: What makes spaces within cities special? In pursuit of an answer, they return to Renaissance Europe and the grand squares of Siena, Venice and Paris. To explain their passing involves an examination of technology, the organisation and activities of the state, the changing nature of commerce, the privatisation of city space and the rise of modernism. But despite the relative homogenisation and privatisation of the modern city, Beattie and Lehmann suggest that special places can emerge through a combination of planned environments, scripted activity patterns and unexpected and unintended behaviours.

While concerned primarily with the nature and use of the built form, this architectural view is not unlike that taken by Brian McLoughlin, an urban and regional planner, as he too mobilises the relationship between social structures and individual agency as a framework in which to examine the management of Melbourne during the 1980s. Like Berry, he situates the city in a global economy of investment and disinvestment, but to this framework adds the roles of local populations, differentiated by various class, locality and professional interests. From this assessment he concludes that while Melbourne was primarily shaped by global capital, there were other 'frameworks of power' which exerted considerable influence over the form and nature of the city.

If these six chapters in Part 1 have been concerned mainly with the ways in which Australian cities as a whole have evolved and functioned, Part

2 reduces the scale to consider elements of these cities in greater detail. In particular, the suburb, the shopping centre and the house are scrutinised by writers coming from history, planning, architecture, sociology and literary studies. As well as drawing on a range of disciplines, Part 2 also traverses a number of theoretical terrains. Some of the diverse elements of postmodernism are taken up again and used to consider the house and literary representations of the suburbs, while the artful empiricism of the historian and the critical eye of the qualitative sociologist are applied to suburbia.

The special nature of the Australian suburb is established by Graeme Davison while its contested reality is explored by the sociologist Lyn Richards. Thus, in Chapter 7 Davison examines the history of the Australian suburb. He observes how the free-standing house on a substantial block of land originated with the British gentry, but its extension across space and social group was facilitated by colonial governments, the private land market, a number of ideologies, the local class system and a gendered separation of home from work. The assumption by centralised authorities of responsibility for servicing these suburbs, Davison argues, has been important for producing relatively low levels of social polarisation. However, the high economic, social and environmental costs of continued suburbanisation have impelled a serious reconsideration of this form of housing and a turn by governments towards higher-density living. One argument often used to support such a shift is the social isolation experienced by those—especially women with young children—who live in suburbs. This suggestion is critically evaluated by Lyn Richards in her examination of recent studies on Melbourne's outer suburbs.

In her evaluation of the Australian Institute of Family Studies' investigation into Berwick, Richards questions whether the newspaper summary of the report—that all is well in suburbia—is accurate. To do so, Richards considers the methodology of this study, the assumptions of the researchers and invokes her own qualitative and long-term study of another outer-Melbourne suburb. From this she concludes that the story is a multi-dimensional one, one related to what is asked and by whom and the diverse expectations and realities of suburban dwellers. How such living patterns have changed in relation to an essential household activity—shopping—is discussed in Chapter 9 by Peter Spearritt.

Spearritt considers the changes in our shopping habits from corner store, home production, delivery and market, to self-service and the suburban shopping mall. Driven by patterns of personal mobility, technology and capital centralisation, these changes impact dramatically on our daily lives not only because we all have to shop, but because we are increasingly subjected to retail advertising, more of us are employed in retailing, more of our leisure time is spent in shopping-entertainment complexes and our very identity is now connected to what we buy and how. Desire is no longer just for a house in the suburbs, but is realised in the process of buying things for that house and all who live in it.

If retailing has followed the population into the suburbs, something else is now happening which appears to be a reversal of this very long trend. For, as Renate Howe discusses in her historical overview of the inner suburbs, they have undergone a transformation from crowded and polluted slums into highly-sought-after, revalorised environments for a new middle class of inner-city dwellers. This process of gentrification, driven by the socio-economic changes described by Berry, Johnson and McLoughlin, is now transforming the inner precincts of all major Australian cities. The transformation does not, however, completely displace all those other groups and characteristics which have long characterised the inner city.

How such areas and the cities themselves have been imagined is discussed by Frances Devlin Glass as she examines a number of literary representations of Australian suburbs in Chapter 11. Thus, Sydney and Melbourne, undergoing massive growth, physical improvement and social polarisation in the late nineteenth century, provide the setting in which a number of urban writers eulogise the bush. Such work builds on a long pastoral tradition in the West, one which was complicated for post-Second World War writers by the massive suburbanisation of the population. However, if writers of this latter era—such as Patrick White and Barry Humphries—depict the suburbs as boring wastelands, those of more recent times—imbued with the experiences and philosophies of the postmodern city—see in the city *and* its suburbs sites of divergent meanings, fractured experiences and a population united, not by suburban uniformity, but by idiosyncratic diversity.

In describing the work of writers like David Malouf, Ania Walwicz and Jeannie Baker as postmodern, emphasis is placed on their writing styles, their fractured images and the ways they plumb the depths of a multicultural city. In a somewhat different use of a postmodern theorist, Michel Foucault, the planner Margo Huxley considers the ways in which urban environments are built, represented and used. In this examination, she critically invokes archaeological studies of past cities to suggest that a reading of such items which directly links maker to intention and use, is simplistic and naive. Further, drawing on studies by Foucault of places built for ease and incarceration, she suggests that use can well be freed from intention. As a result, Huxley argues that some feminist studies of the city and suggested alternatives—which require wholesale demolition or new building—are not only overly pessimistic and unrealistic, but deny the creative possibilities of existing environments. While recognising that contemporary Australian cities are built by and for men, Huxley sees scope within existing physical structures and regulations for women to achieve less oppressive social and spatial outcomes.

In a further exploration of the possibilities offered by postmodern theorising, the architect Mirjana Lozanovska explores the psychoanalytic notion of abjection in relation to the 'othering' of the migrant house in Australia. She argues that the experience of overseas migration to Australia involves a separation from home and the rebuilding of another. In a way not unlike the separation of an infant from its mother, migrants evacuate the motherland

and often the mother tongue in their move to another place, into a new language and a different symbolic order in which they are lesser or 'other'. This order, language and tongue are seen by Lozanovska in patriarchal terms, though the maternal/'other'/migrant woman remains within this order to disrupt it. This disruption occurs especially through the migrant house which, in its obvious, external difference, challenges dominant aesthetic norms, while its internal organisation offers places, not unlike those suggested by Huxley, in which the mixed and fractured identity of the migrant can be expressed.

Through immigration, the global and the local are brought together and connected in the Australian suburb. However, as other chapters have shown, this connection also takes economic, ideological and other social forms. In the mediation of the structural imperatives which shape population movements, the place not only of the locality but of people within it is crucial. In the creation of landscapes, various representations are also constructed to make real the nature of suburban dreaming. Such too is the aim of the following chapters.

References

Berry, M. (1983), 'The Australian city in history: Critique and renewal', in L. Sandercock & M. Berry (eds), *Urban Political Economy. The Australian Case*, Allen & Unwin, Sydney, pp. 3–33.

Glynn, S. (1970), *Urbanisation in Australian History, 1788–1900*, Nelson, Melbourne.

House of Representatives Standing Committee on Aboriginal and Torres Strait Islander Affairs (1992), *Mainly Urban: Report into the Needs of Urban Dwelling Aboriginal and Torres Strait Islander People*, AGPS, Canberra.

McCarty, J. W. & Schedvin, C. B. (eds) (1978), *Australian Capital Cities. Historical Essays*, Sydney University Press, Sydney.

National Population Council Migration Committee (1990), *Immigration and Housing in the Major Cities*, AGPS, Canberra.

Chapter 1 | The British nineteenth-century industrial city
Roy Hay

In what senses, if any, was the British nineteenth-century industrial city the precursor of the Australian city of the nineteenth and twentieth centuries? Such a question presupposes that there was a unique and individual type of industrial city in the United Kingdom, but as this essay will demonstrate, that is not self-evident. As later chapters of this book show, Australian cities were not homogeneous either, although they shared certain characteristics. Moreover, the British industrial cities of the nineteenth century were not necessarily typical of cities in general, and differed in many crucial respects from pre-industrial cities. It is at least arguable that Australian cities may have drawn more from pre-industrial models than they have from British industrial cities of the nineteenth century. (For a brief introduction to some theories of urban growth, see Hudson 1992, pp. 153–5.)

A close study of British industrial cities in the nineteenth century is rewarding if only because it throws up a point of reference for any understanding of the Australian city. Like all their contemporaries, Australians were conscious of the images projected of the British industrial city, for good or ill, and they often took those images to heart as they developed their own living spaces. What is often forgotten is that Australia was a highly urban society almost from its inception. By the end of the nineteenth century the level of urbanisation in Australia was only exceeded by that of England, Wales and Scotland. Australia had a higher proportion of its population in cities than the United States of America, or Germany or France (see Figure 1.1). The overwhelming majority of the white population of Australia came from Great Britain and Ireland, or were descended from people who had done so, and they congregated disproportionately in cities. Why this happened and the form it took requires explanation.

Figure 1.1 Percentage of population dwelling in cities at the latest census, 1899

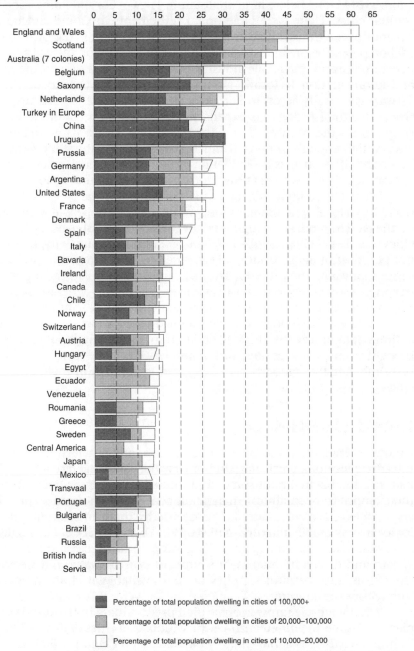

Percentage of total population dwelling in cities of 100,000+

Percentage of total population dwelling in cities of 20,000–100,000

Percentage of total population dwelling in cities of 10,000–20,000

Source: Weber (1967 [originally published 1899], frontispiece)

Pre-industrial cities

Cities existed long before industrialisation. The Greeks and Romans had substantial cities. There were large urban settlements in China and in South America over a thousand years ago. In Europe, London had grown to over a million people before industrialisation took hold. London thrived as a centre of commerce and small-scale industry, but primarily as the centre of the court and administration. Its location in the south-east of the country on the River Thames gave ready access to European trade. Surrounded by highly productive agricultural regions, its expansion depended on a continual influx of people from the countryside for the death rate within its boundaries was always high enough to prevent much growth from natural increase. Other European cities, such as Paris, Vienna or Berlin, were much smaller, but still substantial. They too were at the centre of rich agricultural regions.

What placed limits on the growth of pre-industrial cities was the productivity of local agriculture. As long as the majority of people were required on the land to produce enough food for their own subsistence, the growth of cities was always circumscribed. When agricultural productivity, that is, output per head of agricultural workers, rose in Europe from the seventeenth century onwards then the opportunity appeared for a larger proportion of the population to live in urban areas and engage in non-agricultural pursuits. Improvements in transport, domestic and international, reinforced this process, allowing bulky foodstuffs to be supplied over a wider range, particularly at times of local scarcity. The Malthusian trap, which saw population growth brought to an end by famine, wars or pestilence, seemed to be broken for the first time. A higher proportion of this growing population could now live in cities.

Industrial cities

Unique to England in the late eighteenth and early nineteenth century was the emergence of a particular kind of city, the industrial city. Cities always had industrial activities of some kind located within their boundaries, but these tended to be small-scale handicraft activities dominated by practitioners in skilled crafts, who passed their knowledge on to artisans and produced for local aristocratic or luxury markets. What was new about the English industrial city was the emergence of large-scale industry based on the factory system and driven by inanimate sources of power—water and steam—derived from the plentiful supplies of coal available at strategic locations throughout the country.

What were the impressions which predominate in the minds of people who visited the nineteenth-century industrial cities of Britain? Richard Dennis's *English Industrial Cities of the Nineteenth Century* (1984) is a modern historical geography, which contains a representative sample of contemporary reactions, many of which found their way into subsequent discussions on the nature of the nineteenth-century industrial city.

Dennis's account is striking in that the impressions of contemporary observers of the industrial city in England show that there was not a single pattern of urban development. There were different forms of industrial city and the variations related to the economic and social structures of the places concerned. For example, there is a contrast between Birmingham and Manchester which appears in the contemporary comments (see Figure 1.2). Birmingham has modern industry, but it is organised differently from that in Manchester. Its units of production are smaller, there is a greater variety of industry, and there appears to be a different set of class relationships in existence. Manchester appears as a single-industry city, dependent on the cotton trade, dominated by large factories and with the population divided on the one hand, into a small group of capitalists who own the mills and, on the other, the mass of the people who work in them. As later researchers have shown, this simple picture needs considerable modification.

Dennis also notes the displacement of workers from housing in the centre of cities as urban land values rose. Owners of factories and offices could afford the rents for central urban land, so workers' housing was located further afield. Dennis does not mention another displacement which occurred as the factory owners and other members of the upper middle class moved out into the suburbs in which they built substantial houses, instead of 'living over the shop', which was common in the early days of industrialisation or in the smaller-scale industries which survived into the industrial era.

Contemporary observers compared and contrasted Manchester with other cities, such as Liverpool. The latter was a seaport as well as a manufacturing town and some of its urban problems—cellar dwelling, overcrowding, unemployment—were on a par with those in Manchester, even if they tended to be less obvious than those of the latter city. There is a suggestion that the social structure of Manchester was more complex than that of the smaller factory towns which surrounded it. These smaller centres, which were primarily concerned with the production of cotton goods, had the most stark contrasts between the classes. Manchester as a trading and administrative centre was slightly less polarised. Finally, Dennis notes the different patterns of housing occupation. In Birmingham, it is argued that one family tends to occupy one dwelling, while in Manchester multiple occupancy is more common.

Manchester

So why should we study Manchester in order to understand the nature of cities in Australia? To answer this question a little background is necessary. The city of Manchester is located in the north-west of England. It was one of the major towns of the old county of Lancashire, second only in size to Liverpool, the port city at the mouth of the River Mersey (see Figure 1.2). Both of these conurbations were much smaller than the capital, London, which had a population of over a million people at the time of the first census of England and Wales in 1801. Liverpool and Manchester had 82 000 and 75 000 respectively. However, both grew very rapidly in the next century and had increased their population by a factor of ten by 1921, while London had increased by seven times. The most rapid rate of growth for Manchester and Liverpool came in the first half of the nineteenth-century when their populations increased by nearly four times in forty years (see Table 1.1).

Figure 1.2   Major cities in the British Isles

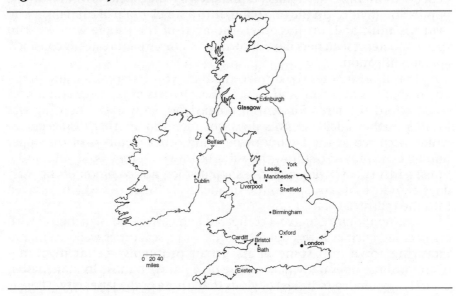

Table 1.1   Population of British cities 1801–1931

Town	1801	1821	1841	1861	1881	1901	1921	1931
Bath	33	47	53	53	52	50	69	69
Birmingham*	71	102	202	351	546	760	919	1003
Exeter	17	23	31	34	38	47	60	66
Liverpool*	82	138	299	472	627	685	803	856
Manchester*	75	135	252	399	502	645	730	766
Oxford	12	16	24	28	35	49	57	81
Sheffield	46	65	111	185	285	381	491	512
York	17	22	29	40	50	78	84	94
Greater London	1117	1600	2239	3227	4770	6586	7488	8216

* Including environs (Figures of populations in thousands)
Source: Mathias (1969, p. 451)

It was not just its size or its rate of growth which makes Manchester worth our attention. Manchester was the prototype 'shock city' of the early industrial revolution in Great Britain. It was the place where the 'Dark Satanic

Mills' were to be found in abundance. It was a centre of poverty, oppression, disease and squalor on a mass scale. It was the subject of the most damning criticism by social investigators like Friedrich Engels, the collaborator and supporter of Marx, in his book *The Condition of the Working Class in England* published in 1844. To know what was wrong with urban life during the early industrial revolution, we must study Manchester.

Manchester existed long before industrialisation began. There was a settlement on the site of modern Manchester in Roman times, seventeen hundred years before the industrial revolution. It was a substantial mercantile and commercial centre in the seventeenth century, engaged in local, national and even some international trade. It was, therefore, not a city created but transformed by the industrial revolution, so a study of it lets us see the impact of industrialisation on an urban centre (Redford 1956).

Manchester was a city which faced many, if not all, of the problems of rampant, unchecked industrialisation and population growth. In Manchester, as Dennis (1984) and Marcus (1974) make clear, a modern capitalist class structure emerged. A sharp division existed between an affluent bourgeois class, the factory masters, who owned the means of production on the one hand, and the proletariat, the factory workers, who had only their labour power to sell on an open market, on the other. Unlike Birmingham, where gradations between employers and workers were less distinct, or London, which had a large middle class and a traditional aristocracy, Manchester appeared to be a two-class city.

Another characteristic feature was the dependence on a single, fast-growing industry, but one whose cycles of prosperity and depression could affect the lives of all who lived in the area. Manchester was synonymous with the cotton trade. Even today the cotton goods sections of Australian department stores are labelled simply 'manchester'. The cotton industry dominated the life of Manchester as a production centre and as the focus of a trading network (Lee 1972).

Finding accommodation for the burgeoning labour force required for the cotton industry led to the fast erection of substandard housing which turned quickly into urban slums, and to the cramming together of immigrants into tightly packed areas of the city. Urban amenities failed to keep pace with the growth in demand. Water supply, sewage disposal, police services and urban government all lagged behind the expanding needs of the urban population (Vigier 1970).

Because Manchester was the earliest city to experience these social disasters, it was also one of the earliest to confront and to tackle many of the revealed problems. Some of the solutions, attempted solutions and failures may have lessons for us even today.

What was Manchester like before the industrial revolution? Well, it was not a sleepy hollow, but rather a bustling city heavily engaged in the textile industries, including wool and linen from domestic, that is, local English, sources of supply. Later it traded in what were referred to as 'Manchester cottons', which were mixtures of wool and cotton, linen and flax imported from the Middle or Near East in the seventeenth and early eighteenth centuries. This industry claimed protection from cheap Indian cotton goods which found a ready market in Britain in the eighteenth century as disposable incomes began to rise. This is interesting in view of Manchester's later reputation as the home of free trade (Redford 1956).

Manchester's industry was organised on the domestic system, that is, the work was done by spinners and weavers in their own homes, sometimes on their own account, but more often under a putting-out arrangement. A merchant would buy the raw materials and distribute it to the workers to make up. Then the yarn or cloth would be collected and sent on to the next stage, whether for making up into clothes or for sale in home or overseas markets.

Work under the domestic system was governed by the demands of trade, involving long hours and an irregular pattern of work, 'hunger and a burst', with 'St Monday' (Thompson 1965, p. 357) as the day when the goods might be taken to the market for sale. In the eighteenth century this system was transformed by the growth of a new system of production associated with the industrial revolution, the factory system. Its growth has been seen as inspired by two elements.

The most popular interpretation among economic historians is that the scale of the new technology and its capital requirements led to the emergence of the factory system. All the cotton inventions and innovations—with the exception of the spinning jenny—such as Arkwright's water frame, Crompton's mule, Roberts's automatic and power looms, required inanimate sources of power: first water, then steam. They were relatively expensive items, so the investment had to be recouped by using them for long periods and at high speeds. Hence it made economic sense to group them together in factories to use the power in a single location and exploit any other economies of scale.

The second, less popular, interpretation is that the centralisation of workers stemmed from the imperative to control the workers and reduce transaction costs. In this argument, the emphasis is on the need to keep track of the processes of production, prevent embezzlement and raise productivity. It was better to employ children and women, not because they were cheaper, but because they were more malleable and subject to industrial discipline than adult males (Jones 1994).

But there was more to the growth of Manchester than the factory system. Transport improvement and the dredging of the River Irwell, provided a link with Liverpool, and boats of up to sixty tons were able to ply the river. Turnpike roads linked river and city. The Bridgewater Canal, on the estate of the third Earl of Bridgewater, enabled coal for industrial power and domestic heating to be brought from mines to the city. Food supplies too could be drawn from a larger hinterland. Such improvements led to the growth of other trades taking advantage of location, freedom from guild restrictions and new sources of power and labour (Owen 1977).

Population growth was a mixture of natural increase and migration. This was part of a European phenomenon, but strongly accentuated in England and particularly in the north-west. Most births occurred within marriage, and although illegitimacy may have increased a little, this was still true of the late eighteenth and early nineteenth centuries. So the critical factor was a fall in the age at marriage. Women were at risk of becoming pregnant over a longer time and, hence, had larger families. Modern research suggests that a rise in the birthrate was responsible for two-thirds of the growth in population, and this makes sense when we look at the mortality rate as cities grew. There was little sign as yet of the major medical or environmental improvements which were to have such important effects later (Wrigley 1983).

It was not just natural increase which explains the phenomenal growth of Manchester. The city absorbed more migrants in the first half of the nineteenth century than Canada or Australia. Where did they come from and why? A major source was immigration from Ireland as rapid population growth there outstripped the ability of the agricultural system to feed it. Numbers flowed in throughout the first half of the nineteenth century, but there was a major influx after the potato famine in 1846. The Irish formed ten per cent or more of the total population. They had a major social impact according to contemporary observers such as J. P. Kay (Kay-Shuttleworth 1971) and Engels (Engels 1958).

But most migrants to Manchester came from the surrounding countryside in Lancashire and the neighbouring counties of Cheshire, Yorkshire, Staffordshire, Cumberland and Westmoreland. Manchester creamed off a substantial proportion of the natural increase in population of the areas around it. Most migration was relatively short-distance movement—here was no mass movement from the south of the country to the north as was once thought. Arthur Redford described the movement as like throwing a stone into calm water, with the ripples spreading outwards (Redford 1976).

The attractions of Manchester

Why did people flock to Manchester? As with all migrations there were push and pull factors. Certainly there was poverty in the countryside and job opportunities may not have kept pace with the growth in population, though the evidence is that people were not being driven off the land by enclosure and new farming methods, as Marx and many early writers thought. The new systems used as much if not more labour than before. It was not until 1851 that the population in England's rural areas began to fall absolutely, long after the maximum periods of growth of Manchester and Liverpool.

Despite the later horror stories, towns like Manchester did have attractions. There was the prospect of escaping rural isolation and narrowness, the chance of employment in the burgeoning new industries, the opportunities for wealth which these appeared to bring about—as in any lottery the odds may have been long, but there were many gamblers, and once the gamble was taken, it was very hard to return to the old ways and the old locations. For many young women employment in the textile industries was to provide an independent source of income, though not necessarily equality of opportunity with their male contemporaries. Considerable debate exists about whether technological change was skewed in favour of males, but there is no doubt that women formed a majority of the labour force in the expanding cotton industry (Hudson 1992, pp. 225–33).

So what formed the centre of this attraction? The cotton industry, the new growth industry of the industrial revolution, was the driving force of Manchester's growth. Though it started as a small industry, uncompetitive with that of India and having to be protected by tariffs, by the late eighteenth century it was developing so rapidly that at its peak early in the nineteenth century it contributed around seven per cent of Britain's Gross National Product and had overtaken the woollen industry as the leading textile industry of the country. A whole series of changes and natural advantages were responsible. The climate of Lancashire, damp and temperate, was conducive to the spinning and weaving of the delicate cotton fibre. (Manchester is a place where you can wear out an umbrella in a year!)

The phenomenal growth of the cotton industry in and around Manchester and Glasgow, in Scotland, can be attributed to improvements in cotton growing and preparation, particularly the invention of the cotton gin in the south of the newly independent United States of America; cheaper transatlantic shipping, first with sailing ships and later with steam and iron and steel traders; the improvement of port facilities at Liverpool and the merchant activities there; overland transport to Manchester and the surrounding towns, like Oldham, Salford (soon to be incorporated within Manchester itself); the new technology of water and, later, steam power; and, very importantly, ample supplies of capital, through the highly developed English banking system, and labour (Lloyd-Jones 1988).

Manchester, its problems and the remedies

So Manchester grew at an almost unprecedented rate from the late eighteenth century, drawing inquirers who marvelled at its awesomeness in both positive and negative respects. Two of the most famous social commentators of the nineteenth century draw on Manchester for much of their critique of the industrial city—James Kay (later Kay-Shuttleworth) and Friedrich Engels, who was heavily influenced by Kay's work. Both concentrated on the deficiencies of Manchester's social organisation. Kay was a medical man who worked as a doctor in Manchester and was one of the first to note and develop the links between appalling environmental conditions and poverty and ill-health. He argued that the conditions under which the mass of the industrial workers lived were actually bringing about the moral, social and economic degeneration of themselves and their society. He blamed the Irish for much of the problem, but it is arguable that they were as much the victims as the cause of the ills described. Yet Kay was clear in his own mind that the commercial system was not the villain, believing that it was possible to reform the system so that the undoubted benefits which it brought about could be more evenly shared. An improvement in civic institutions, better government and policing of the city were necessary to achieve this.

Engels was much more politically concerned, believing, on the basis of his experience of Manchester, that only the revolutionary overthrow of the existing class structure would bring about the emancipation of the workers. Using reports by Kay and many others, Engels believed that he had shown how the factory system and its class structure of owner-entrepreneurs, on the one hand, and wage-slaves, on the other, gave rise to the particular slum conditions and poverty of Manchester. Because there was little or no connection between the two groups in society, he could see no prospect of peaceful accommodation between them or social reform, but only violent confrontation. Evidence of this seemed to be provided by the Peterloo massacre of 1819 and the Plug Plot Riots of 1842 (Marlow 1969).

The historian Steven Marcus gives a sympathetic account of Engels's approach, and tries to show how Engels learned to read the urban landscape and interpret it (Marcus 1973, pp. 257–63). Marcus concludes that Engels's work is an example of the application of theoretical reasoning to a particular set of social circumstances, revealing the reality behind the facade of appearances in the urban environment of Manchester.

In contrast, the introduction to a modern edition of Engels, translated and edited by W. H. Chaloner and W. O. Henderson (Engels 1958), is highly critical of Engels's methodology and presentation. They argue that his deficiencies do as much to obfuscate the reality of nineteenth-century Manchester as they do to illuminate it.

Engels and Kay represent the poles of the argument about urbanisation and urban improvement. For Kay, investigation, institutional reform and then the application of remedies derived from study is the way forward. For Engels, it is only the application of political power which will bring about reform.

It has to be said that the Manchester experience supports Kay rather than Engels. In the first half of the nineteenth century the reform of local government in English cities, including Manchester, slowly got under way. It ran parallel to the reform of national government, in which Manchester played a part. The Reform Bill of 1832 was very much a charter for the middle classes of England and Wales, and it presaged the development of a range of reform movements, including the Anti-Corn Law League which eventually convinced a Tory Prime Minister, Sir Robert Peel, to remove tariffs on imports of wheat. This was a victory for the manufacturing lobby, since it was designed to reduce wage costs by making food cheaper. Manchester was seen as the home of the free trade movement, with Richard Cobden and John Bright as the leading figures. On the other hand, Manchester merchants and manufacturers were involved in the reform of factory conditions and the restriction of the hours of work for women and children. Leading manufacturers who set themselves high standards were prepared to support legislation which would prevent their production being undercut by the output of sweatshops (Kidd & Roberts 1985).

At a local level, the reform of city government, the introduction of a police force, the setting up of bodies to oversee the supply of water and to remove nuisances, improvements in medical and educational services all came about in the first half of the nineteenth century. These were assisted by an improvement in statistical knowledge pioneered by the Manchester Literary and Philosophical Society of 1781 and the later Manchester Statistical Society. These reform groups were driven by an almost messianic zeal and it is fascinating to observe how important religious concerns were in the process of reform. For Kay, among others, it was a struggle between good and evil.

Nevertheless, this was no simple triumph of disinterested knowledge over social problems. There were enormous political battles, even if not the ultimate class struggle which Engels predicted. Given the division of classes in Manchester, there was much opposition to civic reform from interests of one kind or another. Many benefited from the rents of overcrowded tenements and houses, many had an interest in the supply of limited services. Others who had moved out to the newly created suburbs to the south and west opposed the expensive reform of local government. The shibboleths of 'free trade' were often used to prevent or hinder sanitary and environmental reform on the grounds that this would be an interference with the liberty of 'economic man'.

Manchester reform was piecemeal, unplanned and sporadic, with many gains and many steps backward. The successes of one generation often remained to become the problems of the next. Urban pollution was not removed in the nineteenth century. As a student in Manchester in 1959 I can remember driving in Oxford Road from one streetlight to the next in a pea-souper fog, unsure which side of the road the next streetlight was on. The villas of the early Victorian entrepreneurs were later converted into twentieth-century sweatshops for a revived domestic industry based on immigrant labour from the West Indies and Pakistan (Wood 1974).

Yet reform there was, and Manchester pioneered much of the urban reform of the nineteenth century just because it was the first city to experience the problems. When local supplies of fresh water were exhausted or polluted by industry or because of the growing population, it drew on supplies from the Lake District and North Wales. This in turn was to give rise to environmental issues in another generation.

Housing controls were introduced to prevent the worst excesses of unplanned construction. These then led to overcrowding in other areas and rises in rents, necessitating the further extension of municipal powers. Throughout the nineteenth century, the issue of the appropriate scale of the local authority to undertake civic government was a continual source of debate as problems transcended existing powers and boundaries (Fraser 1979; Waller 1983).

Piecemeal and unspectacular reform occurred, often bitterly fought, with vested interests stopping or diverting its course at every step of the way. Democratic institutions gradually emerged after long battles with oligarchic power structures. Of course, there were setbacks. Major problems remained or changed form—poverty and misery did not disappear in the nineteenth century. The great public buildings and the rhetoric of urban achievement cannot hide some appalling squalor and distress in Manchester—nobody ever called it 'Marvellous Manchester', like 'Marvellous Melbourne'—but there was reform of many of the worst abuses of the first industrial city.

As Otto Henderson makes clear in his highly critical assessment of the work of Engels, the latter's devastating critique did force its way into the consciousness of the next generation of citizens of industrialising society in late nineteenth-century Germany (and he might have added urban Britain and Australia, as well) so that the 'social question', or how to deal with the problems of industrial urban society, were never again to disappear from the political agenda (Engels 1958). This was a legacy which Australia inherited, the belief that urban problems could be tackled. The reform may have been undertaken to head off the revolution as Engels predicted, or it may have been undertaken for other reasons, but judging by results it succeeded.

So Manchester not only experienced the worst excesses of early industrialisation and rapid urbanisation, but like some other English industrial cities it began the slow process of dealing with these problems. The attempted and partial solutions appeared as models to be adopted, adapted or avoided when Australian cities began to experience some similar problems in the second half of the nineteenth century. For this reason, if for no other, it makes sense to contrast Manchester with the Australian cities of the nineteenth century.

Australian cities originated in different ways from Manchester. Inevitably they could have no prehistory as mediaeval villages growing into commercial towns. What implications did this have for their geographical location, spread and development? Did Australian cities have a similar industrial base to Manchester or did they draw on a more diverse commercial background? Did they combine the economic bases of both Liverpool, the port city, and Manchester, the industrial city? Were the social structures of Australian cities similar to Manchester's? Was the polarisation of social classes as marked? Did Australian cities face similar problems of poverty, overcrowding, health and sanitation, and urban government as Manchester encountered? Were the processes of civic reform, therefore, similar or different? (Statham 1989). These questions, as well as others, will be explored in later chapters.

References

Dennis, R. (1984), *English Industrial Cities of the Nineteenth Century: A Social Geography*, Cambridge University Press, Cambridge.

Engels, F. (1958), *The Condition of the Working Class in England in 1844*, trans. W. H. Chaloner & W. O. Henderson (eds), Stanford University Press, Stanford.

Fraser, D. (1979), *Urban Politics in Victorian England: The Structure of Politics in Victorian Cities*, Macmillan, London.

Hudson, P. (1992), *The Industrial Revolution*, Edward Arnold, London.

Kay-Shuttleworth, Sir James (1971), *The Moral and Physical Condition of the Working Classes Employed in the Cotton Manufacture in Manchester*, Shannon, Irish University Press, Dublin.

Jones, S. R. H. (1994), 'The origins of the factory system in Great Britain: Technology, transaction costs or exploitation,' in M. Kirkby & M. E. Rose (eds), *Business and Industrialisation*, Routledge & Kegan Paul, London.

Kidd, A. J. & Roberts, K. W. (eds) (1985), *City, Class, and Culture: Studies of Social Policy and Cultural Production in Victorian Manchester*, Manchester University Press, Manchester.

Lee, C. H. (1972), *A Cotton Enterprise, 1795–1840: A History of M'Connel & Kennedy Fine Cotton Spinners*, Manchester University Press, Manchester.

Lloyd-Jones, R. (1988), *Manchester and the Age of the Factory: The Business Structure of Cottonopolis in the Industrial Revolution*, Croom Helm, London.

Marcus, S. (1973), 'Reading the illegible', in H. J. Dyos & M. Wolff (eds), *The Victorian City: Images and Realities*, vol. 1, Routledge & Kegan Paul, London.

Marcus, S. (1974), *Engels, Manchester, and the Working Class*, Random House, New York.

Marlow, J. (1969), *The Peterloo Massacre*, Rapp & Whiting, London.

Mathias, P. (1969), *The First Industrial Nation: An Economic History of Britain 1700–1914*, Methuen, London.

Owen, D. E. (1977), *Canals to Manchester*, Manchester University Press, Manchester.

Redford, A. (1956), *Manchester Merchants and Foreign Trade*, Manchester University Press, Manchester.

Redford, A. (1976), *Labour Migration in England, 1800–1850*, 3rd edn, edited and revised by W. H. Chaloner, Manchester University Press, Manchester.

Statham, P. (ed.) (1989), *The Origins of Australia's Capital Cities*, Cambridge University Press, Melbourne.

Thompson, E. P. (1965), *The Making of the English Working Class*, Gollancz, London.

Vigier, F. (1970), *Change and Apathy: Liverpool and Manchester During the Industrial Revolution*, Massachusetts Institute of Technology Press, Cambridge, Mass.

Waller, P. J. (1983), *Town, City and Nation: England, 1850–1914*, Oxford University Press, Oxford.

Weber, A. F. (1967), *The Growth of Cities in the Nineteenth Century: A Study in Statistics* (originally published by Macmillan, New York, 1899), Cornell University Press, Ithaca.

Wood, C. M. et al. (1974), *The Geography of Pollution: A Study of Greater Manchester*, Manchester University Press, Manchester.

Wrigley, E. A. (1983), 'The growth of population in eighteenth century England: A conundrum resolved', *Past and Present*, vol. 98, pp. 126–32.

Bibliography

Ashton, T. S. (1977), *Economic and Social Investigations in Manchester, 1833–1933: A Centenary History of the Manchester Statistical Society*, Harvester Press, Hassocks.

Cannadine, D. (1980), *Lords and Landlords: The Aristocracy and the Towns, 1774–1967*, Leicester University Press, Leicester.

Cannadine, D. (ed.) (1982), *Patricians, Power, and Politics in Nineteenth Century Towns*, Leicester University Press, Leicester.

Cannadine, D. & Reeder, D. (eds) (1982), *Exploring the Urban Past: Essays in Urban History*, Cambridge University Press, Cambridge.

Davies, A. (1992), *Gender and Poverty: Working-class Culture in Salford and Manchester, 1900–1939*, Open University Press, Buckingham.

Dyos, H. J. & Wolff, M. (eds) (1973), *The Victorian City: Images and Realities*, Routledge & Kegan Paul, London.

Faucher, L. (1969), *Manchester in 1844: Its Present Condition and Future Prospects*, trans. with notes by a member of the Manchester Athenaeum, 1st edn, new impression, Cass, London.

Langdon, J. & Morris, R. J. (1986), *Atlas of Industrializing Britain 1780–1914*, Methuen, London.

Little, J., Peake, L. & Richardson, P. (eds) (1988), *Women in Cities: Gender and the Urban Environment*, Macmillan Education, Basingstoke.

Messinger, G. S. (1985), *Manchester in the Victorian Age: The Halfknown City*, Manchester University Press, Manchester.

Roberts, R. (1978), *A Ragged Schooling: Growing up in the Classic Slum*, Fontana, London.

Scola, R. (1992), *Feeding the Victorian City: The Food Supply of Manchester, 1770–1870*, Manchester University Press, Manchester.

Waller, P. J. (1981), *Democracy and Sectarianism: A Political and Social History of Liverpool 1868–1939*, Liverpool University Press, Liverpool.

Williams, B. (1976), *The Making of Manchester Jewry, 1740–1875*, Manchester University Press, Manchester.

Williamson, J. G. (1990), *Coping with City Growth During the British Industrial Revolution*, Cambridge University Press, Cambridge.

Chapter 2 | # Nineteenth-century Australian cities
Lionel Frost

The development of the Australian economy during the nineteenth century was part of a transnational process of white settler colonisation. While large areas of land suitable for primary production existed in Australasia, Latin America, southern Africa, Canada and, above all, the United States, substantial amounts of capital and labour were needed for these to be exploited successfully. At the same time, Europe was industrialising but had a short supply of land and resources which were needed to feed its growing industrial workforce and supply raw materials to its factories. The surplus labour and capital generated by industrialisation provided a solution, as European settlement and investment opened up new lands which were farmed to produce surplus food and raw materials. Furthermore, Europe's demand for resources encouraged its nation states to scramble for new territory to add to their empires. During the half-century before the First World War, imperialist Europe conquered Africa, Oceania and much of Asia.

Of course, European interest in establishing new overseas colonies did not begin in the nineteenth century. Before the so-called 'age of discoveries', conventionally dated as beginning in the 1490s with the voyages of Columbus and da Gama, Europeans had for centuries obtained high-value goods, such as spices and silk, from Asia through overland traders. Transoceanic voyages opened up opportunities for maritime trade with Asia and the Pacific, the Americas and Africa (see Jones, Frost & White 1993). During the sixteenth century the indigenous population of most of the Americas was swept aside by European colonists. The Spanish conquistadors fought with superior military technology and had the advantage of the use of horses, but the real killers were smallpox and measles to which the indigenous population had no resistance. The Aztec and Inca civilisations were largely destroyed and the native population of the Caribbean became extinct. But in Asia and Africa, Europeans were held in check by lack of a swift means of overland transport and by tropical diseases. Europeans enjoyed considerable superiority at sea, especially in gunnery, but their movement inland was restricted. 'In 1800, after three centuries of lurking offshore, Europeans could only claim a few footholds in Asia and Africa, mainly harbors and islands' (Headrick 1988, p. 5).

Two new developments during the nineteenth century increased the capacity of Europeans to conquer other lands. First, technologies were developed which improved Europeans' speed of movement inland and their firepower. This involved the application of steam power and iron to ships, riverboats and railroads; new communications technology, notably the submarine cable which provided fast transfer of military information; improved firearms, which helped to suppress the indigenous populations; and new medicines which reduced the impact of tropical diseases on Europeans (see Headrick 1981).

Second, the industrialisation of Europe created a growing demand for raw materials which Europe could not provide itself, such as cotton, tin, rubber and palm oil, and for resources such as wool, timber, meat and grain which could be obtained more cheaply from regions of new settlement. Wealthy European consumers demanded tropical products such as sugar, tea, coffee and cocoa. As Europeans applied their surplus labour and capital and transplanted their institutions and technology to the colonies and regions of new settlement, a world economy developed based on the exchange of production inputs and finished goods from Europe for the resources of the New World and the tropics.

Towns were indispensable for the spread of European settlement and the economic growth which resulted. In newly settled regions they were bases for the settlement of the surrounding hinterland. In art and literature, the mythic heroes who tamed and developed these lands are rural ones such as the cowboy, rancher and homesteader in the United States, the gaucho in Argentina and the bush worker in Australia. A similar bias prevailed in American historical writing after the formulation of Frederick Jackson Turner's 'frontier hypothesis' in 1893. For Turner, the frontier—the margin between occupied and unoccupied land—shifted westward because of the taking up of free land by brave, resourceful and practical pioneers. Towns were founded later, as a final stage in the settlement process. However, a number of subsequent case studies of frontier settlement revealed that towns played a more important role than Turner suggested. Richard Wade (1959) found that the settlement of the Ohio Valley was spearheaded by an 'urban frontier' of towns which were founded in advance of the establishment of agriculture. Several studies of settlement west of the Mississippi confirmed that 'the establishment of urban communities ... stimulated rather than followed the opening of the West to agriculture. As vanguards of settlement, towns led the way and shaped the structure of society rather than merely responding to the needs of an established agrarian population for markets and points of distribution' (Reps 1979, pp. ix–x). These towns were part of a global urban system which was the driving force for international flows of commodities, services, capital and labour. London was the centrepiece of this urban system, while in each individual region economic life was dominated by a very large city which was a centre for commodity and capital markets and often political power. In London and these regional metropolises, crucial decisions about the direction and distribution of these flows were made. (for a study of Chicago's impact on its region, see Cronon 1991). Smaller towns provided primary producers with transport, banking and other services which were essential for successful commercial production. Europe's colonial outposts—established towns like Cairo, Delhi and Shanghai, or new ones such as Calcutta and Hong Kong— became focal points for European shipping, railroad and communication networks and for the operations of European merchants and financiers. Towns were both producers and consumers within the world economy, providing production inputs and specialised services, as well as a source of demand for food, building materials and other services as their population expanded. It was the world economy which gave these towns their wealth and purpose.

The first Australian towns were convict settlements. In 1788 Sydney became an 'instant city' with the arrival of a thousand or so convicts and soldiers. In later years a number of other convict settlements were established, including Hobart in 1804 and Moreton Bay, later called Brisbane, in 1824. The towns' demand for food and various services provided economic opportunities for the non-convict and ex-convict population (Statham 1989). While the convict towns had imperial and administrative origins, Melbourne, Adelaide and Perth were founded by free settlers for commercial purposes. Western Australia (1829) and South Australia (1836) were independent colonies settled with the permission of the British government, but Melbourne was settled in 1835 by pastoralists from Van Diemen's Land (Tasmania) who acted independently without formal authority. Until 1851 the Port Phillip District, as Victoria was first known, was run by the New South Wales government. Queensland was part of New South Wales until 1859.

Though the Australian capitals were not all founded for the same purpose, they soon developed a common commercial function as part of the world economy. The grasslands of south-eastern Australia are not especially fertile and the cost of inland transport was initially high. However, these disadvantages were offset by the fact that large areas of cheap land could be used for the production of wool. As Yorkshire woollen mills were converted to factory production, their need for raw materials created a strong demand which encouraged the creation of new wool-growing regions outside Europe. From as early as the 1820s, wool became Australia's major source of export income. The high value of the commodity meant that growers could bear the cost of inland transport. For a modest annual fee, squatters could occupy huge areas of land and establish large-scale, capital-intensive woolgrowing enterprises which required comparatively little labour. The labour-intensive services which were needed to get wool to market, such as transport and processing, were performed most efficiently in an urban setting. Most of the labour necessary for the export of wool was needed in cities, rather than on the pastoral run. The seaport capitals of the new colonies became financial centres which channelled British investment to pastoralists and were the head-quarters of merchants who arranged exports. By 1851, Sydney, Melbourne and Adelaide, with populations of 54 000, 29 000 and 18 000 respectively, had emerged as substantial and important towns.[1]

Australia's wool industry 'was probably the most capitalistic form of primary production in the world at that time' (Bate 1978, pp. 1–2). The owners or providers of the factors of production—land, labour and capital—exchanged them with others in the expectation of profit. People specialised and interacted with each other in ways which were to their mutual advantage. Squatters took up sheep runs to increase the size of their flocks and the woolclip; their annual licence fee provided revenue for the colonial government. Pastoralists borrowed to finance expansion of their operations; British investors and local banks and merchants regarded such lending as a good and profitable investment. Pastoralists who were well-established could sell off part of their flock to those just starting out. Shearers and shepherds offered their services in return for good wages—without such labour profitable wool production would have been impossible. In the towns a wide range of specialist occupations provided goods and services which were needed by the rural economy and by other urban inhabitants. Underlying the countless transactions involved in the Australian rural and urban economy was the strength of the British demand for wool.

While the economy which white settlers built was a capitalist one, that of the indigenous population was based on custom and self-sufficiency. To the Aborigines, notions of private ownership, money, the profit motive, price signals and overseas trade were unknown and unfathomable. Aborigines used the land intermittently and in cooperation with other members of the tribe, moving on when food supplies were exhausted. 'Towns'—permanent settlements with private property—were a foreign concept. There was hypocrisy in the rampant capitalism of white settlers, as Henry Reynolds points out:

> In Aboriginal eyes the whites were invaders who came preaching the virtues of private property; people who talked much of British justice while unleashing a reign of terror and behaving like an ill-disciplined army of occupation once the invasion was effected; fornicators who pursued black women in every fringe camp on the continent but in daylight disowned both lovers and the resulting offspring. (Reynolds 1981, p. 199)

To European settlers, the Aborigines and their way of life contradicted everything they understood by 'progress':

> The blacks did not till the soil, they knew nothing of metals and had no animal husbandry. In fact they were so innocent of the mainsprings of European culture that they were despised as ignorant savages. People who felt mastery over the earth were bound to treat them as irrelevant and expendable. (Bate 1978, p. 1)

There was a clash between the values of the nomadic, customary indigenous peoples and those of the sedentary, capitalistic invaders. Land was crucial to the economic well-being of both white and black Australia, but the former needed it to be privatised to maximise the rate of return on investment. The result was an unequal confrontation which was typical of newly settled societies. Superior firearms and the spread of lethal European diseases meant that indigenous peoples were rarely able to offer much resistance to settler capitalists. Reynolds estimates that as many as 20 000 Australian Aborigines were killed in frontier violence before federation (Reynolds 1981, p. 20).

A case can be made that Australian towns played a crucial role in the subjugation of the indigenous population. The number of white settlers and their concentration in towns reduced food supplies quickly and exposed a large part of the Aboriginal population to European bacteria (Martin 1989, p. 50). The most violent confrontation was in the bush, where squatters were staking out sheep runs. As wild food supplies dwindled because of white hunting, the Aborigines killed sheep and cattle. Initial tolerance and trust disappeared as a result of violence and theft. For whites, what made the land worth fighting for was the chance to share in the profits being generated by the growing world economy.

Aborigines sought refuge from frontier violence by moving close to towns. This was ironic, as in many settler societies towns were fortified to keep hostile natives out. Blacks drifted to towns in search of food, either scavenged or obtained through begging, prostitution or casual work (Reynolds 1981, pp. 193–7). They generally lived in fringe camps at the edge of towns but sometimes lived closer to the centre, as was the case in Adelaide where they camped in the parklands. In these camps serious problems of poverty (disease and malnutrition) and vice (alcoholism and drug use) soon developed. In pre-modern Europe, towns were built compactly and it was normal for people of different classes, religions and races to live close together. Outcasts such as noxious traders, prostitutes and the chronically ill were banished to the edge of town by their inability to afford town rents, but their presence there generally seems to have been tolerated. But in the late eighteenth and early nineteenth century, British society began to express a preference for living in the privacy, tranquillity and respectability of a suburban setting rather than in a closely packed city. British migrants brought this preference with them to Australia but found that it was contradicted by the presence in towns of blacks, who were seen as noisy and immodest people. White demands to have the Aborigines expelled from towns or prevented from moving into them increased (see Hamer 1990, pp. 216–20). For instance, there was a forcible round-up of Aborigines in Melbourne in 1840 (Cannon 1990, p. 68). As the towns grew, fenced properties covered hunting lands, fishing waters became fouled and the Aborigines abandoned their traditional gathering places close to towns. As David Hamer writes in his comparative study of towns and frontier settlement in North America and Australasia: 'it was not long before indigenous peoples, under the weight of many pressures, of which disease and alcoholism were especially significant, began to disappear from towns or to become marginal presences, confined to the outskirts both of the towns and the minds of the townspeople' (Hamer 1990, p. 221).

During the gold rushes Australia experienced very rapid rates of population growth: from 1850 to 1861 the total population roughly trebled, from just over 400 000 to almost 1.2 million. The major goldfields lay in the new colony of Victoria and between 1851 and 1871 Victoria's share of the Australian population increased from 19 to 44 per cent. By 1861 Melbourne had grown at an average rate of 15.7 per cent per annum over the previous decade to become one of the great cities created by European colonisation. Its population of 125 000 was more than double that of San Francisco, which had also been stimulated by gold discoveries, and was exceeded by only seven contemporary cities in North America. Sydney (population 96 000) was also a major city. As the capital of Australia's major wheat-growing region, Adelaide also benefited from the goldfields market.

The gold rushes also created scores of new towns close to the diggings. Only Ballarat and Bendigo grew into large towns: by 1871 they had populations of 47 000 and 29 000 respectively, making them the next largest cities in Australia after Melbourne, Sydney and Adelaide. But if we add up the population of the other, smaller goldfield towns, it is apparent that in Victoria there was a significant degree of urbanisation outside Melbourne. In 1871 the population of Victorian gold towns with at least 500 inhabitants totalled 146 000, thus constituting 'a remarkable balancing force' with Melbourne's population of 191 000 (Bate 1988, p. 57). The towns and settlements officially classified as belonging to Mining Districts in the 1871 Census of Victoria had a total population of 265 000. While the growth of the major cities was rapid during the gold rush period, the total population growth of small towns and farming areas was faster, resulting in a situation of de-urbanisation. Between 1851 and 1871 the proportion of the Victorian population living in towns with at least 2 500 inhabitants fell from 48 to 43 per cent. In Australia as a whole the percentage fell from 40 to 37. By the time the population of the goldfields and their towns began to grow more slowly during the 1860s, people were living and working away from the capital cities to an extent which has not been matched since. Melbourne's share of Victoria's population fell from 38 per cent in 1851 to 23 per cent in 1861.

One of the effects of the gold rushes and the immigration which they stimulated was the creation of an electorate which demanded that crown lands be made available for small family farms rather than be used as large pastoral estates. Land legislation which was designed to bring about this result was supported by government railway building and irrigation projects to assist farmers. This failed to create a prosperous yeomanry of small-scale, intensive farmers, but successful methods of farming were nonetheless developed, based on larger holdings and land-extensive methods.[2] The railway system gave farmers improved access to domestic and overseas markets, but also gave metropolitan merchants and manufacturers an overwhelming advantage over their small-town competitors. Businesses could reduce their transport and distribution costs by locating in the capitals, which were usually the hub of their respective colony's rail network. Large markets and cheap labour provided economies of scale for big city firms, thus reducing the costs of introducing new technology. It was possible for metropolitan firms to conduct business with customers in country areas by receiving orders by telegraph and dispatching goods by rail. Even the most efficient small-town producers struggled to match the prices charged and range of products offered by metropolitan firms.

As Bate notes, although the population of Victorian gold towns declined or stabilised after around 1871, they still contributed positively to economic activity, 'with better factories, greater horsepower, bigger houses, more handsome public buildings, superior facilities and an increasingly skilled workforce' (Bate 1988, pp. 57–8). Nevertheless, there is no doubt that during the 'long boom' from around 1860 to 1890, Australia's population and economic life came to be increasingly centred on its capital cities. From 1861 to 1891 the major capitals increased their share of their respective colony's population: Melbourne from 23 to 41 per cent, Sydney from 27 to 35 per cent and Adelaide from 35 to 42 per cent. Brisbane's share of the Queensland population rose from 14 to 24 per cent in the 1880s. During the 1870s Sydney, Adelaide and Brisbane each grew at a rate of more than 5 per cent per annum, as did Melbourne, Sydney and Brisbane in the 1880s. Construction of urban housing and infrastructure and the manufacture of producer and consumer goods for the urban population became important components in the total level of investment (see Butlin 1964). Technological change in agriculture was encouraged by urban demand and this technological change created jobs in the cities and provided inhabitants with cheap food. The big cities also prospered because their population growth was due mostly to in-migration. In the 1870s, 75 per cent of Adelaide's population increase resulted from in-migration and in the 1880s the respective figures for Melbourne and Sydney were 70 and 56 per cent. Migrants stimulated economic growth because they were generally of working age with few dependants and their education had been provided by other regions. They usually arrived with money to spend and so added to the total level of demand for goods and services.

The growth of the Australian capitals and the rising share of the total population living in them worried contemporary observers. Cities were widely seen as inherently unproductive, while the countryside was regarded as the source of all wealth. There was considerable concern about a perceived imbalance between the urban and rural population, especially what the New South Wales government statistician, T. A. Coghlan, called a 'most unfortunate', 'abnormal aggregation' of population in the capitals (quoted by McCarty 1970, p. 112). Australia has been a heavily urbanised nation from a very early stage in its history and N. G. Butlin is basically correct in saying that the urban percentage was greater than in other new regions such as the United States and Canada. But this is not to say that Australian cities were *abnormally* large or that their size retarded economic growth in general (Butlin 1964; Frost 1991; McCarty 1970).

Before the gold rushes Australian cities were in a dire physical condition. In 1839 Adelaide was described as 'a seedy collection of shacks, tents, and stores, its streets muddy scratches through the grass, its squares a tangle of gum trees and wombat holes' (Whitelock 1985, p. 36). When the Sydney Municipal Corporation was established in 1842, fifty years of virtually unplanned growth had left the city with severe problems. 'Most roads were no more than tracks. No water or sewerage had been laid on ... Building regulations were minimal and often honoured in the breach' (Fitzgerald 1992, p. 39). In Melbourne, attempts to dam the Yarra River to increase supplies of drinking water led to severe flooding in 1839, 1841, 1842, 1843, 1844 (twice), 1848 and 1849. After the last of these floods it was proposed that a water reservoir be constructed outside the city at Yan Yean, but this was not finished until 1857. The Yarra itself was heavily polluted with animal carcasses and other wastes. Like Sydney and Adelaide, the town was unsewered. The streets were unlit and in poor condition: two children drowned in gullies in Elizabeth Street in 1842 (Cannon 1991, pp. 95, 102, 113, 126).

During the gold rushes urban conditions were chaotic. Geoffrey Serle has suggested that in 1852 Melbourne was the world's most expensive city to live in (Serle 1970, p. 119). Wages were high but excess demand for housing and food drove up rents and prices. Many people stayed in Melbourne for only a short time on their way to the diggings, but those who sought work in the capital had to reduce living costs by accepting lower standards of shelter. South of the Yarra, a district of tents and shanties known as Canvas Town appeared quickly. Not many of the new arrivals planned to stay very long in the goldfields towns. Most were prepared to live cheaply in primitive conditions. The gold towns were rough, raw, cosmopolitan places. Ballarat was 'as noisy, smelly, bustling, and congested as an Asian market, as wild as an American frontier town, as wealthy as London's Lombard Street, and as seamy as the back alleys of Naples' (Bate 1978, p. 96). In 1852, a *Sydney Morning Herald* reporter contended 'that a worse regulated, worse governed, worse drained, worse lighted, worse watered town of note is not on the face of the globe; ... in a word, nowhere in the southern hemisphere does chaos reign so triumphant as in Melbourne' (*Sydney Morning Herald* 1852). That was strong condemnation indeed, because in the previous year the *Sydney Morning Herald* had published an excellent series of articles describing Sydney's foul and poorly built physical environment (*Sydney Morning Herald* 1851). Despite these dismal conditions, Australian cities were spared major epidemics, such as cholera and typhus which struck Europe in the 1830s and 1840s.

Frontier towns were like tinderboxes and were vulnerable to fire disasters. For instance, many Californian gold towns suffered several major fires during the late 1840s and early 1850s. Australian gold towns were ripe for burning as well:

If someone had tried to invent a street that would burn like a torch, he
[sic] could have done worse than take over Main Street [in Ballarat]. Like
old London, which had burnt so well in the Great Fire of 1666, Main
Street was a mass of buildings with scarcely a space in between them. In
the mid-fifties [1850s] walls and ceilings were lined with canvas and calico,
and even in quite solid structures flimsily papered-over palings were the
usual partitions between rooms. Flames from unstable candles and oil
lamps waited greedily for the chance to spread, stoves and fireplaces lacked
proper hearths and chimneys, and large stocks of gunpowder, paint and
turpentine were bound to encourage fire. (Bate 1978, p. 111)

Miraculously, no Australian town suffered a multi-building fire comparable to those experienced in many other cities throughout the world (Frost
& Jones 1989, pp. 333–47). In Melbourne, there was a peak of minor fires in
the first half of the 1850s, but all were thankfully extinguished before developing into conflagrations. Wide streets acted as firebreaks, so that fires were
confined to single blocks (Wilde 1991, p. 211).

Though the absence of major fires and epidemics meant that the problems created by the way in which Australians built their cities were not as bad
as they might have been, it remains clear that Australian cities at the end of
the 1850s were poorly built and short of decent housing and infrastructure.
N. G. Butlin calculates that in 1861 one-third of the total population lived in
substandard impermanent housing, such as tents and shanties. In Victoria
the proportion was almost one-third (Butlin 1964, pp. 215–17). One of the
main features of the subsequent 'long boom' was a demonstrable improvement in the physical condition of cities. The housing stock grew more quickly
than the rate of population growth and the average house became larger and
better equipped (see Frost 1991, ch. 6). This improvement was mainly the
result of the achievement of rates of economic growth and living standards
which were equalled by few, if any, contemporary nations.

Yet it should not be overlooked that the effects of earlier city-building decisions exerted an abiding influence on the built form of Australian
cities. For instance, Sydney's constricted town site and absence of planning influenced land use and patterns of commuting. A lack of open space
for railways forced most people to live compactly and within walking distance of where they worked. Sydney lacked efficient public transport
throughout the nineteenth century and its suburbs were slow to develop
as a result. On the other hand, Melbourne, Adelaide and Perth were 'born
decentralised' because their town sites were located inland and railways
were soon needed to provide a link with distant port towns. These three
cities were planned in a way which provided ample open space for rail
lines and termini. Efficient networks of railways and tramways helped to
open up new commuter suburbs. Sites close to the centre were purchased
quickly by speculators, so that when people needed land for housing or
business use, they tended to move to cheaper suburban areas (Denholm
1989, p. 183). During the 'long boom', Melbourne, Adelaide and Perth

would become suburban cities par excellence. Nineteenth-century Australian cities had a common economic function as components of the world economy, but their capacity to open up and develop new suburbs varied because of differences in siting and planning.

Notes

1   The population figures in this chapter are derived from the relevant census data. Capital city populations are from McCarty (1970).
2   For a fuller discussion, see Frost (1992).

References

Bate, W. (1978), *Lucky City: The First Generation at Ballarat, 1851–1901*, Melbourne University Press, Carlton.

Bate, W. (1988), *Victorian Gold Rushes*, McPhee Gribble/Penguin, Ringwood.

Butlin, N. G. (1964), *Investment in Australian Economic Development 1861–1900*, Australian National University Press, Canberra.

Cannon, M. (1990), *Who Killed the Koories?*, William Heinemann Australia, Melbourne.

Cannon, M. (1991), *Old Melbourne Town: Before the Gold Rush*, Loch Haven Books, Main Ridge.

Cronon, W. (1991), *Nature's Metropolis: Chicago and the Great West*, W.W. Norton & Company, New York.

Denholm, T. (1989), 'Adelaide: A Victorian Bastide?', in P. Statham (ed.), *The Origins of Australia's Capital Cities*, Cambridge University Press, Cambridge.

Fitzgerald, S. (1992), *Sydney 1842–1992*, Hale & Iremonger, Sydney.

Frost, L. (1991), *The New Urban Frontier: Urbanisation and City-Building in Australasia and the American West*, New South Wales University Press, Sydney.

Frost, L. (1992), 'Government and economic development: The case of irrigation in Victoria', *Australian Economic History Review*, vol. 32, pp. 47–65.

Frost, L. E. & Jones, E. L. (1989), 'The fire gap and the greater durability of nineteenth century cities', *Planning Perspectives*, vol. 4, pp. 333–47.

Hamer, D. (1990), *New Towns in the New World: Images and Perceptions of the Nineteenth-Century Urban Frontier*, Columbia University Press, New York.

Headrick, D. R. (1981), *The Tools of Empire: Technology and European Imperialism in the Nineteenth Century*, Oxford University Press, New York.

Headrick, D. R. (1988), *The Tentacles of Progress: Technology Transfer in the Age of Imperialism, 1850–1940*, Oxford University Press, New York.

Jones, E., Frost, L. & White, C. (1993), *Coming Full Circle: An Economic History of the Pacific Rim*, Westview Press, Boulder.

Martin, G. (1989), 'The Founding of New South Wales', in P. Statham (ed.), *The Origins of Australia's Capital Cities*, Cambridge University Press, Cambridge.

McCarty, J. W. (1970), 'Australian capital cities in the nineteenth century', *Australian Economic History Review*, vol. 10, pp. 107–37.

Reps, J. W. (1979), *Cities of the American West: A History of Frontier Urban Planning*, Princeton University Press, Princeton.

Reynolds, H. (1981), *The Other Side of the Frontier: Aboriginal Resistance to the European Invasion of Australia*, Penguin, Ringwood.

Serle, G. (1970), *The Golden Age: A History of the Colony of Victoria 1851–1861*, Melbourne University Press, Carlton.

Statham, P. (1989), 'Introduction: Patterns and perspectives', in P. Statham (ed.), *The Origins of Australia's Capital Cities*, Cambridge University Press, Cambridge.

Sydney Morning Herald (1852), 4 November.

'The Sanitary State of Sydney' (1851), *Sydney Morning Herald*, 1 February–5 April.

Wade, R. C. (1959), *The Urban Frontier: The Rise of Western Cities, 1790–1830*, Harvard University Press, Cambridge, Mass.

Whitelock, D. (1985), *Adelaide from Colony to Jubilee: A Sense of Difference*, Savvas Publishing, Adelaide.

Wilde, S. (1991), *Life Under the Bells: A History of the Metropolitan Fire Brigade, Melbourne 1891–1991*, Longman Cheshire, Melbourne.

Chapter 3 | The political economy of Australian cities[1]
Michael Berry

The recent upsurge of interest in the urban among historians and economic historians has either resulted in little or no progress beyond the 'biographical' outputs of earlier local and regional historians, or has led to the reification of the urban in a manner which dissociates the urban problematic from the (class) structural determinants of social life and social change. As always, an inadequate historical conceptualisation of 'class' coheres with an inadequate analysis of urbanisation.

It should be clear that these conclusions are not theoretically innocent. The arguments on which they rest have been organised from within a perspective forged by contributors to the 'new urban sociology', more particularly by Marxists like Manuel Castells. The author also accepts the imperative directing the work of Connell and Irving (1980): Australian history must be approached through class analysis and the latter can only be carried out by confronting historical reality. This position demands an historical study of urbanisation in class terms. However, the reverse side of the same coin requires class analysis to develop a spatial dimension. In commending the relevance of modern urban social theory to historical research, an American historian has concluded:

> Recent writings by geographers, architects and urban planners ... all suggest that the historians may be missing something important in the process. Space is socially produced, they say, and for this reason is not politically or socially neutral. The shape of urban and regional space, they insist, not only reflects the nature of class relations in any society, but also powerfully determines new social outcomes. The quality as well as the shape of urban space, for example, is also held to be historically specific. The nature of public space in the late medieval or early modern city, therefore, will differ from public space shaped, for example, under a system of monopoly capitalism. This is because in a regime of commodity production, space too is a commodity in a way that it was not before, and this is seen to have crucial economic and political consequences. (Amsden 1979, p. 13)

In this passage there is still a tendency to oppose class and space as independent categories. Nevertheless, it does stress the need to relate the spatial organisation of society to its class structuring. The urban is not a trans-historical category frozen in meaning; cities evolving in a world increasingly dominated by advanced capitalism are not simply more populous and densely packed versions of medieval cities. Castells (1977) has offered a useful starting-point for an historical analysis of urbanisation. Redefining the urban question in an historical context entails, he suggests, conceptualising the spatial arrangements or organisation of social life as a product of (or basic element in) the development of social structure. For Castells, the spatial distribution and concentration of populations, and their production, consumption and cultural activities (including the production, consumption and symbolic valuation of the built environment), are only explicable in terms of the dominant social dynamic which, as a Marxist, he identifies as the uneven global expansion of the capitalist mode of production which emerged, historically, in Northern Europe...

The constraints posed by the rise of capitalism in Europe and America loomed largest in the Third World where new patterns of dependence complemented and underwrote development in the advanced countries. A dependent society is one in which the economic, political and cultural structures express and reinforce the class interests of the ruling class(es) in another, dominant society (Castells 1977, p. 44). Clearly, dependence is a matter of degree and can only be established, in any instance, by concrete historical research into the mode of, and success with which, dominant structures have been imposed or, alternatively, repulsed...

Castells distinguishes three forms or types of domination. *Colonial domination* involves the direct political subjugation and administration of dependent territories in order to secure valued resources for the dominant society. *Capitalist-commercial domination* is imposed through trading relations; manufactured goods (and invisible services like shipping and finance) are exported from dominant to dependent societies in return for raw materials, the rate of exchange or terms of trade expressing an unequal exchange by which value is transferred from the latter to the former, as manufactured goods sell above and raw materials below their respective values. *Imperialist industrial and financial domination* arises when capitalists in the dominant society export capital as well as goods to the dependent society. Control is exerted indirectly through the provision of loan capital and directly through the creation of local industries in order to exploit low wages in the dependent societies and circumvent tariff barriers. The precise form which urbanisation assumes will depend on the type of domination ascendant in the context of the particular, historically specific social forces structuring the dominant and dependent societies in question.

Castells attempted to apply this general framework to Latin America, creating obvious difficulties for anyone interested in applying this approach to other historically specific situations—in this case, the Australian. With the partial exception of Argentina, Latin American experiences differ significantly from those characterising and driving Australian development. Australia industrialised earlier, more extensively, but at a smaller scale, prior to the massive internationalisation of production and intensive international division of labour dominant in more recent times. Similarly, the current explosion of Third World industrialisation is reflected in the spectre of de-industrialisation in Australia, most apparent in the decline of traditional manufacturing industries concentrated in the large capital cities (especially Melbourne, Sydney and Adelaide). This suggests the need for caution in attempting to apply the substance of Castells's analysis to the Australian situation; in particular, it suggests the probability that the urban typology he used to guide his analysis of Latin American urbanisation will have to be qualified, supplemented or even replaced for Australian purposes.

Just as an adequate analysis of Australian urbanisation cannot be based on a wider theory of *dependent underdevelopment,* neither can it be easily related to theories of *dominant development* in the advanced capitalist countries or, at least, not without substantial qualification. Thus, Castells's central proposition, namely, the fact of structural changes in advanced capitalism displacing basic contradictions from the sphere of production to the sphere of consumption, and the implications this has for spatial organisation and politicisation of urban life, may not shed much light on contemporary Australian urbanisation and is irrelevant to a study of urbanisation in earlier periods. What is needed is an approach which allows one to grasp the total or global process of capitalist development from the perspective of a theory of *dependent development.* In effect, this calls for a third or 'mid-way' view which would 'fill out' Castells's abstract framework by shifting the focus from the First and Third Worlds to the particular experiences of a small number of societies like Australia, for which development was limited, uneven but present. This entails a focal shift, not a completely different view: *dependent* development implies the existence of relations of domination...

In order to advance this analysis in this direction, it is necessary to start at the most general level of abstraction—the relationship between the process of capital accumulation and the production of spatial forms. In effect, this entails specifying those pre-conditions which must be met if production is to continue on a capitalist basis—that is, if production is to be primarily carried out by a class of property-less wage earners who must sell their labour to capitalists in order to survive. In this context Stilwell (1978) has delineated four functional conditions for continuing accumulation and sought to relate each to the problematic of spatial organisation.

Capitalism requires an ever-expanding market for the increasing volume and variety of the commodities it produces. The incessant competition of individual capitalists leads to continual intensification of the division of labour and the increasing application of technological advances to the production process, which leads, in turn, to a progressive cheapening in the cost of producing commodities and a rapid increase in their output. In order to realise their investments and reap a profit, capitalists must be able to sell their commodities. Historically, one major solution to the problem of markets has been the geographical expansion or penetration of capitalist relations of production and exchange from the few original centres of capitalist production in Northern Europe. This has clearly been an uneven process, both with respect to its form and pace, on the one hand, and its geographic spread, on the other. At the level of exchange, the most dramatic and far-reaching manifestation was the construction—first under British and later German and American hegemony—of an international economic order during the eighteenth and nineteenth centuries. The scale of this expansion can be gauged by the fact that, for the period from 1750 to 1913, the total value of international trade increased fifty-fold (Woodruff 1973, p. 658). However, capitalist penetration also occurred within the borders of the first capitalist nations. In Britain, for example, the new, cheap, factory-produced textiles cut the local (and external) market from underneath the feet of traditional cottage producers in the countryside. Together with the progressive and massive expropriation of tenant farmers and labourers from the land (and, hence, from the means of domestic production), this led to an increasing commercialisation of rural life, culminating in the near-total dissociation of production from the home and reinforcing the drift of the displaced peasantry to the factory towns.

This latter point leads to consideration of the second functional requirement for accumulation, namely, the creation and maintenance of a pool of surplus labour power which acts as a restraint on wage levels. The lower wage levels are, the greater the profits (always assuming that commodities can be sold and profits realised) and the greater the rate of accumulation or growth. Some guarantors of a relative surplus population or 'reserve army of unemployed' are inherent in the dynamic of capitalist development itself—for example, the tendential displacement of labour power resulting from the competitive application of new technology to production, and the temporary waves of unemployment brought about by recurrent economic crises. Other forces leading to a similar outcome are historically contingent or specific to a particular situation or stage of development—for example, the recruitment of female and child labour during the early phases of English industrialisation. Into this second category may be placed those spatial rearrangements which have encouraged the creation and geographic concentration of surplus population at appropriate places for capitalist production. Examples of this type include: the expulsion and drift to the cities of the agricultural population in industrialising England, and the massive waves of European emigration to America during the eighteenth and nineteenth centuries. Stilwell (1978, pp. 23–4) offers two more recent examples—the pervasive 'guest worker' system in Western Europe and the post-war influx of non-English-speaking migrants to Australia, where they have become concentrated in the lowest-paid jobs and the most disadvantaged industrial suburbs of the main capital cities. The direct impact of a continuing flow of temporary or permanent guest workers is to keep unskilled wage levels lower than they would have been had local workers been recruited. More indirectly, the existence of a growing mass of unskilled, disorganised and desperate workers provides an incentive for capitalists to redivide and refine the production process in order to de-skill previously skilled occupations, which, in turn, acts as a general break on wage levels throughout the home economy.

In addition to adequate labour power, capital accumulation requires secure sources of raw materials and means of production. In particular, it requires the satisfaction of a complex and expanding ensemble of *general preconditions of production*, including the provision of extensive and integrated communications and transportation networks expressing, in Marx's terms, capital's attempts to annihilate space by time (Harvey 1975, pp. 11–13). The form, level and spatial patterning of these networks historically reinforced the emerging geographical circulation and concentration of capital, tending in the nineteenth and early twentieth centuries to result in clear-cut patterns of regional and international specialisation. The earliest, most visible and far-reaching examples of geographic specialisation saw key industrial sectors like steel-making, textiles, armaments and shipbuilding tightly concentrated in a relatively small number of centres in the major imperialist powers—that is, the north of England, the Ruhr in Germany and the north-east of the United States—and the complementary concentration of raw material extraction in the periphery. More recently, as Stilwell stresses, the multinationalisation of capital has resulted in large, qualitative changes in the geography of accumulation. The production process has been reconstituted and subdivided on a world scale. Instead of being geographically concentrated within a single factory, as in the early stages of capitalism, the division of labour has become international. Raw materials extracted in one country are refined in a second, enter as semi-finished products in the production processes of a third and are sold in a fourth. In each country, multinational capital faces local workers organised along national lines and the nation state, playing each country off against the rest through the ever-present threat of capital flight. No one group of workers or state in isolation, can exert control over the entire production process. The actual global pattern of production which emerges will reflect the efforts of each multinational corporate group to maximise total profits within the group, whether or not this entails real or book losses on operations in a particular country or region. This, in turn, will depend on the differential prospects for exploiting low wages, loose tax laws, generous subsidies, free infrastructure and a 'favourable' political climate in each country.

A spatial reorganisation of production is also taking place in some advanced capitalist societies. In the case of the United States, Walker (1978a) has argued that regions in the traditional sense—that is, spaces within which most economic decisions are made locally, in the light of local conditions, and most economic consequences are contained, through interlocking linkages or multiplier effects—are fast disappearing. They are being replaced by an uneven 'spatial mosaic' of specialised activities ranged or segregated across space and integrated through the internal administrative control of the large corporation. However, this does not lead to rigid or permanent patterns of regional specialisation. The heightened mobility and penetration of capital leaves it less dependent for profit on any one location. The disruption to accumulation posed by striking workers or an unsympathetic local state in one place can be resolved by shifting production to similar plants located elsewhere. Capital circulates through the institutional form of the large corporate conglomerate, flowing into and out of specific locations according to the profit situation of the group as a whole. The increasing degree of capital mobility, therefore, increasingly secures the necessary delivery of processed raw materials and intermediate (producer) goods within the corporate group; to a lesser extent, it also increases the reliability of supply of basic producer goods to other capitalists outside the group.

The fourth and most basic functional requirement for accumulation is the reproduction of capitalist social relations, notably, the capital—labour relation in production. Social conditions must be generated which ensure that sufficient workers deliver themselves up to the point of production, resigned to selling their labour-power in exchange for a money wage—willing, therefore, to give up control over the uses to which their labour-power is put and, consequently, to give up any claim on the product of their labour. The main spatial dimensions to this problem (for capital) have already been noted in the discussion above of the geographical creation and concentration of a relative surplus population and the multi-regionalisation of production on the intra-national and international scales. However, the movement of labour and capital across space does more than keep wage levels down and the means of production secure. It also strategically weakens any group of workers or state authority bound to a particular territorial base vis-a-vis capital, thereby removing or reducing the economic and political basis for a society ordered by alternative—that is, non-capitalist—relations of production...

The geographic generalisation of capital also allows capitalists to prey on the parochial, racist and xenophobic sentiments of different cultural groups. Inter-regional and inter-national differences and conflicts among workers (often stemming from pre-capitalist times) mystify the nature of capitalist exploitation and further weaken working-class consciousness and unity. It is precisely the capacity to forge working-class cooperation across space, in order to oppose the multinationalisation of capital, which these divisive ideological currents help destroy.

In summary, *places* are locationally specific ensembles of 'usual effects' or 'use-values', differentially effective with respect to the process of capitalist production:

> *From the perspective of capital* , concrete places contain a specific ensemble of the material of nature, a built environment, labour power, members of other classes, various commodities, etc., as well as the specific constellation of social relations into which these spatially-situated people have entered amongst themselves and with their environment. These social

relations are conditions and forces of production as far as capital is concerned, i.e. they affect labour productivity, time of circulation, and so
forth. (Walker 1978a, p. 29, italics added)

There are two related problems inherent in any attempt to apply directly analysis pitched at this high level of abstraction to concrete instances.
Any such attempts almost inevitably assume a functionalist cast: what is good
for capital comes to pass. Moreover, a consideration of functional imperatives
does not automatically lead to an understanding of historical sequence or
development, rather the reverse. Functionalism, especially when linked to a
structuralist perspective—the normal form in which it has emerged in modern social theory—threatens to obliterate historicity, confining analysis to
the synchronic or static level (Hobsbawm 1972, p. 277; Giddens 1979, p. 3).
What is needed is an analytic approach which derives the changing spatial
forms of social organisation from the nature of capitalist relations of domination or exploitation but in a way which ties the determination of particular,
historically contingent spatial outcomes to the crisis-ridden, class-structured
process of capital accumulation. This, it was suggested earlier, was the promise (if not the product) of Castells's work...

In order to move from a static consideration of functional requirements
to an understanding of historical process, one needs to concentrate on the
dynamic of capital accumulation, the object of Marx's mature work. The bare
outline of this dynamic is as follows. Individual capitalists are constrained by
the logic of their position to 'accumulate or perish'. In an unregulated, competitive world, capitalists are forced to defend their profit margin by changing
the labour process in order to improve labour productivity, which, in turn, is
generally secured by the ever-increasing application of machinery and other
forms of fixed capital at the expense of workers. The unintended, overall
outcome of this competitive war is a chronic tendency for the general or
average rate of profit to fall. This tendency results in recurrent economic crises whenever the actual rate of profit falls below a level sufficient to encourage
individual capitalists en masse to re-invest profits already realised. In other
words, the historical process of capital accumulation is inherently discon-
tinuous or crisis-prone. However, the very process which creates this tendency
also calls forth various 'counter-tendencies', making the actual historical career of the average rate of profit—and, hence, the overall process of capital
accumulation—highly problematical and uneven in time and across space.

This suggests that it is necessary to conceptualise historical development in terms of the crisis-prone process of capital accumulation grasped as a
contradictory unity. Spatial reorganisation is a necessary and central element
in this overall process: for instance, most of the examples relating social structure to spatial form noted above can be treated as counter-tendencies.
However— and this is crucial—there is no logical connection between (or
institutional mechanism ensuring) the historical unfolding of the restructuring process and the satisfaction of the functional imperatives discussed above.
In fact, the reverse is true; there is a logical 'disconnection' which strongly

predisposes the system to historical malfunction. This follows from the two basic contradictions inherent to the capitalist mode of production (Harvey 1978, pp. 102–3), namely, the production of unintended and dysfunctional (from the point of view of capital in general) aggregative effects of competition *within* the capitalist class, and the tendency towards intensification of conflicts *between* the dominant capitalist and subordinate working class. These are explicable at the most abstract level of analysis in terms of the overriding opposition of the increasingly social or cooperative nature of reproduction of material life and the private appropriation of the product (as profit). Individual capitalists are 'encouraged' by the coercive force of the law of competition to act primarily in terms of their own, particular, often short-term, interests. The overall and unintended outcome of this war of all against all will often be unfavourable, sometimes disastrous, for the common or joint interests of all capitalists. Thus, if left to themselves, capitalists as a group will tend to overwork workers to the point of physical extinction (so destroying the very basis of their profits and social dominance), chronically under-house them, provide inadequate medical care and education, and by geographically concentrating large numbers of workers in factory towns or port-cities, provide favourable conditions for the emergence of increasingly large, well-organised and militant working-class organisations.

This last point reflects the force of the second contradiction. Capitalism is a system of social reproduction in which a small group who collectively own the means of production effectively control the process of (re)production and are thereby able to appropriate an increasing proportion of the material product of the direct producers (the workers). The fact of exploitation—or to use Harvey's words again, the continual infliction of violence on workers—pervades all spheres of social life, severely constraining the overall life-chances of workers and partially, unevenly, but inexorably filters through to the level of individual consciousness—a necessary, but not sufficient, condition for emerging class-consciousness and action. Thus, in any concrete historical instance, capitalists as a group may not be able to organise the necessary structural readjustments to ensure future capital accumulation and continuing profit, either because they do not know what adjustments are necessary or cannot cooperate in bringing them about, or because workers stop them from so doing. In the latter case, disruptive or 'dysfunctional' opposition may break out in the workplace, at the communal or domestic level, within the political sphere (that is, through the concrete interventions and non-interventions of state agencies) or at the ideological level.

Glimpsed as an overall process, and within broad constraints, capital accumulation proceeds with a certain law-like regularity expressed through the irregular, anarchic, seemingly random recurrence of economic crises. The actual form assumed by the crisis-prone course of capitalist development depends on the manner in which intra- and inter-class struggles unfold. At the global level, the uneven spatial and temporal penetration of capitalist relations of production in the face of persisting pre-capitalist modes of production has resulted in the emergence of highly complex and differentiated patterns of class struggle which must be grasped through careful historical analysis guided, but not determined *in total*, by an understanding of the logic of capitalist development in general. This task necessarily leads to a consideration of the successive stages of capitalist development and raises the vexing problem of periodisation.

Most contemporary Marxists distinguish between the earlier appearance of competitive capitalism and subsequent emergence of advanced or monopoly capitalism, however much they disagree over the specification of each form and the manner in which the former developed (or degenerated) into the latter. Wright (1978) has recently advanced an influential analysis which further subdivides this basic distinction into six developmental stages: primitive accumulation, manufacture, machino-facture (or 'modern industry'), monopoly capital, advanced monopoly capital and state-directed monopoly capital. Each period or stage is characterised by a dominant form of class structure—a dominant articulation of the forces and relations of production—which establishes structural limits or constraints within which the accumulation process proceeds. Progressive developments in the forces and relations of production, the outcome of incessant competition between individual capitalists (or capitalist blocs in the later stages), on the one hand, and the development of class struggle, on the other, raise obstacles or impediments to the smooth reproduction of conditions necessary for accumulation to proceed in its existing form (stage). However, the very contradictions which give rise to impediments also (gradually) induce structural changes in the form of accumulation itself, which temporarily move the process of accumulation back within the structural limits to reproduction imposed by the *new* forces and relations of production. Accumulation can then proceed in its restructured form until new impediments threaten chronic crisis, and force restructuring to a higher phase, and so on. Wright suggests that the basic impediment which arose in the period of modern industry was the tendency of the rate of profit to fall, brought about by a rising organic composition of capital and an increasingly well-organised and militant working class. The 'structural solution' to this impediment was the increasing concentration and centralisation of capital (facilitated by recurrent economic crises) which ushered in the monopoly stage of accumulation. The impediment which increasingly came to dominate this later stage, according to Wright, was a strengthening tendency for the mass of surplus value extracted in production to exceed the prospects for profitably reinvesting it, manifested in increasingly prolonged crises of realisation or 'underconsumption', which resulted, in turn, in the growth of state intervention in the economy (at this stage, primarily in the sphere of exchange).

Wright's analysis clearly focuses on developments internal to the capitalist 'centre'—that is, to those nation-states which first underwent capitalist development—and especially on British and North American experiences. However, he explicitly integrates the analysis described above with an historically grounded theory of the changing forms of imperialism. Thus, the restructuring forced by developing impediments is necessarily seen to 'spill over' the national boundaries of the capitalist centre and involve the integration and reorganisation of peripheral societies in the light of the crisis tendencies driving the former's development. The success of restructuring at the centre will critically depend on the manner and extent to which the periphery can be integrated into the capitalist world system. In short, Wright's framework allows us directly to address the problem with which we started, namely, how to grasp the historically specific development of dominance-dependence relations on a world scale. Wright explicitly restricts his attention to developments in the centre (Wright 1978). He is concerned, above all, to distinguish and historically situate the different forms of imperialist domination of periphery by centre by relating them to the staged unfolding of crisis tendencies in the latter; each stage of capitalist development calls forth 'emergent' or typical forms of imperialist domination which reflects the dominant impediment, state of class struggle and evolution of state interventions which characterise life at the centre. Thus, Wright is able to argue that in the stage of modern industry, the high tide of competitive capitalism, the tendency of the rate of profit to fall—fuelled by a rising organic composition of capital and rising wages in the centre—led both to an increasing concentration and centralisation of capital and the intensification of labour-saving innovations within the centre *and* the increasing export of capital to the periphery in order to secure cheaper raw material supplies.

As a total theory of dependent development and underdevelopment Wright's analysis falls short. It offers only half the story, a framework by which to understand the external forces which constrain but do not totally determine peripheral development or lack thereof. The other half of the story would require us to shift our vantage point from centre to periphery, to focus on internal developments there in the light of the historically specific impact of external forces originating in the former. The individual histories of particular dependent societies will, therefore, differ according to the stage at which, the manner in which, and the degree to which they were integrated into the capitalist world system. This raises the possibility of accounting for widely differing forms of dependence and, therefore, widely differing degrees of development and underdevelopment outside the capitalist centres of Northern Europe, the United States and Japan—a vital advance if one is to understand the peculiar developmental trajectory of Australia.

If it is properly interpreted and extended, therefore, it is Wright's framework, rather than his substantive analysis, that provides a suitable basis from which to apply and develop the general and highly abstract approach to dependent urbanisation. However, it must be admitted that few attempts have actually been made to *apply* such an analysis, to relate, consistently and coherently, evolving spatial form to the staged development of capitalism. Gordon (1978) and Walker (1978b) are exceptions. Since their analyses focus on processes or urban and regional development in the United States, they provide only comparative benchmarks for other analyses which must focus on the social production of space in relatively dependent societies like Australia. In the latter context, only Mullins (1981) and Stilwell (1980) have begun to discuss the questions raised here.

One can now develop the analysis of general stages of capitalist development into a tentative periodisation as a prelude to its application in the case of Australia, by relating Wright's framework to the recent resurgence of interest among Marxists in 'long waves' of development. The stages of capital accumulation pertaining to the capitalist centre could be interpreted in terms of the four long waves of expansion and decline propounded by Mandel (1975). The latter's explicit periodisation can then be used chronologically to locate these stages, thereby orienting analysis of the manner in which crisis tendencies have actually unfolded in the dependent society in question. It is also tempting to interpret the expansive phase of Mandel's long wave as the period in which the structural adjustments forced by the dominant contradictions or structural constraints characterising the previous stage are relatively successful in re-establishing the conditions for intensified accumulation; conversely, the declining phase of a long wave can then be seen as the period in which new contradictions intensify to the point of forcing new readjustments which (can) eventually lead to the emergence of conditions favourable to a new long-term upswing.

It is now possible to specify, albeit schematically, the necessary framework for a Marxist analysis of Australian urbanisation. This framework is more fully developed elsewhere (Berry 1983).

Figure 3.1 draws together the elements discussed above, in the context of—and from the point of view of—the development of Australian capitalism. The four stages of Australian accumulation are specified by the four long waves of expansion and decline in the capitalist centre. The pattern and pace of development in each stage is conditioned by structural constraints deriving from the particular manner in which Australia has been integrated into the world capitalist system, expressed through the particular or characteristic mode of domination defining Australia's place in that system. Crisis tendencies which strengthen at the centre, as development there changes from an expansionary phase to the long swing down, force structural 'solutions' or changes both within the centre economies and in their (dominance) relation to dependent societies of the periphery and semi-periphery. These structural changes re-establish favourable conditions for a new, long, upswing at the centre (or have done so in the past) and a 'new' pattern of dependent development (and underdevelopment) outside it; in this sense one can talk about the movement from one developmental stage to another, in both the centre and periphery. The problem here focuses on the way in which these processes unfold in space; with each stage of development one can identify the characteristic pattern of spatial organisation—or the characteristic mode of urbanisation—which expresses or contains it. Each mode of urbanisation at the periphery can also be seen as one element in the set of structural solutions

Figure 3.1 Stages of Australian urbanisation

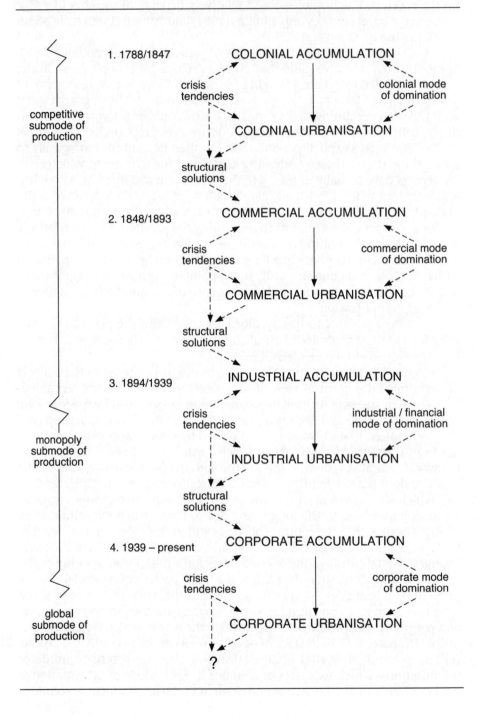

at the centre which smooth the transition to a new stage of development, thereby recasting the structural constraints on peripheral developments including the spatial form in which such development unfolds.

Thus, in the first stage, the form and pace of colonial development was initially ordered through direct economic and political controls imposed by the imperial state. Development was severely constrained by shortages of supplies, capital and labour, and was spatially concentrated on the colonial administrative centres, notably Sydney. However, intensifying crisis tendencies within British capitalism during the declining phase of the first long wave, freed capital which was (partly) switched to the colonies, initiating pastoral expansion and the associated growth of commerce, encouraging, in turn, the further generalisation of capitalist relations of exchange and production. These changes in the nature of colonial accumulation were reflected, 'on the ground', in the creation of new port-cities and the extensive spread of pastoralism, as the colonies began to perfect their new role in the world economy and formed part of the overall 'solution' to the structural problems which beset British capitalism. Historically, these changes in economic and political relations between Britain and its colonies reinforced 'internal' changes in British forces of production, following the spread of mechanisation and rise of heavy industry sufficient to spark a long upswing in British capitalism and an explosive increase in international trade. These developments—in addition to the immediate and longer-term effects of the mid-century gold discoveries—encouraged large inflows of capital and free labour to Australia where development was constrained within limits imposed through international trading relations, managed by British merchant and financial capitalists and their colonial agents.

The consolidation of this second phase or stage of colonial accumulation entailed a degree of spatial reorganisation as the proliferation of small townships followed pastoral and mining expansion, and the capital port-cities grew and internally differentiated, reflecting the scale and concentration there of the commercial, financial and administrative functions tying the colonies into the capitalist world system. This pattern of international specialisation was further reinforced during the long swing down of British capitalism in the third quarter of the century. British capital was again switched to the colonies and tightly concentrated into the pastoral and public infrastructural sectors. Locally accumulated capital also fed through to the built environment, notably the housing sector; wider economic diversification was constrained by the competitive superiority and bulk of British exports, the priorities of British and colonial financial capital and the political and ideological controls tying Australia into the imperial system, all of which contributed to the making of the Australian ruling class. The physical construction of the built environment, in the context of hardening international specialisation, reflected and reinforced the spatial concentration and centralisation of capital and labour in the capital cities. Rapid suburbanisation, of an increasingly speculative nature, characterised growth in those cities during the 1870s and 1880s, as profitable alternatives for colonial accumulation disappeared in a (capitalist) world suffering a pronounced and general decline in average profit rates.

British investment in Australia was more than a short-term reaction to the build-up of idle capital at home. As Australia grew and prospered, markets expanded; Federation, by breaking down inter-colonial trading barriers, reinforced population growth, urban concentration, relatively high wages and improved communications. However, in reaction to increasingly severe competition from German and American industrial capital, the form of British investment in Australia began to change in the twentieth century in favour of direct investment in Australian industries. That is, with the demise of free trade internationally and the retreat to Empire of British capital, generally, from the late nineteenth century onwards, the latter increasingly maintained its dominance by setting up local branches or taking over Australian firms, in order to forestall or pre-empt the incursions of other foreign traders. In Castells's terms, dominance–dependence relations were increasingly constituted through the mode of industrial/financial rather than commercial, domination.

This is not to argue that one mode of domination totally replaced another—as a literal reading of Figure 3.1 would suggest. International trading relations continued to remain vital determining factors in Australian development, as they are today. Only a small proportion of British capitalists trading with Australia relocated production there; lower British wages, preferential tariffs within the Empire, the indebtedness of Australian governments to British moneylenders and the indirect coercive powers of the British state all limited the range and rate of economic diversification in Australia, especially in the manufacturing sector (Cochrane 1980, p. 43). Nevertheless, within these very real constraints, significant diversification and growth did occur, especially after the First World War, in mining, agriculture and manufacturing. The significant role of public infrastructural investment—for example, electrification for industrial and domestic uses—was increasingly directed towards supporting or facilitating Australian production in all sectors, but particularly in manufacturing, rather than (just) the flow of goods internationally. The fact that these developments were limited and uneven in effect is hardly surprising. Australia continued to remain dependent in crucial respects—for example, on high technology goods, foreign capital and the need to export traditional goods—though the particular form of dependence was changing in the manner suggested. Increasingly, foreign and local industrial capital (including the mining and agricultural sectors as well as manufacturing), rather than merchant capital, determined the directions of Australian development.

In the context of the third long downswing of capital accumulation in the capitalist centre, and within the constraints just noted, new manufacturing industries—notably, electrical goods, chemicals and automobiles—as well as established industries like steel and textiles, developed in Australia in the inter-war period, largely reflecting the interests and priorities of British capital. These industries were concentrated primarily in Sydney and Melbourne, close to markets, labour, government and transport, encouraging further de-velopment there and requiring the large-scale provision of urban infrastructure by the State governments. This was, in turn, largely financed by British loan capital. Conversely, heavy capital-intensive investment in the mining and agricultural sectors in order to maintain international competitiveness dis-placed rural labour, reinforcing the significant drift to the capital cities. Within those cities, industrial location tended to intensify pre-existing patterns of differentiation and segregation, while the rising use of cars and trucks facili-tated continuing suburbanisation. This emerging pattern of industrialisation was sharply checked during the Great Depression as the effects of crisis at the centre were transmitted to Australia by plummeting international primary-product prices and the halt in British loans, which, in turn, partly checked the rapid overall rate of metropolitan growth.

Economic recovery, culminating in the Second World War, signalled the final collapse of British hegemony in the world economy. Thereafter, Australian dependence on American (and later Japanese) trade and capital inflow rapidly intensified. Moreover, not only did the geographical source of dominance-dependence relations change—so, too, did their form. New in-dustries, in areas like chemicals and electronics, revolutionised production methods, reduced production costs and increased average profit rates; due to the huge capital and skill requirements necessary to research and develop these high technology products and methods, they were (quite literally) mo-nopolised by capitalists in the central economies. Consequently, other capitalists, especially those outside the centre, have become increasingly de-pendent on them for access to the technologies necessary to maintain competitiveness. In addition, foreign (direct) investment has been increas-ingly directed towards securing *control* over, rather than mere minority ownership of, key sectors of the Australian economy.

This gradual transformation to what might be termed 'the corporate stage of accumulation', has occurred in line with changes in the nature of the capitalist mode of production itself. Gibson and Horvath (1983) have intro-duced the term, 'submode of production', to capture these internal transformations in both the dominant conditions of exploitation of labour by capital and the form of competition between capitalists to appropriate profits. The chronic tendency towards the concentration and centralisation of capital had, by the 1930s, resulted in a significant though uneven degree of monopolisation within the boundaries of national economies constituting the capitalist world. The decisions—including the location decisions—of large capitalists were now significant factors in determining the distribution of capi-tal and labour over space, nationally and within fairly clearly defined regional boundaries. Nevertheless, with monopolisation of significant areas of the national economy, the seeds of breakdown in this familiar pattern of spatial organisation were sown. The internal organisation of monopolistic capitalist enterprises, where the division of labour is intense and hierarchically ordered, has led to the fragmentation of production over space in the form of multi-plant operations, and the separation and locational specialisation of the sales, financial and managerial functions as well. Some urban scholars have seen in this process the destruction of regions in the traditional sense. However, this process has only fully developed with the internationalisation of capitalist production in its current phase—that is, with the organisation of production and redivision of labour on a global scale through the institutional form of the transnational corporation. The spatial form assumed by these current developments in Australia is most obvious in the mining sector, where the 1970s resources boom had involved the channelling of hundreds of millions of dollars of foreign capital into previously remote areas of the continent. The growth of new mining towns has raised the phenomenon of the boom town, familiar elsewhere in the world (Markusen 1978). Foreign mining capital has also had an impact on existing townships, as in the case of Sale in the Gippsland region of Victoria, following the development of Bass Strait oil, and Portland in the south-west of the State, as a result of Alcoa building an aluminium smelter there. However, it is precisely in cases like these, where skilled labour (especially managerial), technology and inputs are often imported and profits are moved around the corporate group globally in order to avoid taxation, that the traditional claims pointing to the intra-regional growth effects of such activities are highly suspect. Questions concerning the local distributional effects of resource developments must also be faced, as the cost of and, therefore, access to housing and other services threaten to favour newcomers associated with the project over existing residents.

However, it is in a consideration of developments centred in the existing metropolitan areas that the most far-reaching and serious implications of the current stage of capital accumulation arise. The fragmentation and global coordination of production have resulted in the real threat of significant de-industrialisation in Australia. Increasingly mobile capital moving out of the local manufacturing sector—previously concentrated in the capital cities, especially Melbourne and Sydney—has raised the prospect of deep-seated and rising structural unemployment, on the one hand, and a reorganisation of the industry which does remain, in the direction of an enforced national specialisation, further de-skilling, increasing technological dependence and greater effective independence from state regulation, on the other. Recent developments in the international automobile industry, including the concept of 'the world car', illustrate this twin prospect. Continuing economic decline of the capital cities is likely to be reinforced by the indirect effects of the process on public policy. The Federal and, especially, State governments are increasingly constrained to redirect expenditure to 'productive' uses— that is, to activities and services which attract and facilitate foreign investment under the new global conditions for the valorisation of capital. Inevitably, this has led to a run-down of services elsewhere—to a decline in policies favouring national capitalists and petty bourgeoisie and a savage attack on 'the social wage', notably health, housing, education and social welfare. The other major destabilising effect of current global developments on Australian urbanisation follows from the tendency for foreign capital (and idle local capital) to switch into the built environment for both production and consumption, and out of the sphere of production into speculative real estate transactions, especially in response to falling average profit rates in a period of intensifying crisis. This general tendency lies behind the over-development of city centres, the gentrification of the inner suburbs and the speculative property price spiral in the upper-class suburbs of the (mainland) capital cities, all visible during the 1970s and 1980s.

Note

1   First published in L. Sandercock & M. Berry (1983), *Urban Political Economy: The Australian Case*, this is an extract from M. Berry's chapter 'The Australian city in history: Critique and renewal' (pp. 15–32) edited by Louise C. Johnson and then to the Deakin University style.

References

Amsden, S. (1979), 'Historians and the spatial imagination', *Radical History Review*, vol. 21, Fall.

Berry, M. (1983), 'Urbanisation and social change: Australia in the twentieth century', in S. Encel et al. (ed.), *Australian Society: Introductory Essays*, Longman Cheshire, Melbourne.

Castells, M. (1977), *The Urban Question*, Edward Arnold, London.

Cochrane, P. (1980), *Industrialisation and Dependence: Australia's Road to Economic Development*, University of Queensland Press, St. Lucia.

Connell, R. W. & Irving, T. H. (1980), *Class Structure in Australian History: Documents, Narrative and Argument*, Longman Cheshire, Melbourne.

Gibson, K. D. & Horvath, R. J. (1983), 'Aspects of a theory of transition within the capitalist mode of production', *Environment and Planning D: Society and Space*, vol. 1, pp. 121–38.

Giddens, P. (1979), *Central Problems in Social Theory*, Macmillan, London.

Gordon, D. (1978), 'Capitalist development and the history of American cities', in W. Tabb & L. Sawers (eds), *Marxism and the Metropolis*, Oxford University Press, New York.

Harvey, D. (1975), 'The geography of capitalist accumulation: A re-construction of the Marxian theory', *Antipode*, vol. 7, no. 2.

Harvey, D. (1978), 'The urban process under capitalism: A framework for analysis', *International Journal of Urban and Regional Research*, vol. 2, no. 1.

Hobsbawm, E. J. (1972), 'Karl Marx's contribution to historiography', in R. Blackburn (ed.), *Ideology in Social Science*, Fontana, Bungay, Suffolk.

Mandel, E. (1975), *Late Capitalism*, New Left Books, London.

Markusen, A. (1978), 'Class, rent and sectoral conflict: Uneven development in Western U. S. boomtowns', *Review of Radical Political Economics*, vol. 10, no. 3.

Mullins, P. (1981), 'Theoretical perspectives on Australian urbanisation: 1. Material components in the reproduction of Australian labour power', *Australian & New Zealand Journal of Sociology*, vol. 17, no. 1.

Stilwell, F. J. B. (1978), 'Competing analyses of the spatial aspects of capitalist development', *Review of Radical Political Economics*, vol. 10, no. 3.

Stilwell, F. J. B. (1980), *Economic Crisis, Cities and Regions*, Pergamon, Sydney.

Walker, R. (1978a), 'Two sources of uneven development under advanced capitalism: Spatial differentiation and capital mobility', *Review of Radical Political Economics*, vol. 10, no. 3.

Walker, R. (1978b), 'The transformation of urban structure in the nineteenth century and the beginnings of suburbanisation', in K. R. Cox (ed.), *Urbanisation and Conflict in Market Societies*, Maeroufa Press, Chicago.

Woodruff, W. (1973), 'The emergence of an international economy, 1700–1914', in C. M. Cipolla (ed.), *The Fontana Economic History of Europe*, vol. 4, part 2, Fontana/Collins, Glasgow.

Wright, E. O. (1978), *Class, Crisis and the State*, New Left Books, London.

Chapter 4 | The postmodern Australian city
Louise C. Johnson

If Australian settlements have been variously characterised as colonial, mercantile, industrial, suburban and corporate, the contemporary city presents a new set of possible labels. The period since the early 1970s has been described by many as heralding a different era of urban form and life. From this time, significant changes in the global economy—such as the diffusion of micro-electronics, greater capital mobility, the growth in the power and reach of the mass media, the rise of finance capital and new international and local divisions of labour—are seen as underpinning an economic and cultural revolution. The resulting *postmodern city* is the subject of this chapter.[1]

Postmodernism is a highly debated and difficult term to define. It has been used to describe an architectural style (Jencks 1986), an historical era characterised by major changes in the global social, spatial and cultural economy (Jameson 1984; Harvey 1989a; Soja 1989; Rose 1991) and a philosophical revolution involving a crisis and reconceptualisation of dominant social-scientific forms of representation (Owens 1983; Lyotard 1984; Soja 1989; Flax 1990; Nicholson 1990; Doherty & Graham 1992; Cosgrove & Domosh 1993; Smart 1993). This chapter will look in more detail at these various meanings of the term before considering its use in describing Western cities and its applicability to contemporary Australia. To do so I will explore whether the proposed Multifunction Polis (MFP) and the apparent increase in social and spatial polarisation in some Australian cities constitutes a shift to a postmodern urban era. From these examples, I conclude that there are indeed elements of the postmodern city in Australia, but that these components are not all present at one place, but are diffused across parts of cities and the continent. We may indeed be in a postmodern era, but whether we are living in postmodern cities remains unclear.

The postmodern city of style

In urban design, the International School of Modernist Architecture produced a global proliferation of remarkably similar steel and glass office towers, airport lounges, high-rise housing blocks and hotels (Giedion 1941; Frampton 1980; Relph 1987; Harvey 1989a). Such structures defy local conditions, heritage and the resident populace, elevate the architect to the status of hero and follow the dictums of the machine age. In contrast, for Charles Jencks, 'Post-Modern' architecture involves a 'double coding' of the modern with other styles drawn from the past, the local environment or vernacular tradition (Jencks 1978, 1981, 1986; Rose 1991). In addition, postmodern buildings are populist—in the dual sense of respecting and incorporating popular culture and local traditions into their design and involving the community in their creation. They are also playful, eclectic and alive with metaphor, ambiguity and asymmetry. In the postmodern building there is collage, collision, pastiche and humour and a veritable cacophany of styles (Jencks 1978, 1981; Jameson 1984; Calinescu 1987; Rose 1991; Wilson 1991; Ley 1993).

For the cultural theorist Frederic Jameson, an archetypical postmodern building is the Bonaventure Hotel in Los Angeles (described, however, by Jencks as 'High Modern'). Built by the architect/developer John Portman—whose other work includes various Hyatt Regency Hotels around the world—the Bonaventure is a popular place frequented by large numbers of people. However, it is not easily entered or exited, as doorways are not on the street or clearly demarcated. For Jameson, such a trait makes this a 'total space, a complete world, a kind of miniature city (constituting) a new and historically original hypercrowd' (Jameson 1984, p. 81). In this place, myriad escalators, elevators and mini-environments produce both a sense of motion and total disorientation—not unlike that produced in many large shopping centres (see Morris 1988a).

For another observer of Los Angeles, Mike Davis, this hotel also represents the darker side of contemporary life. For Davis, there has been a social polarisation accompanying the shift to global capitalism which has produced a need to fortify the citadels of capital and conspicuous consumption. The Bonaventure Hotel, with its mirror glass facade, elaborate security, obscure entrances and self-contained opulent worlds, thereby asserts its physical and social distance from the mass of child, racialised and immigrant labour on which the boom economy of Los Angeles rests (Davis 1988, 1990).

Surveying the same hotel, the geographer Edward Soja confirms its social and symbolic value:

> … the Bonaventure has become a concentrated representation of the restructured spatiality of the late capitalist city: fragmented and fragmenting, homogeneous and homogenizing, divertingly packaged yet curiously incomprehensible, seemingly open in presenting itself to view but constantly pressing to enclose, to compartmentalize, to circumscribe, to incarcerate … The Bonaventure both simulates the restructured landscape of Los Angeles and is simultaneously simulated by it. (Soja 1989, pp. 243–4)

In its design, symbolic meanings and look, the Bonaventure Hotel of Los Angeles is therefore seen by some as typifying postmodern style. In the social relations of its creation and operation, it is also read as an expression of contemporary social, economic and political life—of *postmodernism*.

Postmodernisation: The process of creating the postmodern city

Frederic Jameson typifies late capitalism (after Ernest Mandel 1975) in terms of multinational corporations operating a decentred, global communications network. Accompanying this new economic order is a different culture—the society of the media, an architecture of pastiche and the city of spectacle (Jameson 1983, 1984). The shift, then, is a total one, embracing economics as well as culture and society.

This economy has been described not only as postmodern, but also as post-industrial (Bell 1973; Allen 1988; Allen & Massey 1988), disorganised capitalism (Lash & Urry 1987; Urry 1988), post-Fordist (Piore & Sabel 1984; Cooke 1988; Murray 1988; Mathews 1989), New Times (Murray 1988; Hall & Jacques 1989; Hebdige 1988, 1989) and flexible accumulation (Harvey 1989a, 1989b; Scott 1988; Christopherson 1989; Storper & Walker 1989).

Though working in different countries, writers such as Alan Lipietz (1982), Michael Piore and Charles Sabel (1984), Allen Scott (1987, 1988), David Harvey (1989a), Philip Cooke (1988) and John Mathews (1989) see the globalisation of finance capital and an extension of microelectronic technology into a newly reorganised workplace—be it industrial or service—as the fundamental economic changes of the last twenty years. In such analyses, the period before 1970 is characterised by mass production within dedicated plant (in, for example, the car, whitegoods or textile industry) for and by unionised, relatively well-paid workers supported by a high level of state provided services. This era of Fordism came into crisis in the 1970s, to be gradually replaced by post-Fordism. In this new regime of accumulation, the assembly line is replaced by customised batch-production, worked by flexible, multi-skilled operatives creating goods for a highly differentiated market. The electronics which makes such production possible, also allows the physical separation of conceptualisation from execution and of the various stages of the production—across the city, country and the globe.

There is a great deal of ongoing debate about whether such changes are actually occurring and if production systems of the 1970s and 1990s across the Western world can be characterised in such a way (see Gertler 1988; Pollert 1988; Schoenberger 1989). Discussion also rages around the social and political consequences of this post-Fordist scenario (see, for example, Graham 1992). However, accepting for the moment that such economic and technological changes are occurring, what then are some of their spatial manifestations?

For those writing within the Fordist/post-Fordist literature—in Australia, Britain, Europe and North America—there have been the following manifestations.

- Deindustrialisation of some areas (of a city, a region, even countries) and the service-based redevelopment of others (such as 'sunbelts', 'silicon valleys', technolopolises) along very different organisational and technological lines. Such a deconcentration of population and production to rural or suburban locations forces competitive counter-strategies of redevelopment from the abandoned city (Harvey 1989a, 1989b; Zukin 1991).

- A differentiation of global cities into those housing the international headquarters of large manufacturing, financial and trading firms and accommodating the increasingly integrated producer services used by such corporations—such as those serving their legal, advertising and real estate needs—and lower-order cities which compete to support the command and control activities of international firms locally (Huxley & Berry 1990; Sassen 1991; Berry & Huxley 1992).

- Within these cities, the subsequent creation of new classes of workers, a shrinkage of the traditional middle class and a burgeoning unemployed group, all of whom congregate in particular precincts. The well-paid, technologically skilled, service worker occupies the desirable suburbs, inner-city apartments and regenerated historical areas (Castells 1989; Mingione 1991; Fainstein, Gordon & Harloe 1992). These are increasingly protected by elaborate surveillance systems and surrounded by physical markers and barriers (Davis 1990; Marcuse 1993). They, in turn, are served by the part-time, casualised workforce—often racialised and feminised—who, along with the unemployed, live contained in decaying urban spaces.

In Britain, Philip Cooke has taken such general observations and highlighted their local manifestations. Thus, he has compared the modern and postmodern in terms of economic regimes, State actions and spatial relations across British cities and regions. For him, modernisation—occurring from 1945 to 1975—was supported by an interventionist State, was evenly spread across the country and led to a convergence of income and employment variation between regions and groups. As a consequnce there was the creation of three emblematic socio-economic spaces which expressed the 'transient ascendancy' of the Labour voting class:

- older Victorian industrial areas which were rejuvenated and not just allowed to die as market imperatives would have dictated;

- new towns and development zones which were created as symbols and actual spaces of a regional and class egalitarianism; and

- the peripheral suburban and inner-city public housing schemes.

In contrast, postmodernisation involves an appeal to the market as the vital mediator of all social and economic relations, a rolling back of the welfare state, a weakening of established workplace solidarities and the elevation of the private over the public in the provision of cultural and social goods. In socio-spatial terms, these changes have been associated with growing regional and social disparities; a reorientation of production to customised output for niche markets; economic development in new areas of privatised consumption in, for example, the outer-London sunbelt; a growth in the insecurity of the labour market, with an expansion in the casualised, part-time and informal economy; and a concomitant expansion in the service class, especially those employed in banking, finance, insurance, business services and research and development (Cooke 1988, pp. 482–4).

The new era of flexible/disorganised/post-Fordist accumulation is therefore seen by a number of writers to have both revolutionised production and marketing as well as the specific urban economies in which they are placed. For many, what has also accompanied these changes have been new ways of experiencing and comprehending this society.

Postmodernity: The death of the meta-narrative and the unified self

In his analysis of the historical geography of Western cities, regions and states, Edward Soja connects economic to cultural and philosophical changes, focusing on the ways in which space and time have variously dominated interpretative frameworks (Soja 1989). Thus he delimits a number of phases in capitalist development. The third phase, dating from the 1920s, he sees as dominated by historicism. The preoccupation with the temporal (apparent in Marxism and the social sciences)—with progress, certainty and rationality—accompanying Fordism, changes in the late 1960s when capitalism undergoes its fourth modernisation to create a regime of flexible accumulation. For Soja, postmodernism—with its concern for the decentred subject, spatiality, contradiction and indeterminacy—is the appropriate way to apprehend this new phase of capitalist development.

Associated with analyses of the changing economic foundations of Western countries and their cities, then, there has been an alteration in the ways these societies have been represented and theorised. This, in part, has occurred as a result of the different experiences of living in postmodern cities, by reflections on the technologies suffusing them and from an inability of pre-existing bodies of philosophy to understand them.

Reflecting on this writing, on her own experiences of urban Britain and on contemporary film and literature, Elizabeth Wilson writes, in a way recalling those observing the Bonaventure Hotel in Los Angeles:

> In postmodernism the city becomes a labyrinth or a dream. Its chaos and senselessness mirror a loss of meaning in the world. At the same time, there may be an excess of meaning: the city becomes a split screen flickering with competing beliefs, cultures, and 'stories'. This play of unnerving contrasts is the essence of the 'postmodern' experience ... Everything is the same and nothing is quite real. (Wilson 1991, p. 136)

For Wilson, the contemporary city is a place of contradictions—between sameness and difference, excitement and fear, pleasure and danger—mediated by media and computer technologies which fragment its experience and representation. In such a place individuals become decentred and disoriented, yet also potentially free to experience the many possibilities now open to them. This is so particularly for women as they occupy a place where, though subject to forces impelling containment and regulation, they also have many more opportunities to offer resistance and realise desires. In the postmodern city, then, she sees many opportunities for self-expression, meaning and autonomy for women (Wilson 1989, 1991).

Reflections on the technology which has produced the flattened, everywhere-but-nowhere imminence of the city and the media image, has been critical to two other philosophers of the postmodern condition. Thus Jean Baudrillard has focused on the ways in which the new media technologies, their saturation coverage of the globe and ubiquity in the household and individual experiences, have effected the ways in which we apprehend the world (see Baudrillard 1989). In one effort to make sense of these changes, Baudrillard divided history since the Renaissance into three dominant 'orders of appearance'. The last of these, 'simulation', sees reality overtaken by its images and ruled by the language of systems technology and advertising (Baudrillard 1983). From such a communications invasion, emerges the primacy of the *simulacrum*, an image, a copy of something—be it a television picture of a war fatality, an exhibition home or a rainforest atrium in a corporate building—which has no original, no actual referent.

Considering the impact of computer technology, not on the media but on the sciences, universities and research practice, Jean Francois Lyotard concludes that knowledge, increasingly contained in data banks, is *the* commodity of the era and the main means by which power is achieved (Lyotard 1984, 1986). Further, such knowledge no longer comprises a series of universal certainties endorsed by the state but is more and more a limited story, an indeterminate fiction. He writes:

> Postmodern science—by concerning itself with such things as undecidables, the limits of precise control, conflicts characterized by incomplete information ... catastrophes, and pragmatic paradoxes—is theorizing its own evolution as discontinuous, catastrophic, non-rectifiable, and paradoxical ... It is producing not the known, but the unknown. (Lyotard 1984, p. 60)

As a consequence, 'the grand narrative has lost its credibility' (Lyotard 1984, p. 37), so that science, and other bodies of knowledge, no longer has legitimate means of unification and accreditation. Such a conclusion sends deep reverberations throughout the Western intellectual tradition which, since the Enlightenment, has built philosophical, scientific and moral certainties upon the ability of reason to triumph in the creation of overarching theories of the human condition.

If science has been so revealed, in the realms of history, Michel Foucault, through his inquiries into the minutiae of the everyday—rather than the great wars or political leaders—has concluded that historical subjects are created by the discourses and power relations in which they are engaged. Studies of the institutional practices and textural regulations which construct sexualities, the prisoner and the mental patient lead to a view of people, not as heroically individualised, but as historically and discursively constituted subjects (Foucault 1973, 1977, 1979).

This turn to the ways in which language, the media, power and discourses constitute people and their multiple identities, has become one of the focal points of postmodern inquiry. From it have arisen studies of the city as an array of texts—regulatory codes, signs and systems of meaning—which are inscribed on its various parts (bodies, buildings, events), as well as the city, as created by those with particular interests and powers (see, for example, Morris 1988a, 1988b, 1992; Huxley 1989a, 1989b; Johnson 1989, 1993; Game 1991; Tett & Wolfe 1991; Watson 1991; Duncan & Ley 1993; Freestone 1993; Grosz 1993).

The exposure of the quest for meta-narratives—theories of the whole of human society—as unrealistic, redundant and deceptive was forced not only by reflections on technology and the postmodern condition but also by those engaged in claiming spaces for marginalised groups.

Thus, for example, feminism exposed the partiality of much Western thought as women documented its patriarchal preoccupation with the experiences of men. Many feminists critiqued the ways in which philosophy, political theory and social science purported to be about the human condition, when in fact it was built upon unrecognised and unacknowledged masculine assumptions and prioritised male interests (see, for example, Pateman & Gross 1986; Gunew 1990). Within feminist thought there has been a further move away from seeing women as a unified group—defined by either biological or common social experiences of oppression (see Firestone 1979; Daly 1978; Rowland 1988)—towards a recognition that this discourse emanated primarily from white, middle-class, heterosexual, Anglo-American women. Such a feminism, while purporting to be universal, was itself partial (Gunew & Yeatman 1993). In addition, women of colour and from the Third World argued that such a feminism was not only the voice of the Anglo-West, but that, in constituting the unified white Western woman as its subject and norm, such work rendered them marginal, invisible and problematical (see hooks 1982, 1990; Amos & Parmar 1984; Awatere 1984; Huggins 1992). Not only was this politically unacceptable, but it denied notions of a postmodern subject who was diverse, fragmented and multiple in her experiences and oppressions. As Judith Butler wrote:

> ... the insistence upon the coherence and unity of the category of woman has effectively refused the multiplicity of cultural, social, and political intersections in which the concrete array of 'women' are constructed. (Butler 1990, p. 14)

In such a view, women as some sort of unified group do not exist except through the various discourses and power relations which construct them. Feminism itself is one such discourse and therefore it is inevitably intersected by others concerned with race, sexuality, ethnicity and so on. The deconstruction of a fixed identity—derived from liberatory politics—thereby meets the fragmented, discursively constituted, postmodern subject. How such subjects create and relate to the contemporary Australian city is the subject of the following pages.

Finding the postmodern city in Australia

The postmodern has been described above in three related ways: as an architectural style; as a process of global, national, regional and urban restructuring of political, technical, economic and social relations; and as a body of theory responding to and challenging earlier grand narratives. Even within such broad characterisations, some diversity has been exhibited, though this account has not dwelt on the many debates and disagreements which exist. I have also taken a stand to define what some would argue is not definable. For the very quest to delimit boundaries, to fix meanings of the postmodern and to test out the veracity of its characteristics could be viewed as a modernist project without legitimacy in this postmodern world.

However, in view of the pervasiveness of the postmodern in urban and regional studies, architecture and social theory —dare one suggest that it has become a dominant meta-narrative?—it would seem appropriate that some sort of empirical exploration of the term occur. What, then, could be examined in the Australian context?

From the preceding discussion, a number of common threads can be distilled which singly/together/in combination could constitute the/all/some parts of the Australian city as postmodern.

New architectural styles and practices

These include, the not wholly consistent notions of, double coding, pastiche, humour, metaphor and the vernacular in the form of buildings; a respect for and integration with the locality and the local population in their situation; but also elements of surveillance, security, fortification, fragmentation, disorientation and hyperspace in their occupation.

Do such stylisitic elements typify the newly rebuilt inner-city precincts of Sydney or Melbourne? Are the new fringe or affluent suburbs of Perth, the Gold Coast or Canberra increasingly walled and watched over by elaborate surveillance systems?

Situation in a decentred global network of hypermobile multinational capital

While a colony for most of its white history and then economically dependent on Britain, the United States and Japan—is the era of capital globalisation altering these relationships? Can the office boom of the late 1980s and coastal resort developments be related primarily to the globalisation of Japanese finance capital? And what of recessionary times? Could the indebtedness of the United States, England's European orientation and an inward-looking Japan, undermine the economic foundation of the postmodern era or city?

Location within a nation state dominated by a pro-market, noninterventionist strategy

Pointing to Thatcher's England and Reagan's United States, those critical of economic rationalism, the winding back of the welfare state and the extension of deregulation and private enterprise into previously public areas of concern, are key theorists of postmodernisation. However, with the passing of these regimes, are such anxieties still valid and are they applicable to Australia?

De-industrialisation and post-Fordist re-industrialisation

When examining the Australian economy and landscape as a whole, there is evidence of a decline in manufacturing, measured in terms of employment and investment levels (though export performance points in another direction). There is also some indication within manufacturing and in newer industries, such as aerospace and biotechnology, of new ways of structuring organisations—with, for example, flatter management structures, more team rather than assembly-line production—and in marketing, away from mass production towards batch manufacture for niche markets. But how significant are such developments, are they really new and how are they impacting on our cities?

Rise of the service sector and the service class

Supposedly accompanying post-Fordist re-industrialisation is the burgeoning of new classes of workers engaged in areas like business services, tourism and recreation. Can the growth of places like the Gold Coast and Cairns be seen in these terms? What of these workers within older cities in Australia?

Social and spatial polarisation

This is argued to be occurring on a global scale—as the First World is more and more differentiated from the Third World—but also regionally within countries and cities, in the creation of sunbelts (like the Queensland coast), high-technology precincts (around major research universities), sunrise-industry agglomerations (such as biotechnology around the Monash Medical Centre, telecommunications and business services in Sydney).

Polarisation is supposedly also occurring within cities as the burgeoning service class (secure, well paid, skilled, male? white? Anglo?) living in fortified suburbs or inner-city apartments, is served by an increasingly disorganised working class (of men and part-time women?) and a burgeoning underclass of unemployed and the waged poor of casualised and underemployed (migrant and female?). The latter groups are confined to the outer suburbs or poorly serviced and stigmatised regions of the city, such as Melbourne's and Sydney's west (but see Powell 1993).

Heightened competition between cities for hypermobile capital and command and control functions

This is variously expressed in desperate battles for corporate headquarters and high-level services, the urban spectacle (such as a trade fair, the Olympics, the Grand Prix), the differentiation of cities symbolically from each other (for example, Melbourne as the sports capital, Adelaide as an arts city, Sydney as the international city), state subsidisation of urban redevelopment (such as Darling Harbour in Sydney [Huxley & Kerkin 1988], Brisbane's expo site, Docklands in Melbourne) and the revalorisation of derelict buildings (seen in inner-city gentrification and warehouse conversions).

Different experiences in and modes of representation of the city

Is living in Australian cities in the 1990s different from the 1960s and 1970s? Are such differences related to new technologies, industries, social polarisation, the growth in the service sector, architectural styles and practices?

How are such experiences and the cities themselves being researched, fictionalised and theorised? Are there new ways of studying the city emerging from postmodern theorising?

It is not possible to consider all of these elements of the postmodern city, though other writers in this book do take up some dimensions (such as Berry, Devlin Glass, McLoughlin, Huxley, Spearritt and Lozanovska). Space will permit a brief examination of only two dimensions here:
- what looks to be a clear attempt to create a postmodern city in Australia—the Multifunction Polis; and
- changes in the economic structure of our cities and their greater social polarisation.

The Multifunction Polis: A postmodern city?

In January 1987 a proposal was first raised by the Japanese Minister for Trade with Australia's Minister for Industry, Technology and Commerce for a city of the future to be built on Australian soil. With Australian interest declared, *A Multifunctionpolis Scheme for the 21st Century: Basic Concept* was developed by Japan's powerful Ministry of International Trade and Industry (MITI) (Leisure Division) (1987). In this document, a 'Pacific Era' of economic and social dominance was prefigured. So too was the need for greater cooperation between Japan and Australia to remake the city into a place where new social and technological trends could achieve their maximum economic and human potential. In this city of the 'Fifth Stage' (the preceding ones being typified by the increasing separation of home from work and leisure), there will be a combination of the 'Biosphere' (managed in terms of conservation and sustainability), the 'Technopolis' (advanced industrial and service industries located in innovative buildings and served by state-of-the-art infrastructure) and the 'Renaissance' city (where domestic life, social care, work and leisure are integrated) (See Figure 4.1). In this new city there would be an emphasis on international exchange (of people and ideas), mutual stimulation through 'high-tech' and 'high-touch' industries, technical innovation and a need, in the light of an ageing population, to expand educational opportunities for adults. Specifically, the MITI document points to biotechnology (in relation to agriculture and livestock), new materials and rare metals (such as polymers, ceramics, titanium, aluminium and fibre-reinforced alloys) and computer software, as new industries which could be developed in the city. In addition are the 'high-touch' industries encompassing convention services and those creating a 'resort life'. These new industries would be served by a research-based medical and health care system, an education and training system, information systems and a high-technology transport system (MITI 1987).

The MITI document recognises the two imperatives driving this idea as Japan's massive trade surplus and highly valued currency. Other writers have added to this list, noting the falling quality of life for Japanese workers, failure of internal 'technopolises' to achieve success or to deal with internal problems (of high-cost land and regional and interdepartmental rivalries), the move to counter emergent trade blocs in Europe and North America with one focused on the Pacific and expansionist capital keen to secure Australian material and human resources (Rimmer 1989; Huxley 1990; McCormack 1990a; Morris-Suzuki 1990; Berry & Huxley 1992). In short, the MFP is seen by both proponents and critics as representing a new phase in the global expansion of Japanese capitalism.

Why Australia was chosen as an appropriate site for such a city was related to its political stability, high educational standards, skilled labour, solid infrastructure, time-zone similarity and relative proximity to Japan and, critically, its abundant land and natural resources. For those enthusiastic businesses and politicians in Australia (the only ones to have a place on the various

Figure 4.1   Multifunction Polis aims

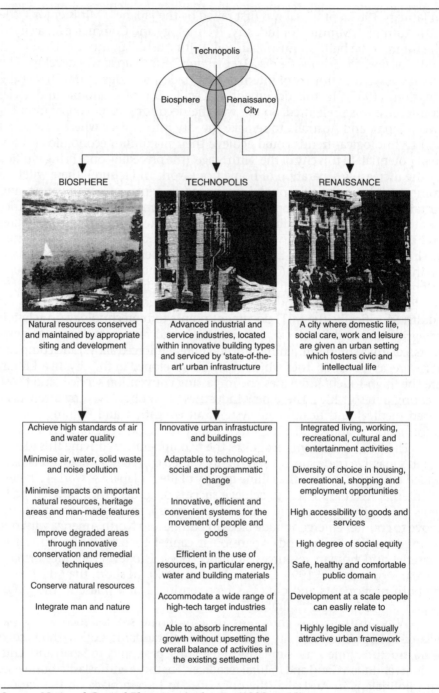

planning bodies overseeing its development), the idea offered the chance to access Japanese capital, technology and markets, to achieve closer integration with one of the economic powerhouses of the globe and to stimulate the restructuring of the Australian economy away from manufacturing towards high-technology, sunrise industries (Brown 1989; Jones 1989; McCormack 1990a).

If such was the initial plan, subsequent developments were embroiled in regional and national politics and dogged by controversy. The main issues were social—whether the MFP was desirable and would form an elitist and racially exclusive enclave with massive internal social divisions; political— the disparity in power of the two main players, whether it was to be a multi-lateral or bilateral undertaking, in the different visions of the project held by Japan and Australia, the secret and non-collaborative nature of its evolution; economic—the degree of public support for basically a private, profit-oriented project, its cost and economic feasibility; and whether it would be environmentally sustainable (Juddery 1989; Self 1989; McCormack 1990b; Mover & Sugimoto 1990; Nittim 1990; Sugimoto 1990; ACOSS 1991; Inkster 1991; MFP Working Group 1991).

Finally to be accommodated on 3000 hectares of reclaimed land—at the moment a swamp and industrial waste dump—in Adelaide's suburb of Gilman, this city of 20–100 000 inhabitants (80 per cent of whom would be foreigners) still does not have any more than a name, a site, a large injection of public money and a mountain of consultant and other reports to prove its existence. For, as more than one critic has observed, the MFP is a moving, amorphous phantom, a set of contradictory ideas rather than a thing (Lonsdale 1991).

But it is not just in its elusive and contradictory nature that the MFP constitutes a postmodern city. In its economic and social structure, it is envisaged, by both its promoters and critics, as expicitly postmodern. Some highlight its focus on leisure and the environment, others point to its sponsorship by large multinational companies (including the ANZ Bank, Qantas, CRA, the AMP Society, IBM, and AWA as well as eighty-six large Japanese companies involved in finance, construction and engineering, on the various management boards), emphasis on high-technology industries, networks, privatised space and its highly skilled, technocratic, expatriate and temporary service class. In such a place, the role of education is critical but also international in scope, utilitarian and commercial in purpose and computer-driven in its formulation and acquisition. The MFP thereby heralds a society created at the behest of and held together by global, interactive, information technology—in ways theorised earlier by Baudrillard and Lyotard (see also Lonsdale 1991).

In its very non-existence, in its debated, vague and contradictory image and in its planned form, operation and structure, the Multifunction Polis does seem to be an Australian postmodern city. However, the MFP may never actually be built, as Japanese and Australian business interests withdraw in the 1990s. However, it is also perhaps too easy to single out an intention for such scrutiny. For plans are often futuristic, with their ultimate realities often bearing little resemblance to the initial proposals or to existing Australian cities. What, then, of present cities and their social structures? Do they evince some of the characteristics of class composition and social polarisation noted to be part of the postmodern city?

Social and spatial polarisation of the Australian city

Despite the ease of asking the question: Are Australian cities becoming more socially polarised?, it is an extraordinarily difficult one to answer. Ever since there have been observers of the Australian city, the existence of social extremes of wealth and poverty have been noted (see, for example, J. S. James [1877] 1969; Henderson, Harcourt & Harper 1970; Hollingworth 1983). It could well be argued that Australian cities were far more socially and spatially divided in the nineteenth century than in the late twentieth century, with historians of both Sydney and Melbourne drawing convincing portraits of the horrors and opulence of these two cities, especially in the aftermath of the 1893 depression (see, for example, Davison 1978; Kelly 1978; Johnson 1984; McCalman 1984; Davidson 1986; Fitzgerald 1987).

However, the argument about the existence or otherwise of the postmodern city focuses primarily on the period between 1970 and 1990. While there is clearly a need for a longer historical perspective on this question, in pursuing the issue of social and spatial changes in contemporary Australian cities, it is first necessary to retrace the argument and establish whether there has been a notable decline in manufacturing and an increase in the service sector. From a consideration of occupational and employment data from 1970 to 1990 (see Australian Bureau of Statistics 1971, 1986, 1991–2) it is apparent that there has been a massive decline in the proportion of the workforce in manufacturing (from 23.2 to 14.5 per cent, though the fall in number was only from 1.2 to 1.1 million). Correspondingly there was a disproportionate rise in those engaged in various services, especially in community services (from 10.8 to 18.9 per cent), finance, property and business services (6.9 to 11.5 per cent) and in recreation, hospitality and personal services (from 5.1 to 8.1 per cent). The other significant shift, usually not mentioned by those theorising about the shift to a post-Fordist economy, has been the expansion in the number of women in the workforce, especially in those service occupations which have shown the most growth.

In the occupational structure, the proportion of those involved in trades, process working and labouring declined (from 32 to 28 per cent) while there were notable rises in professional and technical work (from 10 to 15.5 per cent) and for those in the clerical (16 to 18.6 per cent), sales (8 to 9 per cent), service, sport and recreation areas (7.3 to 9.7 per cent). This is work which is more likely to be part time and perhaps without good career paths.

From such figures, it does indeed seem that the Australian economy is moving away from industry towards services. Whether these changes have been associated with a greater social polarisation in Australian cities has been investigated in a number of recent works. Thus, for example, in Adelaide, two studies have concluded that certain areas within the city have sustained high levels of unemployment and these also accommodate populations with low incomes, have high numbers of single-parent households, a falling proportion of women in the paid workforce and high levels of public housing. Those areas of the city which are the more affluent have not been as hard-hit by these changes (Forster 1986; Baum & Hassan 1993). For Sydney, Frank Stilwell similarly observes, using the 1981 and 1986 censuses, how those households residing in high-status, high-income areas have continued to enjoy high material standards of living while low-status areas have been most affected by structural change and have suffered a further lowering of their living standards (Stilwell 1989). Evidence from the Institute of Family Studies Living Standards survey, conducted over 1992, also found significant increases in income inequality over 1986 to 1991 in both Sydney and Melbourne. The average incomes of families with dependent children were 21 per cent more unequally distributed across local government areas in 1991 by comparison with 1986 in Melbourne; the corresponding figure was 18 per cent for Sydney (Burbidge 1994).

A study by Stilwell and Hardwick on Sydney's local government areas (LGAs) used the 1966 census and court crime statistics to generate an array of indices of social wellbeing (Stilwell & Hardwick 1973). Recalculating some of these measures from the 1986 census (Australian Bureau of Statistics Census 1986)—the percentage of employers in the workforce, the proportion of people with tertiary education and the percentage of people in each LGA born in non-English speaking countries— tends to confirm the view that social divergence between these areas has increased. Thus, for example, in 1966, there were only two local government areas, Woollahra and Ku-ring-gai, which had more than 8 per cent of its population registered as employers. In 1986, there were four suburbs: Ku-ring-gai, Hunters Hill, Mosman and Baulkham Hills. At the same time, the number of areas with less than 3 per cent of employers rose from nine to eleven—all of them in the far west of the city. Similarly, in education levels, Ku-ring-gai was the only LGA with more than 14 per cent of its population with a tertiary qualification in 1966, but in 1986 it was joined by Woollahra, Willoughby, Mosman, North Sydney, Lane Cove and Leichhardt, registering both a growth in the number of people with such qualifications and their spread through the upper north shore of the city as well as the gentrification of (parts of) inner Sydney. On the measure of ethnicity there was a massive increase across the whole city, though the growth in the range from 1966 (from 5.2 per cent to 27.9 per cent) to 1986 (8.5 per cent to 42.2 per cent) points to greater levels of non-English-speaking concentration in certain parts of the city, especially in the west and some inner city municipalities. Such figures confirm the applicability of Soja's observations on Los Angeles as a racially and ethnically polarised city (Soja 1989) to Sydney, but they do not lead to any further conclusions about racial division and tension. On the contrary, research to date suggests the opposite occurs in areas of Sydney with high levels of non-English-speaking migrants (see Dunn 1993).

Sydney, Adelaide and Melbourne, therefore, are cities where social and spatial divisions have intensified since the 1960s and 1970s. This is particularly so when the economic indicators of employment, education level and unemployment are used. The ethnic diversity of Sydney has also increased though, on this scale and at this level of generality, little more can be said. It is extremely difficult to speculate on the consequences of such polarisation in the absence of detailed empirical studies. These cities are variously situated in a national economy moving from manufacturing to services, an economy which has also seen a massive growth in women's employment in the service sector. Such patterns are variegated in their regional manifestations, with places like the Gold Coast and Canberra having far larger service sectors than Sydney, Geelong or Whyalla. Which is the most postmodern as a consequence? Further, what of the contradiction of *empirically testing* a notion like a postmodern social order, when such techniques continue the illusion of universal truth which has been successfully challenged by postmodern philosophy? The difficulty of measurement, regional disparities and the ongoing slippery nature of key terms makes it difficult to make clear-cut conclusions from this inquiry.

Conclusion

In general, though, it seems that some elements of the postmodern city can be discerned in Australian cities. There has indeed been a decline in manufacturing and a disproportionate rise in the service sector nationally. Further, when Sydney, Adelaide and Melbourne are examined, it seems that, in economic terms, they are more socially polarised now than in the 1960s. Whether such patterns can then be explained in the terms offered by analysts of the post-Fordist economy is an enormous analytical and political question. If, together with the fanciful heterotopia of the Multifunction Polis, such trends constitute the burgeoning postmodern Australian urban experience, remains, like the terms themselves, a contestable proposition.

Note

1   I wish to acknowledge the helpful comments of Kate Kerkin on an earlier draft of this chapter.

References

Australian Bureau of Statistics (1986), *Census of Population and Housing*, AGPS, Canberra.

Australian Bureau of Statistics (1971, 1986, 1991–92), *Australian Yearbook*, AGPS, Canberra.

Australian Council of Social Service (ACOSS) (1991), *Social Justice and the MFP: The ACOSS Response to the MFP-Adelaide Proposal*, ACOSS Paper no. 45, ACOSS, Surry Hills.

Allen, J. (1988), 'Towards a post-industrial economy?', in J. Allen & D. Massey (eds), *Restructuring Britain. The Economy in Question*, Sage & The Open University, London.

Allen, J. & Massey, D. (eds) (1988), *Restructuring Britain. The Economy in Question*, Sage & The Open University, London.

Amos, V. & Parmar, P. (1984), 'Challenging imperial feminism', *Feminist Review*, vol. 17, pp. 3–20.

Awatere, D. (1984), *Maori Sovereignty*, Broadsheet, Auckland.

Baudrillard, J. (1983), 'The ecstasy of communication', in H. Foster (ed.), *Postmodern Culture*, Pluto, London, pp. 126–34.

Baudrillard, J. (1989), *America*, Verso, London.

Baum, S. & Hassan, R. (1993), 'Economic restructuring and spatial equity: A case of Adelaide', *Australian and New Zealand Journal of Sociology*, vol. 29, no. 2, pp. 151–72.

Bell, D. (1973), *The Coming of the Post-Industrial Society*, Penguin, Harmondsworth.

Berry, M. & Huxley, M. (1992), 'Big build: Property capital, the state and urban change in Australia', *International Journal of Urban and Regional Research*, vol. 16, no. 1, pp. 35–59.

Brown, R. (1989), 'A DITAC view of the Multi-Function Polis proposal', *Australian Planner*, vol. 27, no. 2, pp. 8–13.

Brownmiller, S. (1975), *Against our Will. Men, Women and Rape*, Penguin, Harmondsworth.

Burbidge, A. (1994), Preliminary calculations from the Australian Institute of Family Studies Family Living Standards Survey, n.p.

Butler, J. (1990), *Gender Trouble. Feminism and the Subversion of Identity*, Routledge, New York & London.

Calinescu, M. (1987), *Five Faces of Modernity*, Duke University Press, Durham, NC.

Castells, M. (1989), *The Informational City*, Basil Blackwell, Oxford.

Christopherson, S. (1989), 'Flexibility in the US service economy and the emerging spatial division of labour', *Transactions of the Institute of British Geographers*, new series, vol. 14, pp. 131–43.

Chodorow, N. (1979), 'Mothering, male dominance and capitalism', in Z. Eisenstein (ed.), *Capitalist Patriarchy and the Case for Socialist Feminism*, Monthly Review Press, New York & London.

Cooke, P. (1988), 'Modernity, postmodernity and the city', *Theory, Culture and Society*, vol. 5, pp. 475–92.

Cosgrove, D. & Domosh, M. (1993), 'Author and authority: Writing the new cultural geography', in J. Duncan & D. Ley (eds), *Place/Culture/Representation*, Routledge, London & New York.

Daly, M. (1978), *Gyn/Ecology. The Metaethics of Radical Feminism*, Beacon Press, Boston.

Davidson, J. (ed.) (1986), *The Sydney–Melbourne Book*, Allen & Unwin, Sydney.

Davis, M. (1988), 'Urban renaissance and the spirit of postmodernism', in E. A. Kaplan (ed.), *Postmodernism and its Discontents. Theories, Practices*, Verso, London, pp. 79–87.

Davis, M. (1990), *City of Quartz: Excavating the Future in Los Angeles*, Vintage, London.

Davison, G. (1978), *The Rise and Fall of Marvellous Melbourne*, Melbourne University Press, Carlton.

Doherty, J. & Graham, E. (1992), *Postmodernism and the Social Sciences*, Macmillan, Houndmills.

Duncan, J. & Ley, D. (eds)(1993), *Place/Culture/Representation*, Routledge, London & New York.

Dunn, K. M. (1993), 'The Vietnamese concentration in Cabramatta: Site of avoidance and deprivation, or island of adjustment and participation?', *Australian Geographical Studies*, vol. 31, no. 2, pp. 228–45.

Fainstein, S., Gordon, I. & Harloe, M. (1992), *Divided Cities*, Basil Blackwell, Oxford.

Firestone, S. (1979), *The Dialectics of Sex: The Case for Feminist Revolution*, The Women's Press, London.

Fitzgerald, S. (1987), *Rising Damp: Sydney 1870–90*, Oxford University Press, Melbourne.

Flax, J. (1990), *Thinking Fragments. Psychoanalysis, Feminism and Postmodernism in the Contemporary West*, University of California Press, Berkeley.

Forster, C. (1986), 'Economic restructuring, urban policy and patterns of deprivation in Adelaide', *Australian Planner*, vol. 24, no. 1, pp. 6–10.

Frampton, K. (1980), *Modern Architecture: A Critical History*, Thames & Hudson, London.

Freestone, R. (1993), 'Heritage, urban planning and the postmodern city', *Australian Geographer*, vol. 24, no. 1, pp. 17–24.

Foucault, M. (1973), *The Birth of the Clinic: An Archaeology of Medical Perception*, Pantheon Books, New York.

Foucault, M. (1977), *Discipline and Punish. The Birth of the Prison*, Penguin, Harmondsworth.

Foucault, M. (1979), *The History of Sexuality. Volume 1, An Introduction*, Penguin, Harmondsworth.

Game, A. (1991), *Undoing the Social. Towards a Deconstructive Sociology*, University of Toronto Press, Toronto.

Gertler, M. S. (1988), 'The limits to flexibility: Comments on the post-Fordist vision of production and its geography', *Transactions*, Institute of British Geographers, new series, vol. 13, pp. 419–32.

Giedion, S. (1941), *Space, Time and Architecture: The Growth of a New Tradition*, Harvard University Press, Cambridge, Mass.

Graham, J. (1992), 'Post-Fordism as politics: The political consequences of narratives on the left', *Environment and Planning D: Society and Space*, vol. 10, pp. 393–410.

Grosz, E. (1992), 'Bodies/cities', *Sexuality and Space*, Princeton Papers on Architecture, vol. 1, Princeton University Press, Princeton, pp. 241–53.

Gunew, S. (ed.) (1990), *Feminist Knowledge. Critique and Construct*, Routledge, London & New York.

Gunew, S. & Yeatman, A. (eds) (1993), *Feminism and the Politics of Difference*, Allen & Unwin, Sydney.

Hall, S. & Jacques, M. (eds) (1989), *New Times: The Changing Face of Politics in the 1990s*, Lawrence & Wishart, London.

Harvey, D. (1989a), *The Condition of Postmodernity*, Basil Blackwell, Oxford.

Harvey, D. (1989b), 'Flexible accumulation through urbanization: Reflections on "postmodernism" in the American city', in D. Harvey, *The Urban Experience*, Basil Blackwell, Oxford.

Hebdige, D. (1988), *Hiding in the Light. On Images and Things*, Routledge, London & New York

Hebdige, D. (1989), 'New times: After the masses', *Marxism Today*, January, pp. 48–53.

hooks, B. (1982), *Ain't I a Woman? Black Women and Feminism*, Pluto, London.

hooks, B. (1990), *Yearning: Race, Gender and Cultural, Politics*, South End Press, Boston.

Henderson, R. F., Harcourt, A. & Harper, R. J. A. (1970), *People in Poverty*, Longman Cheshire, Melbourne.

Hollingworth, P. (1983), *Australians in Poverty*, Nelson, Melbourne.

Huggins, J. (1992), 'A contemporary Aboriginal women's relationship to the white women's movment', in Deakin University HUA 813 *A Woman's Place in Australia*, Deakin University, Geelong, pp. 16–26.

Huxley, M. (1989a), 'Reading planning politically', *Arena*, vol. 89, pp. 116–32.

Huxley, M. (1989b), 'Massey, Foucault and the Melbourne Metropolitan Planning Scheme', *Environment and Planning A*, vol. 21, no. 5, pp. 659–61.

Huxley, M. (1990), 'The Multifuction Polis: The issues', *Arena*, vol. 90, pp. 43–9.

Huxley, M. & Berry, M. (1990), 'Capital's cities: Polarizing social life', in P. James (ed.), *Technocratic Dreaming*, Left Book Club, Melbourne, pp. 115–28.

Huxley, M. & Kerkin, K. (1988), 'What price the bicentennial? A political economy of Darling Harbour', *Transition*, Spring, pp. 57–64.

Inkster, I. (1991), *The Clever City. Japan, Australia and the Multifunction Polis*, Sydney University Press in association with Oxford University Press, Sydney

James, J. S. (1969 [1877]), *The Vagabond Papers*, edited by M. Cannon, Melbourne University Press, Melbourne.

Jameson, F. (1983), 'Postmodernism and consumer society', in H. Foster (ed.), *Postmodern Culture*, Pluto, London.

Jameson, F. (1984), 'The cultural logic of late capitalism', *New Left Review*, vol. 146, pp. 53–92.

Jencks, C. (1978), 'Why post-modernism?', in 'Post-modern history', *Architectural Design*, vol. 48, no. 1, pp. 11–26, 43–58.

Jencks, C. (1981), *The Language of Post-Modern Architecture*, 3rd edn, Academy Editions, London.

Jencks, C. (1986), 'What is Post-Modernism?', Paper given to Post-Modernism Conference, Northwestern University, Evanston, Illinois.

Johnson, L. (1984), *Gaslight Sydney*, Allen & Unwin, Sydney.

Johnson, L. (1989), 'Geography, planning and gender: An extended review of a planning textbook and its peers', *New Zealand Geographer*, vol. 45, no. 2, pp. 85–91.

Johnson, L. (1993), 'Text-ured brick: Speculations on the cultural production of domestic space', *Australian Geographical Studies*, vol. 31, no. 2, pp. 201–13.

Jones, Hon. B. (1989), 'Introduction', *Australian Planner*, vol. 27, no. 2, pp. 6–7.

Juddery, B. (1989), 'Multifunction polis: Science fiction or reality?', *Australian Business*, 21 June, pp. 58–61.

Kelly, M. (ed.) (1978), *Nineteenth Century Sydney: Essays in Urban History*, Sydney University Press, Sydney.

Lash, S. & Urry, J. (1987), *The End of Organized Capitalism*, Polity Press, Cambridge.

Ley, D. (1993), 'Co-operative housing as a moral landscape: Re-examining the "Postmodern city"', in J. Duncan & D. Ley (eds), *Place/Culture/Representation*, Routledge, London & New York, pp. 128–48.

Lipietz, A. (1982), 'Towards global Fordism', *New Left Review*, vol. 132, pp. 33–48.

Lonsdale, M. (1991), 'A heterotopian polis?', *Arena*, vol. 95, pp. 85–99.

Lyotard, J-F. (1984), *The Post-Modern Condition: A Report on Knowledge*, Manchester University Press, Manchester

Lyotard, J-F. (1986), 'Defining the post-modern', *ICA Documents*, vols 4–5, Institute of Contemporary Arts, London.

Mandel, E. (1975), *Late Capitalism*, Verso, London.

Marcuse, P. (1993), 'What's so new about divided cities?', *International Journal of Urban and Regional Research*, vol. 17, no. 3, pp. 355–65.

Mathews, J. (1989), *Tools of Change. New Technologies and the Democratisation of Work*, Pluto, Leichhardt.

McCalman, J. (1984), *Struggletown: Public and Private Life in Richmond, 1900–1965*, Melbourne University Press, Carlton.

McCormack, G. (1990a), 'And shall the Multifunction Polis be built?', in P. James (ed.), *Technocratic Dreaming*, Left Book Club, Melbourne.

McCormack, G. (1990b), 'Multifunction polis: A change of tack', *Australian Society*, May, pp. 8–9.

MFP Working Group (1991), 'The multifunction polis: A city of contradictions', Submission to the Community Consultation Panel, n.p.

Mingione, E. (1991), *Fragmented Societies: A Sociology of Economic Life Beyond the Market Paradigm*, Blackwell, Oxford.

Ministry of International Trade and Industry (1987), *A Multifunctionpolis Scheme for the 21st Century: Basic Concept*, MITI, Tokyo.

Morris, M. (1988a), 'Things to do with shopping centres', in S. Sheridan (ed.), *Grafts. Feminist Cultural Criticism*, Verso, London, pp. 193–225.

Morris, M. (1988b), 'At Henry Parkes Motel', *Cultural Studies*, vol. 2, no. 1, pp. 1–48.

Morris, M. (1992), *Great Moments in Social Climbing. King Kong and the Human Fly*, Local Consumption Publications, Sydney.

Morris-Suzuki, T. (1990), 'Futuristic cities: Japanese models for Australian followers', *Arena*, vol. 91, pp. 78–91.

Mover, R. E. & Sugimoto, Y. (1990), *The MFP Debate: A Background Reader*, La Trobe University, Bundoora.

Murray, R. (1988), 'Life after Henry (Ford)', *Marxism Today*, October, pp. 8–13.

National Capital Planning Authority (1990), *MFP An Urban Development Concept: A Report to the Department of Industry, Technology and Commerce*, Highland Press, Canberra.

Nicholson, L. J. (ed.) (1990), *Feminism/Postmodernism*, Routledge, New York & London.

Nittim, Z. (1990), 'Of feminist space and Multi-Function Polis', *Refractory Girl*, vol. 35, May, pp. 44–7.

Owens, C. (1983), 'The discourse of others: Feminism and postmodernism', in H. Foster (ed.), *Postmodern Culture*, Pluto, London.

Pateman, C. & Gross, E. (1986), *Feminist Challenges, Social and Political Theory*, Allen & Unwin, Sydney.

Piore, M. & Sabel, C. (1984), *The Second Industrial Divide: Possibilities for Prosperity*, Basic Books, New York.

Pollert, A. (1988), 'Dismantling flexibility', *Capital and Class*, vol. 34, pp. 42–75.

Powell, D. (1993), *Out West: Perceptions of Sydney's Western Suburbs*, Allen & Unwin, St Leonards.

Relph, E. (1987), *The Modern Urban Landscape*, Croom Helm, London.

Rimmer, P. (1989), 'Putting Multi-Function Polis into context: MITI's search for a place in the sun', *Australian Planner*, vol. 27, no. 2, pp. 15–21.

Rose, M. (1991), *The Post-Modern and the Post-Industrial: A Critical Analysis*, Cambridge University Press, Cambridge.

Rowland, R. (1988), *Woman Herself: A Transdisciplinary Perspective on Women's Identity*, Oxford University Press, Melbourne.

Sassen, S. (1990), 'Economic restructuring and the American city', *Annual Review of Sociology*, vol. 16, pp. 465–90.

Sassen, S. (1991), *The Global City*, Princeton University Press, Princeton.

Schoenberger, E. (1989), 'Thinking about flexibility: A response to Gertler', *Transactions,* Institute of British Geographers, new series, vol. 14, pp. 98–108.

Scott, A. J. (1987), 'The semi-conductor industry in South-East Asia: Organization, location and the international division of labor', *Regional Studies*, vol. 21, pp. 146–60.

Scott, A. J. (1988), 'Flexible production systems and regional development', *International Journal of Urban and Regional Research*, vol. 12, no. 2, pp. 171–85.

Self, P. (1989), 'International lessons for an Australian new city', *Australian Planner*, vol. 27, no. 2, pp. 28–32.

Smart, B. (1993), *Postmodernity*, Routledge, London & New York.

Soja, E. (1989), *Postmodern Geographies: The Reassertion of Space in Critical Social Theory*, Verso, London.

Stilwell, F. (1989), 'Structural change and spatial equity in Sydney', *Urban Policy and Research*, vol. 7, no. 1, pp. 3–14.

Stilwell, F. J. B. & Hardwick, J. M. (1973), 'Social inequality in Australian cities', *The Australian Quarterly*, vol. 45, no. 4, pp. 18–36.

Storper, M. & Walker, R. (1989), *The Capitalist Imperative*, Basil Blackwell, Oxford.

Sugimoto, Y. (1990), 'High-tech cities for lonely technocrats', *Arena*, vol. 90, pp. 50–7.

Tett, A. & Wolfe, J. (1991), 'Discourse analysis and city plans', *Journal of Planning Education and Research*, vol. 10, no. 3, pp. 195–200.

Urry, J. (1988), 'Disorganised capitalism', *Marxism Today*, October, pp. 30–3.

Watson, S. (1991), 'Gilding the smokestacks: The new symbolic representations of deindustrialised regions', *Environment and Planning D: Society and Space*, vol. 9, no. 1, pp. 59–70.

Wilson, E. (1989), *Hallucinations. Life in the Post-Modern City*, Radius, London.

Wilson, E. (1991), *The Sphinx in the City. Urban Life, The Control of Disorder and Women*, Virago, London.

Zukin, S. (1991), *Landscapes of Power. From Detroit to Disney World*, University of California Press, Berkeley.

Chapter 5 | Special places: The nature of urban space and its significance

Nick Beattie and Guenter Lehmann

Urban space is one of the most obvious of urban elements. It is shared by all who visit, live or work in the city, irrespective of social, economic, or cultural differences. Aside from the physical elements of the city—the buildings, the topography etc.—it is the most noticeable and the most commonly experienced feature of the city. Urban spaces are where we find most of those experiences that we consider make urban life stimulating, exciting and worthwhile. Urban space, in short, is where 'urban life' takes place.

Yet, how urban space is defined, made, used or perceived is not at all a simple or clear matter. Is it, for instance, simply the 'left-over' or unbuilt space between and around buildings, or is it that which is consciously 'made'? Can it be considered to have its own form and identity, like interior space? When is it a public and when a private space? Who, if anyone, should decide how it is to be used? And what about 'unintended' uses for or in it?

What is understood as 'urban space', how it is used, and how it relates to the public life of the city depend on many factors, especially the cultural setting. Edward T. Hall, an anthropologist, coined the term *proxemics* to refer to the different ways people of various cultures see and use space (Hall 1966). It is important to remember this because we frequently take for granted the various ways we use and define space as personal rather than 'taught' differences.

Thus, various issues related to 'urban space' begin to emerge: designed versus 'leftover' space, cultural determinants of the perception and use of space, public versus private space, intended versus actual uses, and so on. And, finally, what, if anything, makes some urban spaces special?

In order to be called 'urban space'—rather than regarded as just negative or left-over space—space is generally considered to have some geometric and aesthetic characteristics. In this view, space is formed perceptually by the relationship between physical objects and an observer who perceives it. This relationship is primarily determined by sight, but when architectural space is considered, the relationship can also be affected by touch, hearing and smell. Architectural space is a purposeful environment that is delimited by three planes: floor, wall, ceiling. We may regard exterior space as 'architectural space without a roof', thus making the remaining two planes—floor and wall—all the more important (Ashihara 1972). An excellent example of an urban space as 'architecture without a roof' is the Piazza del Campo in Siena, Italy (Figure 5.1): it has a distinct shape, a varied floor and a unified enclosure or wall.

Figure 5.1   Urban space as 'architecture without a roof': Piazza del Campo in Siena

Source: Taylor (1981, p. 52)

However, the notion of 'outdoor space as room' relies heavily on a particular—and traditional—conception of space: that of an entity which has form and identity (Peterson 1980). We can recognise this conception in a famous eighteenth-century map of Rome drawn by Giambattista Nolli (Figure 5.2). It displays the spaces between buildings as volumetric entities, treated—and presumed to be formed—like the interior spaces with which they are linked inextricably:

> ... the inside spaces [become] an extension and completion of the experiences of the street, and at the same time extend their influence outward, molding the character, and in some cases the actual form, of the exterior spaces before them. (Bacon 1992, p. 161)

This traditional conception of space has been largely abandoned by both theory and practice in recent times. Principal architectural theory—shaped by the tenets of the so-called 'Modern Movement'—tends to emphasise space as continuous and fluid, and popular building practice favours the free-standing building—especially evident in the Australian city with the detached house on its 'quarter-acre' block. Both treat buildings as isolated objects instead of parts of the larger 'fabric' of streets, squares and viable open space. Thus, 'urban space' is rarely thought of in terms of a volumetric entity having identifiable shape, specific properties, or connections with other spaces.

Figure 5.2 Detail of Nolli's 1748 map of Rome

Note the remarkable moulding of the open space in front of S. Ignazio by the curved walls of the surrounding buildings, extending the spatial forms of the church interior.

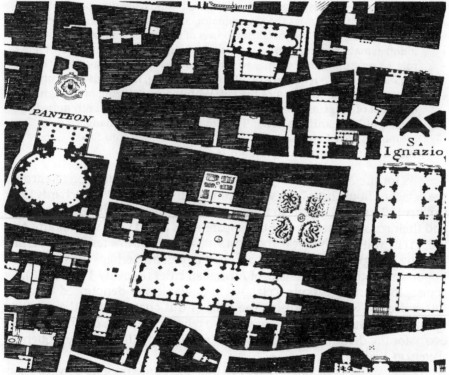

Source: Bacon (1992, p.161)

The failure to consider and exploit the potentially rich relationship between built form and its surrounding spaces has made much of the urban space in our cities banal and unvarying. Moreover, by dismissing differentiation and making everywhere seem the same, forming hierarchies of spaces and imageable spatial arrangements has also been inhibited. These are important since they help define public, semi-public and private domains in the city. Consequently, the prevailing space conception has blurred the important distinction between public and private realms (Peterson 1980). This is considered the greatest loss related to the disregard of the traditional conception of space because cities must be able to support and enrich these two realms of urban life and provide all kinds of spaces for the needs of both. At the same time cities must clearly delineate the public, semi-public and private spaces within, yet preferably keep them proximate. (It has often been said that the ideal in this respect would be to be able to step from a secluded garden straight into a busy street.)

How did all this happen? Besides the acceptance of the idea of the 'isolated object' and the abandonment of urban space as established by the cities of the past, there are a number of other, historic developments which contributed to this state of affairs. Kostof sees it this way:

> The slow demise started more than a century ago ... As progress spread, the piazza died. Newspapers first, and then radio and television, preempted the role of the piazza as the disseminator, and maker, of news. Modern water systems killed the socializing power of the public fountain. A revolution in mass marketing and consumption drained the piazza of its pivotal role in economic life. Crime, which once had been a desecration of *communitas* and so required a ritual public cleansing, now spirited its consequences to the seclusion of the jail. With the neutralizing or outright dismissal of kings, and the laicization of culture, power and faith muted their public manifestations. The royal monument made way for monumentalized abstractions: Louis le Grand turned into Liberty, and then a holed hulk by Henry Moore. (Kostof 1992, p. 181)

As for the Australian city, the reasons for the prevailing preference for the detached house have been well documented (Stretton 1989; Richards 1990; Collins 1993; etc.). They are as much cultural as they are said to be economic, and their consequences are all too apparent. As a bird's eye view of any Australian city will quickly reveal, the most visible result is a low residential density forming an expansive repetitive pattern. It represents perhaps the single most important spatial characteristic of Australian cities (Kemeny 1983, p. 18). Of course, low density is both acclaimed as desirable and denounced as wasteful—a dispute which is outside the aims of this chapter—but the resulting spatial sensibility has meant that we have relinquished the 'distinctions necessary for the definition of place, which requires specificity and uniqueness' (Peterson 1980, p. 99).

One would conclude, therefore, that the contemporary city, or especially the low-density suburb, with its grid street pattern has ostensibly lost the capacity to provide either indelible urban spaces or special places. But is that inescapably the case? This brings us to the first point about special places.

Historically, special places were identified with public spaces in urban settlements; in fact, one could say that human settlement and 'special place' were initially synonymous. The forerunners of permanent human settlements, that is, cities, were sanctuaries and meeting places for rituals (Mumford 1991, p. 16). Thus, as ceremonial centres, they were special places in the best sense of the word. This tradition of gathering and equating special places with public spaces is quite visible in the history of public space in the city. From the very beginning urban settlements have had open spaces that were used for communal gatherings, be they for spiritual reasons, to trade goods or services, or to discuss common affairs. But even in the early history of cities, in the ancient Near East more than three thousand years ago, we find the emerging separation of functions by physically separating the market square from the temple square, as the latter was walled off to emphasise the special nature of this space:

> If we think of the pre-historic urban gathering space, which had many uses, as the prototype that still survives in simple communities everywhere, then we begin to acknowledge how great an act of invention the walling-off of a temple square was. The separation tells us, as it told the residents of Babylon, 'Here something special is going on'. (Crouch 1981, p. 7)

Throughout history we can see the provision of open spaces for specific public activities which—combined with the traditional spatial conception of urban space as an identifiable entity—produced numerous memorable squares and special places, such as the Piazza San Marco in Venice, the Piazza Navona in Rome, the Place Vendôme in Paris, and the already mentioned Piazza del Campo in Siena. Now, it is obviously unfair to judge urban spaces in the Australian city against comparably sized European squares, let alone the celebrated ones. They were created in very different times from our own, often have been built over hundreds of years and have a very rich history. Yet, as we neither have the rich urban history nor make much use of the particular spatial conception but have a seemingly formless, horizontal and repetitive organisation of space, such comparison can at least ask: What special places could we possibly have in our cities and suburbs? How, then, do we make or find meaningful places in our cities?

First, we have to accept that we can hardly expect the vivid, impressive and even dramatic places like the classic European squares, as desirable and as perfect as we may regard them, but may have to look occasionally for meaning in seemingly unremarkable streets or spaces; to find, enjoy and occupy places mentally, so to speak. This possibility is suggested by research that implies that spatial arrangement (a cognitive aspect) is more important than visual organisation (a perceptual aspect) in forming our image of 'places' (Canter 1977, p. 77).

We may consider the more personal meaningful places as 'special places'. Any human settlement will have places that have special meaning to someone and which, therefore, could arguably be called 'special places'. However, such a definition is too broad to be useful and obscures the very notion of 'place' as something special. After all, 'place' itself denotes more than merely location; it implies 'identity', a certain 'atmosphere' or distinct qualities, even if we cannot always articulate any of them easily (Dovey 1991, p. 34). Despite this lack of clarity, the importance of 'place' has received much attention in recent years; it is frequently discussed under the topics of 'sense of place',

'place and placelessness' and so on. This is because of the renewed recognition that a stable and imageable structure of the environment—or place—is important to the sense of identification and the emotional security of city dwellers (Lynch 1960). This image is supported by meaningful personal places. However, to be useful for our understanding of the role of special places in the city, meaning must transcend individual significance and touch society. In other words, 'special places' in the city belong to the public realm, if not always physically in the sense of public spaces, then in the realm of institutions that represent cultural values.

Hence, we can discover a number of possible examples: there are linear street spaces, parks and other open spaces, definite as well as ill-defined 'territories', school yards, arcades, verandas and even backyards. Street spaces can become special, memorable, not only because of some communal activity centred around the street (like shopping) but also by some unique features (such as, a view to a local landmark) or unifying feature (such as trees or a tramline). We all consider places, in themselves perhaps quite unprepossessing, to encapsulate the experience of a district or a city when seen in a particular sequence (the Sunday drive?) and therefore to be shown to visitors. So it may sometimes be a pattern which unifies a series of spatial impressions—including shapes, colours, textures, signs, light—into a cohesive sense of place. In such a 'surprising way seemingly ordinary and unremarkable street places play a powerful role in one's memory of a place and, by extension, one's sense of place' (Oliver 1981, p. 58).

We may also find, for instance, that the commonplace single-family home can provide the interplay of the public and private realms— or community and privacy—we expect of our cities, albeit on a smaller scale. The spatial arrangement between public street and private door, the siting, landscaping and stylistic elements all clearly describe the subdivision: public, semi-public, private (Craig 1986, p. 24). The front garden is the important transitional space: its lawn and flower beds obey the external, or public, order of the streets while the private domain remains implied; the front garden is an object of appreciation for the public while attempting to exhibit private feelings (pride, pretence etc.). Fences follow reasons of appearance and conformity rather than privacy—in other words, the specialness of the front garden is its visual importance over functional uses. The physical evidence of the various domains will be the presence of the veranda or porch; its socialising aspects are well understood and highly regarded in several new urban developments.

And backyards are the most significant spaces which are private in conceptualisation and use, yet have enormous appeal and cultural value; private space, indoor or out, is highly valued in Australia. The preference for big houses on big blocks of land is a vestige of the reaction of newcomers fleeing the overcrowded slums of Europe to a land of abundant space and sunshine (Collins 1993, p. 10). The space around the suburban house—even though often poorly or not at all designed— can be the simplest source of light and air as well as a barrier to sight and sound, and the free-standing house allows the closest relation of inside spaces with the greatest variety of outdoor spaces (Stretton 1989, p. 14). Studies have supported the claim that, consequently, the backyard has become a special place indeed: the prime location for recreation for Australians (Halkett 1976, p. 126).

It becomes apparent that the special places in the Australian city are increasingly in the private domain. This trend of moving traditional street and open space functions into the private sphere has altered significantly the identification with and control of previously collective urban spaces. In some countries undergoing similar changes, new 'centres' often refer to what they have replaced by name in an attempt to rekindle associations: the French new town of Evry outside Paris calls its centre the 'Agora'—the term for the ancient Greek city space; and Columbus, Indiana, in the United States calls its central retail mall 'The Commons'—the collective urban meeting space of the early American city. This may conceal, but does not change, the fact that our social interactions have 'eased into a set of privatized public places unique to our time, including the atrium, theme parks, shopping malls, and those "festival marketplaces" made [so] popular in the United States' (Kostof 1992, p. 185). The spatially dispersed landscape of detached houses has become dominated by a succession of private realms—special or not—and makes the experiences of traditional special, and public, places—and the city centre itself—increasingly rare. The public places unique to our time are becoming more and more privatised (Kostof 1992). Whether they will ever become unique 'special places' or will need to be balanced by the more traditional special places, only time will tell.

A desired balance between public and private space is still reflected in most cities' land-use plans and their provision for public and private uses. Individual blocks for private settings are interspersed with the public areas: streets, reservations for parks, schools and shopping. But intentions of a plan can be modified by use or by appearance: a weed-filled open space will not seem very public even if so indicated in a plan and, conversely, private property may be regarded as visual common space (Craig 1986, p. 22).

Not only do intentions regarding public and private use of space often have unexpected outcomes but there is also a degree of unpredictability about the things that people do in urban open space. In fact people seldom seem to be doing what they are expected to do and it is the unexpected that is most interesting.

To put this in a more systematic way, if one is to observe urban spaces, behaviours, activities and responses, it is unlikely that there will be a neat one-to-one relationship of human and physical phenomena. For instance, even though there are many urban spaces that are used precisely as one would expect, those spaces will also be used for something else. It is equally common to find that the unintended use dominates; streets are used as marketplaces or for car racing (Lygon Street, Melbourne), town squares are used for skateboarding (Melbourne City Square) or purely for circulation from one place to another, and some parks are not used at all.

This is interesting and important. Furthermore, what are the implications of a good fit or a lack of fit between environment and the activities and behaviours that take place? The following section intends to establish that:

- urban space is created for specific purposes;
- irrespective of the purpose for which urban space is designed, people will respond on a number of levels and the behavioural responses influence decisions about what they will and will not do; and
- the behavioural responses are as important as the purpose that was intended for the urban space.

It might be worthwhile thinking about how urban space comes into being at this time in history. There is no doubt that land has a considerable monetary value which is determined by its potential to generate income. Thus, a piece of land in an urban area will potentially earn income through its ability to accommodate development and to attract rent from people who wish to occupy a particular location. They want either to operate a business or to live in a particular location because of its accessibility, its proximity to other locations in the urban area with which the occupier might want to be associated, because of the negative or positive externalities generated by adjacent locations, or the symbolic or prestige value and so on. Many of these factors are complex, some are interdependent but they all have an effect on the cost of land. In creating urban open space, the potential for land to attract income in the normal manner is reduced or forgone.

As one would therefore expect, open space does not generally come into being as the result of whim or accident. However, within the boundaries of urban areas, a large quantity of open space remains in agricultural use or has been agricultural and is now not used at all. The amount of unbuilt land varies from one city to another but it is most likely to be the largest amount of open space in the urban area (Neutze 1977). The next largest quantity of open space is owned by public bodies (government at various levels, utility providers etc.) who have a responsibility to provide infrastructure in the form of roads, power and water reticulation, communication, waste disposal etc. The other major space is provided for recreation in the form of parks and playing fields and originally relates to notions of health (Cranz 1991, p. 118). Of course, some playing fields, no matter what their ownership, provide revenue and prestige as well as supporting a recreation and health function.

In addition, open space is often required to be donated to local government by developers of urban land. This is usually in the form of recreation or public open space, but in business districts it is often required for public access, shopping arcades, public squares or other forms of pedestrian-dominated space. These requirements are embodied in town planning regulations or in development controls and guidelines. Here again the requirement for urban space to be donated would not be imposed lightly and one must accept that the planning authority expects the urban space to provide some advantage to the citizens using the space. The expected advantage might be in the form of recreation opportunities, symbolic value—as in a civic square or in the form of a vista—or visual relief from the pattern of urban development.

Apart from the economic and utilitarian significance of urban space mentioned above, the open spaces and streets of a city are the medium through which a city is known—in the same way as people get to know a building by moving from room to room, gaining an understanding of the opportunities and experiences it has to offer. To gain this understanding, people are constantly observing and responding to the city and its spaces, forming opinions and constructs and evaluating and making decisions that affect the things that they do and where they do them.

Of the various responses and behaviours that people exhibit in urban space, there are a few that are of interest to us at this time. One of the things that people are constantly doing is gathering useful information about their surroundings. Hershberger explains in simple terms that people extract meaning from the people and objects in their surroundings at two levels. At the level of what he calls 'representational meaning', people identify and classify objects according to form, scale, colour, material etc. At the level of 'responsive meaning', people react emotionally, evaluate reflectively and decide what to do and how to behave (Hershberger 1974, p. 147).

Part of that information is retained as a means of getting to know the spatial structure of the city through exploring the urban spaces, and expanding constructs of the layout through assimilating the visual information that is available. This is an essential part of 'wayfinding' and it is well established by Lynch (1960) that in this mode of response people are attuned to a number of elements of the environment: paths, nodes, edges, districts and landmarks. Armed with knowledge of these elements of urban structure, people are able to navigate. Thus we can assume that if those elements are not present, people will be dissatisfied and will have to expend an additional amount of attention on 'wayfinding' and will have less in reserve for the other things that may need to be done. Pocock and Hudson (1978) provide a useful discussion of Lynch's theory and add a discussion about how the pragmatics of wayfinding are expanded to include appraisals of the symbolic values of some significant places that have an identity beyond the memorable qualities of navigational aids. They begin to explore the theoretical framework of the concept of special places that has already been introduced in this chapter. Canter (1977) devotes a whole book to developing that theory. He concludes that a combination of the physical attributes of a place, the activities that it accommodates and the conceptions the people hold of the place contribute to its significance. It is evident that the conceptions are by far the most important and necessary ingredient without which the place will not have special qualities and significance. Many authors have connected the concept of place with concepts of territoriality that have a powerful influence on the way people behave and on the differences in behaviour close to home and far from home. Here we can read the word 'home' in its conventional sense and also as referring to any other place with which a person has a territorial connection.

In addition, it is probably not surprising that people are sufficiently sensitive to so-called 'incivilities' in the urban environment (vandalism, loitering, litter, dilapidation, vacant building etc.) that they are able to associate these indicators with perceived crime rates and feelings of safety and permanence (Perkins, Meeks & Taylor 1992). Similarly, Brantingham and Brantingham (1993) have shown that people use information gathered from the urban environment in selecting the place to commit a crime.

Without going any further into the complexities of human behaviour, it will be useful to look briefly at a way of putting together behaviour, conceptions, function, expectation and space in what has been termed a 'behaviour setting' by Roger Barker (1968). Barker's work includes much that is important to the behavioural scientist but the part that is pertinent to the study of urban space can be introduced with a few simple observations. For instance, allow yourself to fill in as much detail as you can about the activities and behaviours that go with the words 'football match'. Clearly there is not only one football code and there are many levels at which the game is played, however, most Victorians would think about Australian Rules, the particular patterns of play on the field, the arrangement of the spectators, the time of day and the season, the clothing worn by the various groups of people, the food and drink consumed, the time of arrival, the activities and behaviours to be observed before and after the game, and a host of other details. People from other parts of Australia or the world would arrive at other equally consistent images of the complexities of behaviour, activity and response associated with their own brand of football.

The same degree of uniformity and definition would be associated with many other kinds of urban space usage even though the pattern would not, at first glance, be as clearly identifiable. Take, for example, the thing called 'shopping' that is also very common but is apparently not as formally constituted as a football match. Firstly, it does not take place in as specific an environment as a football stadium or ground, nor does it have defined starting and finishing times—or does it? If you try to fill in the same kinds of detail as mentioned for a football match above, it will once again be found that there is a lot that can be identified as being regularly associated with the event. Examine the following analysis.

Football	Shopping
• stadium or field	• shopping centre or street
• patterns of play on the field	• patterns of purchasing activity
• arrangement of the spectators	• window shoppers and socialisers
• Saturday afternoon	• business hours and peak times
• winter	• seasonal variations such as Christmas
• clothing with club colours	• street and business clothes
• football fans, casual observers	• shoppers, workers, bus catchers
• beer, pies and sauce	• food courts, coffee
• activities before and after the game	• parking, trams, preparations, bank

Having carried out a great deal of work on this phenomenon, Barker has identified a number of parameters that are constant and important in the successful combination of events and physical surroundings (behaviour settings). You will be able to identify most of them in the informal analysis of 'football' and 'shopping' above. The parameters are as follows:

- There will be one or more behaviours and activities that will always be present in a particular behaviour setting.
- There will be a degree of correspondence between the physical setting and the activity patterns.
- There will be distinctive starting and finishing times.
- Certain roles will be filled each time a particular behaviour setting occurs. The identity of the role players will change but the role will always be filled.
- Roles fit into a hierarchy according to their ability to influence the proper running of the event.
- There will be forces, mechanisms or procedures to facilitate the correct behaviours and activities and to discourage disruptive behaviours; people who behave inappropriately will be subject to social sanctions; particular equipment or 'props' will be available to reinforce the correct activities; the will of the majority ensures that the correct order of proceedings is observed and so forth.
- There will be an optimum number of people required to make the event successful.

It is evident that at times and in many places people, and especially planners and developers, have lost sight of the relationship between behaviour and environment as discussed above. Cities and their residents have suffered as a result. An interesting and perhaps not very uncommon example of this loss of contact with what people do in urban space is described by Holston (1989, p. 105) in an analysis of Brasilia—the contemporary capital of Brazil built from scratch. He describes how new residents in Brasilia are disappointed and frustrated by the physical attributes of the planned city which they see as not having any of the attributes of city life as they know it. They complain that Brasilia has no streets and no street corners and it is revealed that these two elements of the traditional city have a specific physical configuration in the minds of the citizens and are instrumental in the social life of a city and the means of communication with other members of their community. In fact it is evident that without the expected configuration of street and street corner, a sense of community does not develop.

Continuing the shopping example introduced above, we can examine the changes that have occurred in retailing trade and shopping facilities. The changes can be briefly explained in this way. In the nineteenth century when consumer behaviour and retail distribution were different to what they are today, shopping facilities were divided into two groups: the market for consumables and high street shopping for durables (Davis 1966, p. 251). Davis explains that marketing was seen as a chore and was, wherever possible, left to servants. It was customary to do it frequently and only immediate requirements were satisfied. Shopping was more pleasurable and was done in a leisurely fashion accompanied by socialising with other shoppers, and with shopkeepers who were a mine of news and gossip, and usually included a meal or tea with friends. The shopping trip may or may not have included a purchase and one concludes that the actual shopping was not as important as the trip.

Gayler (1984) presents a picture of how that nineteenth-century pattern of retailing changes through the first half of the twentieth century. The change is characterised by the growth of fewer, larger shops and the clustering of shops into shopping precincts and zones, the emergence of the stand-alone shopping centre, and the development of a hierarchy of shopping centres at regional, local and neighbourhood levels. The trend continued with the development of even larger shopping centres—centres which specialise in particular types of merchandise and centres which specialise in particular forms of retailing such as the factory outlets on the periphery of major cities or even between large cities, but so far only common in the United States.

The development has moved through a period when shopping in the supermarket was reduced to the bare essentials. Consumption was facilitated by placing all goods on display so that consumers could efficiently and quickly complete their purchases without contact with other human beings and in surroundings that did not entice them to stay any longer than was necessary. Instead, contending with shopping trolleys, children and car parking, really only added to the drudgery without any pleasurable experiences to dilute or disguise it. The birth of the supermarket was largely to blame for reducing the act of shopping to the drudgery of collecting essentials and the pain of paying for them, whereas in an earlier time frequent shopping trips to the 'high street' were part of an elaborate ritual of social communication with shopkeepers and other shoppers.

Since then developers have moved towards recognising the full range of things that happen in conjunction with shopping and a lot more recreational opportunities are combined with retail zones in an attempt to entice people to visit more often, stay for longer, feel comfortable taking children and spouses with them, and generally see it as a pleasurable experience rather than as a chore. This may not be altogether noticeable to the general shopper but it is evident when making comparisons between the shopping centres built up to, say, the end of the 1970s and those built and planned more recently. Perhaps the first to make a virtue of shopping as partly recreation was the Festival Market at Sydney's Darling Harbour.

It can be assumed that developers are motivated to provide the added amenity of public access urban space associated with shopping precincts as a result of their recognition or understanding of the behaviour of the people who come to visit the shopping precincts. The behaviours accompany the activity of shopping and are seen to be an important component of the things that shoppers do.

A study by the Department of Environment, Housing and Community Development (1978) showed quite clearly the subtle mixture of leisure and shopping in trips to the Westpoint Shopping Centre in Blacktown in New South Wales. Here, then, may be the development of the twenty-first century special places to replace the piazzas of old.

References

Ashihara, Y. (1972), *Exterior Design in Architecture,* Van Nostrand Reinhold, New York.

Bacon, E. (1992), *Design of Cities,* rev. edn, Thames & Hudson, London.

Barker, R. G. (1968), *Ecological Psychology: Concepts and Methods for Studying the Environment of Human Behaviour,* Stanford University Press, Stanford, Cal.

Brantingham, P. L. & Brantingham, P. J. (1993), 'Nodes paths and edges: Considerations on the complexity of crime and the physical environment', *Journal of Environmental Psychology,* no. 13, pp. 3–28.

Canter, D. (1977), *The Psychology of Place,* Architectural Press, London.

Collins, T. (1993), *Living for the City—Urban Australia: Crisis or Challenge,* ABC Books, Sydney.

Craig, L. (1986), 'Suburbs', *Design Quarterly,* no. 132, pp. 3–31.

Cranz, G. (1991), 'Four models of municipal park design', in S. Wrede & W. Adams (eds), *Denatured Vision,* Museum of Modern Art, New York.

Crouch, D. P. (1981), 'The Historical Development of Urban Open Spaces', in L. Taylor (ed.), *Urban Open Spaces,* Academy Editions, London.

Davis, D. (1966), *A History of Shopping,* Routledge & Kegan Paul, London.

Department of Environment, Housing and Community Development (1978), *The Shopping Centre as a Community Leisure Resource,* AGPS, Canberra.

Dovey, K. (1991), 'Melbourne Docklands and the sense of place', *Picking Winners: Melbourne's Urban Development Game,* Social Justice Coalition, Melbourne.

Gayler, H. J. (1984), *Retail Innovation in Britain: The Problem of Out-of-Town Shopping Development,* Geo Books, Norwich.

Halkett, I. (1976), *The Quarter-acre Block,* Australian Institute of Urban Studies, Canberra.

Hall, E.T. (1966), *The Hidden Dimension,* Doubleday, Garden City, NY.

Hershberger, R. G. (1974), 'Predicting the meaning of architecture', in J. Lang et al. (eds), *Designing for Human Behaviour,* Dowden, Hutchenson & Ross, Stroudsberg, Penn.

Holston, J. (1989), *The Modernist City,* University of Chicago Press, Chicago.

Kemeny, J. (1983), 'The privatised city: Critical studies in Australian housing and urban structure', Occasional paper, Centre for Urban and Regional Studies, University of Birmingham, Birmingham.

Kostof, S. (1992), *The City Assembled: The Elements of Urban Form Through History*, Thames & Hudson, London.

Lynch, K. (1960), *The Image of the City*, Massachusetts Institute of Technology Press, Cambridge, Mass.

Mumford, L. (1991), *The City in History: Its Origins, its Transformations and its Aspects,* (first published 1961), Penguin, Harmondsworth.

Neutze, M. (1977), *Urban Development in Australia,* Allen & Unwin, Sydney.

Oliver, R. (1981), 'Images of special places', in L. Taylor (ed.), *Urban Open Spaces*, Academy Editions, London.

Perkins, D. D., Meeks, J. W. & Taylor, R. B. (1992), 'The physical environment of street blocks and resident perceptions of crime and disorder: Implications for theory and measurement', *Journal of Environmental Psychology,* no. 12, pp. 21–34.

Peterson, S. (1980), 'Space and anti-space', *Harvard Architectural Review*, vol.1, Massachusetts Institute of Technology Press, Cambridge, Mass.

Pocock, D. & Hudson, R. (1978), *Images of the Urban Environment,* Macmillan, London.

Richards, L. (1990), *Nobody's Home: Dreams and Realities in a New Suburb*, Oxford University Press, South Melbourne.

Stretton, H. (1989), *Ideas for Australian Cities*, 3rd edn, Transit Australia Publishing, Sydney.

Taylor, L. (ed.) (1981), *Urban Open Spaces*, Academy Editions, London.

Chapter 6 | **The political city**[1]
J. Brian McLoughlin

This chapter draws out some of the main conclusions to emerge from Part 1.
Preceding chapters have considered various important aspects of the development of the Australian city from the point of view of history, political
economy, architecture, postmodernity and so on. This is not an unrealistic
attempt to pull all that together in a summary, but rather to offer a broad
viewpoint which emphasises the political aspects of urban development.

When I say 'political' I do not wish readers to think only or even primarily of the main organised parties which contest elections, instead I want to
draw attention to the major social groupings and forces which can be shown
to be influential. I am, therefore, thinking of such social formations as the
various 'fractions' of capital, of community organisations and 'social movements', of the state and its bureaucracies and professions, of the political
parties and the law — and much else. I am concerned in particular to estimate
the relative strength of each of these groupings and how 'frameworks of power'
(Clegg 1989) have changed over time—growing, declining, periodic, temporary or enduring as the case may be—in the ceaseless ebb and flow of the
social construction of the built form. My evidence comes largely from Melbourne since the end of the Second World War; a fuller account is to be found
in McLoughlin (1992) and in O'Connor (1993).

Before we tackle the task in more local detail, it is vital to look at the
wider context. For it is now a truism to observe that it is impossible to understand regions, towns and localities without working through the ways in which
far wider forces have been at work in shaping their societies and spaces. It is
useful to consider, in turn, Australia in the global context, Melbourne's changing position in Australia and then to move on to the ways in which various
social 'agencies' have been shaping the social and spatial arrangements within
the metropolitan region.

Australia in its global context

Australia began as a set of British colonies and their role was typical of white-settler 'dependent development' for at least a century, if not longer. Their role within the wider system of the British Empire was to provide primary produce—wool and wheat at first and latterly coal and other minerals—to be remitted, on highly advantageous terms, to Britain. The other side of the coin was that the colonies provided opportunities for the export of surplus capital from Britain, either in the form of material goods (railway engines, textile machinery) or in the form of investment capital through the banking system run from London. This relationship goes a long way to explaining the pattern of settlement being dominated by a small number of port cities, each to become the capital city of an Australian State.

This form of 'core–periphery' dependence was to persist until the Second World War; after this a number of changes began to exert profound influence on Australia (since 1901 a 'Commonwealth' of the British Empire). First, world trade, at least in the capitalist West, came more and more under the influence of the United States, and that country became an increasingly important source of investment capital and cultural hegemony. Secondly, Australia, although retaining an important primary-producer/exporter role, deliberately set about building a manufacturing industry, concentrated on consumer goods, by way of substituting for imports. Though Sydney and Adelaide were important loci for this industrialisation of Australia, it was Melbourne that played the dominant role, and it was in these three cities that the great majority of the workforce, recruited from southern and eastern European countries since the 1950s, made its home.

Thus by the mid-1960s, we had created an Australia which was doubly vulnerable to the evolving nature of world economic organisation. In the first place, the prices of primary products such as wheat, wool and coal themselves became subject to the vicissitudes of a global system of prices and conditions. Secondly, the global organisation of manufacturing — in such things as motor vehicles, clothing, textiles, footwear and other consumer goods — meant a distinct disadvantage for countries with higher wages, trade-union recognition, environmental-protection policies, workers' welfare and similar conditions of production.

A third set of factors relates to the gradual decline in importance of primary and secondary activity and the remorseless increase in the service sector, especially those activities which have been described as 'producer services', that is, those activities which are directly or indirectly related to the servicing of the new global systems of capital accumulation, be they in manufacturing or (increasingly) in property and tourism. So, as the world has been reorganised into a 'global village' of manufacturing, served by a network of 'world cities' which perform the command-and-control functions of the producer-services sector, so has Australia had to deal with some deep and painful transformations in its functions.

This has been particularly difficult for a country doubly cut off — from the old imperial relationship with the 'mother country', Britain, and lacking any special relations with the new 'big brother', the United States. To add to all this, the Federal government has, if anything, exacerbated the country's difficulties by the pursuit of what is called 'economic rationalism' (Pusey 1991). Under the Prime Ministership of Bob Hawke in the mid-1980s, Treasurer Paul Keating shifted macroeconomic policies from the 'corporatism' of 'The Accord' to the 'dry' monetarism associated with Ronald Reagan in the United States and Margaret Thatcher in the United Kingdom. The associated de-regulation of the banking system, the floating of the Australian dollar, and the gradual lowering or elimination of tariff barriers on imports deliberately exposed this small and vulnerable economy to the fierce winds of international trade, currency speculation and unproductive patterns of investment —for example, in central city offices, up-market real estate and tourism — rather than into investment for production and wider wealth-creation. Paul Keating's comments in 1987 about the possibility of a 'banana republic' cannot have helped.

In summary, Australia has become, in the course of the last few decades, a very much weaker economy, with its destiny far more in the hands of the superpowers and the multinational corporations, and less and less able to debate and decide, let alone control, its own economic and social destiny. It may well be a sign of maturity for our leaders to seek to join one or more powerful groups of trading nations in the recognition that 'if you can't beat them, join them', and that the days of dependence on the old Imperial power of Britain and the self-interested paternalism of the United States are long since over.

It is against this background that we must look at the changing role of Melbourne within Australia.

Melbourne's changing position in Australian life

Melbourne was one of the world's great cities. In its heyday, say between 1860 and 1920, it was one of the richest in the capitalist West and, from 1901 to 1927, the unrivalled chief city of the new Commonwealth of Australia. Even today, after a long decline in national and international significance, it is still rated (equally with Seattle/Tacoma and Montreal) as the world's 'most liveable city' by the Washington-based Population Crisis Committee (1991). Nineteenth-century observers marvelled at the cosmopolitan vitality of Melbourne compared with the sleepy provincialism of Sydney. But those days are long gone and it is now an Australian cliché to reverse this view.

What we must understand is the way in which the massive changes affecting the country as a whole (described above) have been and still are bringing about a 're-positioning' of Melbourne within the urban system of Australia.

In demographic and broad economic terms — total population, numbers of jobs, households, proportion of the respective State totals, and so on — we cannot see many great differences between the two largest and most important cities. It is when we dig beneath the surface, especially to reveal the qualitative nature of changes in their respective economies, that the truth emerges.

Sydney's emergence as the chief city dates from the end of the Second World War and particularly from the growth of international air travel on a massive scale. Just as Melbourne was the first stop in the populous and prosperous east (after the landfall at Fremantle) on a sea voyage from Europe, so Sydney is the most convenient major airport for flights from the United States, New Zealand, South-East Asia and Japan, who now form the greater part of our trading partners. But there is pleasure as well as business and Sydney is by far the most popular tourist destination (though it may well be overtaken before long by Queensland — the new international airport at Cairns is a pointer to the trend). The 'image' of Sydney is a major factor in both the locational choice of businesses as well as tourists. International investments have shifted their centre of gravity from manufacturing to property, banking and finance and in all these new areas Sydney has proved a marked favourite. The highly significant 'producer services' sector which includes the making and transmission of images (in the media, and above all, in advertising and telecommunications) has also tended to choose Sydney as its base. In combination, these factors have been the most significant in the emergence of Sydney as the chief business and 'gateway' city of the nation.

But Melbourne's changed role does not necessarily mean a diminution. Many 'second cities' — Lyon, Montreal, Barcelona, Manchester — continue to provide valuable, though necessarily different, roles for their respective countries; roles which the chief city may not perform so well, or does not find particularly useful.

Melbourne has a number of locational and specialisation advantages over Sydney. It is by far the most important transport node in the country. This 'least-cost location' means that for national (rather than international) business, linkages, and all forms of physical communication, Melbourne is unchallenged. It is also a major sporting centre (though this may well diminish as a result of the choice of Sydney for the Olympic Games in the year 2000), having a 'grand slam' tennis tournament, arguably the world's best cricket ground, and the centre of a football code with almost religious devotees.

Melbourne, too, is a major national and international centre for certain aspects of intellectual life. It has world status in medical research, is the headquarters for a number of governmental research institutes (for example immigration, criminology, family studies) and decision-making bodies such as the Australian Council of Trade Unions (ACTU) and the Arbitration Commission. In short, Melbourne is a place which lives to a large extent on reflection, introspection and conflict. It is not surprising that it is the national capital of humour.

But these Melburnian characteristics should not blind us to the fact that it is still, despite recession and tariff cuts, the unrivalled centre of Australian manufacturing with over 320 000 workers out of a national total of 889 000 — that is 36 per cent of the national manufacturing workforce with about 18 per cent of the population (O'Connor 1993). Of course this could represent a disadvantage in that manufacturing is in long-term decline, is highly vulnerable to take-overs and is not likely to yield more jobs even if investment increases. On the other hand, an advanced society always needs some manufacturing capacity, and this is often a focus for research-and-development investment; in both these areas Melbourne is well placed.

Having sketched out the international and national trends which have been influencing the Melbourne metropolitan area as a whole, it is time to turn to the factors which have shaped the internal social and spatial structure of the region.

The roles of capital

Capital in all its forms has had, and continues to have, a very significant influence over the production of Melbourne's built form. But this degree of influence has shifted over the years. In the earlier part of the postwar period it was manufacturing capital whose effects were decisive as Australia, and especially Victoria and New South Wales, converted from primary-production economies to become manufacturing economies in their own right. As I have shown elsewhere (McLoughlin 1992), this change was associated with very high rates of immigration which supplied both a labour force and a market.

However, during the 1970s this growth slowed, and latterly it has faltered. The development of the built form in the 1970s and 1980s came more and more under the influence of wholesaling and retailing capital, where the archetypal contribution was the very large suburban shopping centre and its surrounding massive car parks. This phenomenon is not only to be understood as a movement towards the homes of the suburbanising consumers, but also as the outcome of a deep and wide restructuring of the distribution sector. This involves both horizontal and vertical integration to produce retailing giants which control ever larger shares of the nation's trade and also own or control significant agricultural and consumer-product operations.

So, whereas at one time the typical contribution of manufacturing capital to urban development was the large, new mass-production factories — such as those of Ford at Broadmeadows and General Motors at Doveton — the typical product of the new structures of retailing capital was the giant 'shopping town' in what are, by now, middle-to-outer suburbs — Chadstone, Box Hill, Doncaster, Greensborough, Highpoint City, Northland, Knox, Airport West — a process which continues in the present outer ring of suburban growth. Almost all of these mega-developments were contrary to the prevailing planning-scheme provisions and gave rise to epic legal and statutory-planning struggles.

A rather special form of 'retailing' is the provision of sporting and other entertainment centres, of which a typical 1960s form was the drive-in cinema — now all but extinct — and very large sporting developments such as VFL Park (for Australian Rules Football) at Waverley off the South-Eastern Freeway and the Calder Park Thunderdrome (for car racing) off the Calder Highway on the north-west fringe of Melbourne.

One of the most visible and significant physical-form contributions of recent years has been created by property and finance capital, overwhelmingly in three distinct forms: suburban retailing-and-office complexes throughout the middle ring of suburbs, but especially in the eastern and south-eastern sectors; office skyscrapers in the central business district (CBD) and along St Kilda Road; and multi-purpose 'mega-projects' dominated by office floorspace but also including retailing and recreational uses, hotel rooms, high-price residential apartments and other activities. Examples from the 1980s include the 'Como Project' in South Yarra, the 'Melbourne Central' project on the northern edge of the CBD, the (temporarily aborted) 'Station Pier' proposal in Port Melbourne and a multitude of large-scale proposals associated with such linked development notions as the Very Fast Train, the Multifunction Polis and the (now failed) bid for the 1996 Olympic Games.

Two features of all such forms of investment by property and finance capital are noteworthy. First, a large and increasing proportion of this activity involves overseas ownership and control; all of them involve to some degree the participation and support of the state — almost always the State of Victoria rather than other levels of government. Frequently the projects are joint public–private ventures.

The most enduring and ubiquitous contribution by capital to the production of the built form of the metropolis has been the *construction of private housing*. Whilst in some ways its small scale and extent at any moment makes us overlook its significance, in sum its effects are of enormous importance. If we remove from the analysis the central city and other land uses of regional (or even national) relevance — such as Tullamarine airport, the largest parks, defence establishments and major sewerage treatment works — almost the whole urban fabric of Melbourne, as is the case in all large cities, has been created by suburban housing and car-related development. Furthermore, a lot of the non-residential development — schools, local parks, local roads, shops, community buildings and so on — can be directly attributed in scale and location to the growth of suburbia. Whilst land-use planners can and do have concerns for the small numbers of medium and large-scale developments which shape the urban form, they also have an enduring concern for the very continuous and widespread form of development which leads to the production of the suburban residential milieux. The constitution and size of the agencies responsible — ranging from owner-builders and small speculative developers to a rather small number of 'volume builders' — are, of course, quite small and insignificant when compared with the giant retailers, the office-construction companies and the multi-national property developers. But when we consider the overall effects of the modest makers of suburbia over periods of ten, twenty, thirty and forty years, it is clear that they play an extremely important role in the production of the total built form.

Individuals, households and community politics

The influence of individuals, households, community groups and more formal organisations such as trade unions and environmental lobbies has varied greatly over time and space. Their fortunes, in terms of their effects on urban form, have been mixed. The organised labour movement, as represented in the trade unions, has had quite limited effects, largely because it has not been radically activated in the way that its colleagues in New South Wales were in the 1970s. The Victorian construction unions have never had leaders as charismatic as Jack Mundey who urged that workers become active in issues far wider than merely pay and conditions and develop ethical positions concerning their role in reshaping the living and working environments of others.

But in more recent times, say from the onset of the 1970s, organised community groups have become far more vocal, if not always more effective. Long-established bodies like the Town and Country Planning Association have continued to press for more humane and sensitive policies, whilst left-inclined groups such as Socialist Alternatives for Melbourne have put forward wider strategies for more equitable metropolitan growth. At the close of the 1980s they have been joined by newer organisations which are seeking to unite disparate community and single-issue-based organisations into far wider and cross-class coalitions such as the Rainbow Alliance.

But community politics in Melbourne, as elsewhere in prosperous capitalist societies, has been typified for most of the post-war period by single-issue organisations using *oppositional* tactics directed against specific public and private proposals. Many commentators on the political life of Melbourne point to the classic examples of the fights against high-rise housing and freeway construction. Sometimes the bulldozers were indeed stopped in their tracks and forced to move on, but such total stoppages were rare; settlements which resulted in negotiation and compromise have been the most common results of Melbourne's 'urban social movements'. Concessions have been won which related to the scale, location, timing, content and appearance of proposals. The Como Project in South Yarra was significantly reduced in size and the South-Eastern Freeway downgraded to an ordinary dual-carriageway road in the face of strenuous objections from local residents in both cases. A protracted campaign throughout the late 1980s has resulted in considerable modification to a large redevelopment proposed for the Camberwell Junction shopping centre.

The effectiveness of community groups and labour organisations has been greatest when oppositional, single-issue and temporary. But far more significant 'victories' have been won when such groups acted in alliances, where the limited power of residents, local councillors, trade unionists and others has been greatly augmented by acting in concert.

One of the most stark contrasts between the power of capital, on the one hand, and of ordinary people, on the other, relates to the degree of continuity of their involvement. Capital, in its various forms, is *continuously* active in the shaping of the built environment, by putting in place new investment *and* by withdrawing it; capital, in its ceaseless and restless search for new opportunities, is active all the time. But ordinary people, whether as individuals, households or groups, are involved only on *specific occasions,* when they feel their interests and their quality of life are threatened. They become involved, therefore, only in response to some perceived threat posed by capital or the state. But to leave the matter there is to make one serious omission.

Individuals and households are continuously engaged in the production and moulding of the built form in a number of very important ways. Most obviously, they are the prime movers in the development of the residential portions of suburbia, either as owner-builders or in collaboration with smaller or larger house-building contractors (as noted above). Whilst I do not subscribe to 'consumer sovereignty' theories of urban growth, it is nevertheless clear that households, although constrained in several ways, have exerted considerable influence on the evolution of the suburban environment and, thus, on the overall form of Melbourne. Not only have they produced or bought the subdivisions, the houses and the flats; they have also had considerable influence over the wider local living environments through direct resident actions, or, often more effectively, through their membership of community groups. Or again, they have exercised their control through pressures on, or membership of, local councils. Well-known examples include residents' pressures on local government authorities (LGAs) to adopt or modify certain town-planning policies or development codes, to create local parks, to control car-parking and traffic flows, to plant trees and shrubs and to declare conservation zones — and much else to do with the protection and enhancement of local living qualities. The struggles to retain local schemes, to have Local Development Schemes legalised and to have local provisions inserted in the Melbourne Metropolitan Planning Schemes (MMPS) (see McLoughlin 1992, ch. 15) now appear as one of the success stories of 'community politics' and localism. However, at the time of writing (late 1993) the Victorian (Coalition) government, elected in October 1992, is proposing to make the Planning Act much more 'streamlined' to cut out 'red tape' and 'bumbledom'; this would be praiseworthy did it not seriously threaten the rights of ordinary citizens and confer draconian powers on ministers and their bureaucrats.

The 'state' and the bureaucracies

The state and its bureaucratic apparatus has played a very significant part in the shaping of Melbourne. For the first three decades of the post-war period, the power frameworks were quite diffused — with the Melbourne Metropolitan Board of Works' (MMBW) town-planning, infrastructure and parks divisions playing important roles alongside the advisory Town and Country Planning Board, the influential road planners and engineers of the Country Roads Board (later the Road Construction Authority), the late, unlamented Housing Commission of Victoria and the small new Ministry of Planning.

But since the mid-1970s, the moves towards corporatist structures and agencies have become a major force in Melbourne's growth. The Ministries of Transport, Housing and Planning and Environment and, above all, the setting up by the post-1982 Cain government of the Department of Management and Budget, the Department of Premier and Cabinet, and a high-powered Cabinet Committee charged with that classic of Victorian politics and administration — central coordination — are the crucial developments in this sphere.

The land-use implications of this corporatist trend will be explored later, but for the time being note that one of the key characteristics of such structures is an enhanced ability to control the agenda of debate, to select issues and to legitimate policies and the role of the state in general.

The influence of LGAs has generally tended to be overlooked in the study of Australian politics (see Halligan & Paris 1984, especially ch. 5). Whilst it is certainly true that in comparison with many other rich countries, Australian LGAs are small and limited in their formal powers, in the present study they loom much larger. Some of their most important functions are directly and centrally concerned with the *management of local environments* — with their promotion and protection by means of building and town-planning regulations and, increasingly, with 'urban design' activities. The point I wish to stress is that, when compared with the State apparatus of Victoria, LGAs constitute 'locales' which *lie at the intersections of the power* of local residents, pressure groups, elected councillors and professional officers — all within small areas which are comprehensible and meaningful to their occupiers. Indeed the significance of local identity has long been known to social scientists. One would, therefore, expect that LGAs in Melbourne to have been rather effective in the shaping of their parts of the metropolis and that such effectiveness will be related to the 'goodness of fit' between the various frameworks of power and their jurisdictional areas.

The professions

The town-planners' professional bodies, as such, have been shown (McLoughlin 1992, ch. 13) to be of very limited significance for the shaping of Melbourne, for the setting of agendas or the promotion of particular urban and environmental issues. From the power-frameworks point of view adopted here, the Royal Australian Planning Institute and other town-planning professional associations have been relatively weak. Their major debates have been introspective, even narcissistic, and their control over the labour market — the traditional trade-union function — very limited, at least in Victoria.

Their main influence seems to have been ideological in promoting the virtues of professionalism and in sustaining this by means of propaganda and the system of 'recognising' town-planning courses in tertiary education.

However, some influences can be detected on central ideas embodied in the various 'Marks' of the MMPS which seem to have come from professional points of view. The Mark I 1954 MMPS (MMBW 1954) contained the profession's historic ideas of neat-and-tidy growth, separation of non-conforming land uses and reservations to safeguard future developments. The Mark II Scheme's 'corridors and wedges' strategy is again a representation of quite old-established town-planning and urban-design ideas of linear urban form — found in the famous plans for Copenhagen, Madrid, Washington DC, Paris and many others. The corridor form arose from within the professional cadre rather than the democratic political arena, a point confirmed personally by leading people of the period (Alastair Hepburn, Alan Hunt 1985 pers. comm.). Again, in the early 1980s, the ideas of 'containment' and 'consolidation' came almost entirely from the professional staff of the MMBW, the Ministry of Planning and the Town and Country Planning Board. Most recently, traditional spatial-form notions about 'growth poles', 'satellite towns' and 'twin cities' are being recycled in a major policy-discussion document produced by the Victorian public service professionals (Victoria 1990), but whether or not they know how out-of-date and discredited these ideas are is not clear. This salience of the professionals, not so much *qua* professionals as in their roles as *skilled bureaucrats*, contrasts rather sharply with the very limited role played by the political parties.

The political parties

Land-use planning in Victoria has seldom been sharply politicised in the manner of Britain in the 1940s (under Attlee), in the 1980s (under Thatcher) or in West Germany in the 1970s (under Brandt), where there were clear ideological positions taken over the state's role in promoting and controlling physical development. It is certainly true that in the 1940s town planning was resisted by a conservative State government and only adopted under duress in 1944 and 1949. But since that time, town planning has tended to become and remain a bilateral 'cross-bench' matter. Conservatives and reformers alike have sponsored 'growth' in the 1950s, 1960s and 1970s, containment and economic recovery in the late 1970s and early 1980s, and, as we entered the 1990s, both major parties in Victorian politics were committed to the 'urban boosterism' associated with the Olympic Games, the Very Fast Train, the Multifunction Polis and major redevelopment projects for the Melbourne docks area, the South Bank (of the Yarra), the Jolimont railway yards, Station Pier and many similar schemes. Not only political careers but, perhaps of more enduring significance, senior bureaucratic careers are at stake here in 'shaping Melbourne's future'.

Frameworks of power

When we try to put together these diverse sets of political and social influences on the growth of a city, a 'power-framework' (Clegg 1989) approach to the understanding of human action has much to commend it. By considering the widest possible range of structures and agency over some considerable period, it is possible to gain a grasp of the complexity and the fluidity which characterise the 'urban question' itself. Moreover, it avoids giving any special priority to any particular agency or coalition; these must be discovered empirically for each place and time, as I have tried to do for Melbourne in the postwar period. Frameworks of power in the urban field are constantly shifting and reformulating, like the city itself. Nevertheless, this position does not require one to collapse into 'formless relativism'. Certainly there are general tendencies and phenomena — the over-riding *power of capital* in our society and the dominance of ever-more global and mobile systems of investment and dis-investment; the parallel and perhaps functionally related *rise of corporatism* in the apparatus of the state; the countervailing trend towards *localism* in the defence of turfs; an almost postmodern recovery of *diversity* and heterogeneity in the shaping of urban built form; the *politicisation of the bureaucrats*, cloaked and mystified by *professional ideology*.

Finally, an important general point to note is the possibility of the *conjuncture of power frameworks* — or of course the possibility of *dis*juncture. When, as in postwar Melbourne, power frameworks have been disjunct, and even antagonistic, as was often the case in the State apparatus until the late 1970s, one may expect little coherence in the direction of strategic land-use planning and a tendency for increasingly unified and mobile capital to be able to determine the process. By contrast, when power frameworks tend to conjunction, as we find recently in the case of the 'mega-projects' and 'spectacle' developments, and at most times in the control of land use and urban design in localities, we expect and find a considerable degree of cohesion and effectiveness in the shaping of the local built form.

Conclusion

Cities are humankind's most complex artefact and achievement. The making and remaking, every hour of every day of every year, of a city is, therefore, a most complex process since, as we have seen, every one of its inhabitants is involved. It is also a very conflictual process. Not only are others (nonresident investors and developers with economic rights but few responsibilities) involved, but also the local people are usually deeply divided about what seems desirable in the constant reshaping of the city. We have seen that what seems good to a multinational chemical company may seem totally unacceptable to local residents; a desirable freeway to eastern-suburbs commuters is a terrible environmental intrusion to inner-suburban residents; the bargain-basement offer of a railway-track bed to a (private) road-builder brings out an army of angry rail-users to defend the line.

All this is normal, happening all over the world all the time. That is why this chapter is entitled 'the political city'. The challenge for all of us is to find ways of managing and resolving the conflicts in ways which are fair and seen to be fair. Good cities can only arise in good societies.

Note

1   This chapter draws on material previously published in J. B. McLoughlin (1992), *Shaping Melbourne's Future? Town Planning, the State and Civil Society*, Cambridge University Press, Melbourne, pp. 150–55.

References

Clegg, S. (1989), *Frameworks of Power*, Sage, London.

Halligan, J. & Paris, C. (eds) (1984), *Australian Urban Politics*, Longman Cheshire, Melbourne.

McLoughlin, J. B. (1992), *Shaping Melbourne's Future? Town Planning, the State and Civil Society*, Cambridge University Press, Melbourne.

MMBW (Melbourne and Metropolitan Board of Works) (1954), *Melbourne and Metropolitan Planning Scheme*, 2 vols, MMBW, Melbourne.

O'Connor, K. (1993), *The Australian Capital City Report*, Centre for Population and Urban Research, Monash University, Melbourne.

O'Connor, K., Maher, C. & Rapson, V. (annual since 1988), *Monitoring Melbourne*, Monash University, Department of Geography, Melbourne.

Population Crisis Committee (1991), *Indicators of Urban Quality of Life*, United Nations, Washington DC.

Pusey, M. (1991), *Economic Rationalism in Canberra: A Nation-Building State Changes its Mind*, Cambridge University Press, Melbourne.

Victoria, Government of (1990), *Urban Development Options for Victoria*, Department of Planning and Urban Growth, Melbourne.

Chapter 7 | **The past and future of the Australian suburb**[1]
Graeme Davison

In the early 1990s Australian cities have reached a historic turning point. For over two centuries, our dreams of the good life have been shaped by a cluster of interrelated ideas we may loosely describe as the suburban ideal. The owner-occupied, single-storey house standing in its own garden was the standard of domestic comfort to which most Australians have continued to aspire. When Melbourne was recently assessed as 'the world's most liveable city', it achieved that much-disputed title partly on the strength of its performance by criteria that correlate closely with its highly suburbanised form.[2] The suburb has become so closely identified with popular conceptions of the good life that any move away from it, for example towards urban consolidation, is apt to be viewed as an attack upon people's living standards. How this came to be so, and whether the suburban form of our old cities is an aid, or hindrance, to their continued liveability, is now a subject of more than academic interest.

Today Australians are witnessing perhaps the most significant challenge to their suburban way of life in more than a century. The challenge is posed, most formidably, by the decline of those conditions of economic prosperity and benign technological development which we, along with Americans, have enjoyed during the past 150 years. Economic scarcity and the threat of environmental catastrophe have made the suburban sprawl seem as profligate and dangerous as it once seemed safe and boring. If the tide has turned against the suburban way of life, however, it is not only because we can no longer afford it, but because we have also begun to question the social aspirations and political arrangements that so long supported it. Declining levels and changing sources of immigration, declining fertility and smaller government have produced a new urban agenda in which urban consolidation comes to seem not only more economical and more virtuous, but even more attractive.

In this chapter, I wish to look more closely at the historical forces that made Australia so thoroughly and precociously suburban. What were the ideas of the good life that lay behind the establishment of our suburbs, and why were they so widely adopted? How far were these ideas contested by earlier generations of Australians? Which components of the suburban idea have contributed most to their 'liveability' and popularity, and what value have different groups of suburbanites placed upon them? If, as many planners suspect, Australia can no longer afford—if it ever could—to keep all of them, which should we consider trading off?

The suburban idea: The logic of avoidance

Australia was born urban and quickly grew suburban. From the beginnings of European settlement, a high proportion of the population was concentrated in the coastal towns which served both as ports and, in the case of Sydney and Hobart, as urban gaols. In 1789 when Governor Arthur Phillip drew up the first town plan for Sydney, he required that the streets be laid out:

> ... in such a manner as to afford free circulation of air, and when the houses are built ... the land will be granted with a clause that will prevent more than one house being built on the allotment, which will be sixty feet in front and one hundred and fifty feet in depth. (Arthur Phillip to Lord Sydney 1788, pp. 147–8)

Such an arrangement, he declared, would 'preserve uniformity in its buildings [and] prevent the many inconveniences which the increase of the inhabitants would otherwise occasion thereafter'. It shows too much hindsight to credit Australia's first colonial governor with the invention of that popular Australian institution, the quarter-acre suburban block; but it is significant that, from the outset, Australia's founders anticipated a sprawl of homes and gardens rather than a clumping of terraces and alleys.

Phillip nowhere used the word 'suburb', but his regulations embody some of those aspirations to decency, good order, health and domestic privacy which lay at the heart of the suburban idea. Australia had come into being as a European colony at the very moment when the suburb was emerging as a solution to the urban ills of the Old World. Like a colony, the suburb was a place of escape or refuge, and it was shaped, therefore, largely by the logic of avoidance. The suburb was, in essence, a mirror image of the slum. While the slum was seen as dense, dirty, unnatural, disorderly and disease-ridden, the suburb was seen as open, clean, natural, orderly and healthy.

Four great contemporary ideologies—Evangelicalism, Romanticism, Sanitarianism and Capitalism—strengthened the influence of the suburban idea upon the minds of colonial Australians.

Many of the more respectable colonists had been touched by the influence of the Evangelicals and their call for a revival of the homely virtues. It was the Evangelicals who had most clearly articulated the idea of 'separate spheres' for men and women, and of the suburban home as a kind of temple in which the wife ruled as the 'Angel of the Home' (Davidoff & Hall 1987). The prototype of the modern bourgeois suburb was Clapham, on the eastern fringes of London, where wealthy Evangelicals like the Wilberforces and the Thorntons settled in the early nineteenth century.

The idea of the suburb as a place of peace and refuge also drew inspiration from Romanticism, for the ideal suburb enabled the care-worn city man to repair his battered spirits through communion with the beauties of nature. J. C. Loudon, the British architect and landscape designer who may be regarded as the father of the modern suburb, declared that 'A suburban residence, with a small portion of land attached, will contain all that is essential to happiness'. It enabled the man of business to retire from the cares and clamour of the city into the country 'where [as he said] man may approach the simplicity of nature and attain the enjoyments and pleasures of pristine innocence' (Loudon 1838, p. 8; Fishman 1987; Archer 1988). The garden, therefore, was as important a feature of the suburb as the cottage or villa and the ideal suburb attempted, in its planning and architecture, to evoke something of the peace and solitude of the countryside.

The suburbanite found further reason to escape the city in the warnings which doctors and sanitary engineers were sounding about the deadly pollution of the cities. According to the medical science of the day, there was a direct relationship between death rates and the density of the urban environment. Captain Phillip's concern to promote 'the free circulation of air' and his desire to keep building blocks large and streets wide reflected this belief. Suburbs everywhere, but especially in the environs of the new industrial cities, were promoted as much for their safety as their beauty or social exclusiveness.

In its original British context, the suburb was also promoted as a zone of exclusively bourgeois residence. In the pre-industrial city the elite and the plebs had lived in much the same neighbourhoods, the elite in the grand houses facing the squares and parks; the plebs in the cramped lanes and backstreets. From the early nineteenth century, however, the middle classes began to show a growing fear and fastidiousness towards their working-class neighbours. They sought to insulate themselves, and especially their wives and children, from the uncouth and possibly dangerous life of the streets. Thus began the slow process of class segregation that eventually brought about the distinctive concentric-zones of middle-class and working-class residence that we associate with the late nineteenth-century city. 'Choose a neighbourhood where houses and inhabitants are all, or chiefly, of the same description and class as the house we intend to inhabit, and as ourselves', Loudon advised the prospective suburbanite (Loudon 1838, p. 32). In Australia, as we shall see, this aristocratic impulse was considerably weakened, as the suburb, once the exclusive retreat of the rich, eventually became the dominant pattern of urban life. This did not happen all at once, and throughout the nineteenth century the house and garden ideal had to compete with more traditional styles of urban living focused around the terrace house, the corner shop, the pub and the vigorous social life of the streets.

Why the suburbs grew

Why did the suburbs flourish so luxuriantly in Australia? I think we may detect four crucial influences. Firstly, as we have seen already, the suburban idea arrived with the country's European founders and it was vigorously promoted by the state during the early colonial period. Secondly, it had strong appeal to immigrants who were themselves largely refugees from urban Britain. Australia may be thought of as the farthest suburb of Britain and ambitions for land, space and independence, frustrated in the crowded cities of the homeland, were often realised on the suburban frontiers of Australia (or Canada, the United States or New Zealand). Thirdly, throughout the nineteenth century, Australian suburbanites were able to take advantage of relatively high wages, low unemployment, cheap land and extensive, modern public transport services. Finally, suburbanisation was promoted by Australia's system of strong central government and relatively weak local government. By providing new schools, police stations, suburban railways and other infrastructure, the colonial governments and their successors, the state governments, shouldered many of the costs which would otherwise have had to be borne by the local community. Already in the nineteenth century, therefore, Australians were effectively subsidising suburban growth from their state treasuries. Some current proposals for privatisation therefore reverse more than a hundred years of state support for suburbanisation.

From Phillip onwards colonial administrators were determined to avoid reproducing the evils of Old World cities. Many of the first settlers—the convicts—were products of the slums of London and other large towns, and the authorities feared that, if the colonial towns were allowed to grow unimpeded, and ex-convicts to gather there, the same vicious subculture of crime and licentiousness would begin to pollute the new society. This was one of the recurrent fears expressed by witnesses to Mr Commissioner Bigge's inquiry into the condition of New South Wales in 1919–20. By the mid-1820s, the growth of crime and poverty in places like Sydney's notorious Rocks district convinced some respectable colonists that the attempt to ward off the evils of city life was failing.

The first self-conscious movement towards the creation of villa suburbs in the English style came from the circle of wealthy, often Evangelical, officials and businessmen, known appropriately as the 'Exclusives', who came into political and social prominence under the New South Wales governor, Sir Ralph Darling, in the late 1820s. In 1828 Darling authorised the subdivision of Woolloomooloo Hill, a pleasant rise overlooking the Harbour about a mile east of the town, into special 'villa allotments' with a view 'to the ornament and improvement of the suburbs of Sydney'. Fifteen 8–10 acre allotments were granted to wealthy Exclusives, mostly high government officials, subject only to the condition that within three years they construct villa residences to the value of at least 1000 pounds according to designs approved by the Town Surveyor, 'taking care that the front of the building faced toward Sydney' (Broadbent 1986; Dyster 1989; Kerr & Broadbent 1980). Soon the pleasant slopes overlooking Double Bay were sprinkled with Gothic cottages and Italianate villas, some directly modelled on Loudon's designs. Thus the first Australian suburb was created by government decree as a means of enabling the respectable middle class of Sydney to seek refuge from the dirt, disease and vice of the convict capital.

More remarkable than the aristocratic impulse behind the creation of the Australian suburb, however, was the speed with which it took a more democratic course. Already by the mid-1830s wealthy ex-convicts had begun to build their own villas on private land at Glebe, Balmain and other harbourside suburbs. And very soon real estate agents, those infallible harbingers of suburban development, were inviting 'the mechanics and shopkeepers of Sydney' as well as 'Professional Gentlemen' and 'Opulent Merchants' to enjoy 'repose after the anxiety of business' on a cottage or villa estate.[3] As the other colonial capitals—Brisbane, Melbourne and Adelaide—took shape during the 1830s, they grew along largely suburban lines. The word 'suburb' actually enters Australian parlance through its use by government land agents as a term for those allotments which lay immediately beyond the 'town', that is, beyond what we now describe as the central business district. It is perhaps to this circumstance that we owe the peculiarly Australian habit of referring to virtually any part of the city beyond the central business district as 'the suburbs'.

Australia's suburbs were shaped, decisively, by the successive waves of immigrants who pioneered them. The demand for land, for space and for independence have always been prominent in the aspirations of immigrants to Australia. Many looked back upon the experience of living as tenants in their homeland, and longed to be free of the fear of the landlord and the bailiff. 'What can I gain by going to Victoria?', asked James Ballantyne in 1871, anticipating the question of his British working-class readers. 'He will be able, whether by economy or saving, or through the help of one of the numerous building societies, to secure a comfortable freehold for himself and thus possess what every Englishman glories in—a house which will be his castle', he replied (Ballantyne 1871). But it was not only British immigrants who longed for homes of their own. In postwar Australia immigrants from peasant backgrounds in eastern and southern Europe often acquired their own suburban homes more quickly even than the native-born (Australian Population and Immigration Council 1976, p. 96). It was home ownership, rather than space or family privacy, that these immigrants desired above all, and, in order to achieve it, they were often ready to sacrifice some of the personal space and family privacy that British immigrants held so dear.

Australians have been so inclined to equate suburbanism with the good life that they have too readily assumed that their sprawling cities were a simple proof of their prosperity. When Donald Horne christened Australia 'the lucky country', he pointed to its status as 'the first suburban nation' (Horne 1964, pp. 23–7). There can be little doubt that the high average incomes enjoyed by Australian wage-earners during the late nineteenth and early twentieth centuries contributed strongly to the growth of the suburbs (Butlin 1965, p. 8). Cheap, easily serviced urban land, cheap building materials, inexpensive methods of building construction and plentiful housing finance enabled Australians to purchase or rent more house and land for their wages than their counterparts in Britain or North America. 'A working man in Melbourne no doubt pays more for his house or for his lodgings than he would do in London', Anthony Trollope estimated in 1872; but in Melbourne, he believed, 'the labourer or artisan enjoys a home of a better sort than would be within reach of his brother in London doing work of the same nature, and in regard to house-rent gets more for his money than he would do at home' (Trollope et al. 1967, p. 399). Lionel Frost's recent calculations of late nineteenth-century wage-rent ratios seem to confirm Trollope's view (Frost 1991, pp. 113–17). In the twentieth century, however, and especially over the past half century, the link between living standards and suburbanisation has grown more complex, as Australia's lead as 'the first suburban nation' has been whittled away by other lands, and as gentrification has created alternative styles and standards of urban prosperity.

Throughout their history, Australia's suburbs have relied, more heavily than those of other lands, on the support of the state. By supplying new schools, police stations, suburban railways and other infrastructure the colonial governments and their successors, the state governments, shouldered many of the costs that would elsewhere have been borne by the local community or by private developers. While North Americans paid for most of these services out of locally-based taxation assessed on landed property, colonial Australians paid for them out of general revenues furnished largely from sales of crown lands and customs duties. This had two important effects. Firstly, it lowered the threshold of development costs faced by ratepayers of the brand-new suburb. While the suburb was young, and most of its residents were hard-up, young, first-home buyers, the costs of building local services could be a significant drag upon development, unless the central government came to the rescue. Secondly, by guaranteeing a relatively common standard of state schooling, policing, fire protection etc. across all suburbs, it reduced one of the main motives for class differentiation between them. The Australian suburbanite's choice between one suburb and another may have been a choice between degrees of scenic attractiveness, or between different building codes, but it was not, to the same degree as in other similar countries, a choice between one standard of state schooling and policing and another. It is only if we compare these arrangements and the grosser inequalities between the levels of services in American suburbs, and especially between their inner cities and their suburbs, that we will appreciate how much we owe to this distinctively Australian form of urban political economy. Some current proposals for smaller government and 'user-pays' principles threaten this century-old tradition of state support for a relatively democratic form of suburbanisation.

Realising the ideal: Preferences and trade-offs

From the vantage point of its creators the 'liveability' of the early Australian suburb may be said to have consisted in the satisfaction of five prime wants: domestic privacy; natural, semi-rural surroundings; a healthy environment; private ownership and social exclusiveness. The ideal suburb satisfied all five of these wants, but the value which was placed upon each, and the trade-offs between them, varied a good deal from one country or social class or ethnic group to another.

In general, I think that British and Australian suburbanites have placed a higher value on domestic privacy than Americans. Consider, for example, the continued preference of Australian and British suburbanites for fenced or hedged allotments compared with the American preference for an unbroken sward of lawn between house and house and from the front door to the street. In this sense, the form of our suburbs may reflect more general features of the public life of the two societies, such as the strict Australian and British libel and privacy laws compared with the almost unfettered freedom of American press and television reporters seem to enjoy to investigate people's private lives.

American and British suburbanites, on the other hand, seem to have placed a higher value on social exclusiveness than Australians. When Professor Edward Morris arrived from London to take up the Chair of English at the University of Melbourne in the late 1880s, he was immediately struck by what he called the 'diversity' of Melbourne's landscape: 'A poor house stands side by side with a good house, a cottage, one might almost say a hovel, in close proximity to a palace' (Morris 1888–9, p. 58). Statistical comparisons are hard to make—the data is scarce and seldom collected on a base that makes comparison meaningful—but the few historical studies that have been made tend to confirm Morris's impressions (Fricker 1978, ch. 4). If Australian suburbs were socially less homogeneous than British or American ones, it was probably not just that Australians were less stand-offish than British and American city-dwellers, but that local methods of land subdivision and sale placed fewer restrictions on who could build what. Not everyone approved of these free-and-easy arrangements. A British immigrant, commenting on a proposed model suburb at Kensington near Sydney in the late 1880s, noted how, 'with the silent resolve that imperceptibly moves a well-ordered society', London suburbanites had gravitated to suburbs of a more or less homogeneous class composition. 'Intuitively [he noted] everyone knew his place and dropped into it'. In Sydney, however, 'houses of all sorts and conditions [are] strewn about in a fashion that makes it easier for one to believe that they wandered there of their own accord than that any sane man began in cold blood to rear them' (Blackwell 1889, p. 77). Blackwell was supported by another observer, James Green, who called for more selectivity to be exercised in the development of new suburban estates: 'However estimable in their own spheres of life may be "the butcher, the baker and the candle-stick maker" we do not wish, with all our boasted democracy, to have them elbowing our comfortable cottage or more ornate villa with their miserable shanties ...' (Green 1889, p. 153).

The model suburbs applauded by Green and Blackwell represented an attempt, relatively rare in nineteenth-century Australian experience, to plan suburbs along socially exclusive lines. The Grace Park Estate in Hawthorn near Melbourne was a similar contemporary venture (National Trust, Victoria 1987). Like some comparable experiments in Britain and the United States, these model suburbs were based on leasehold principles and required prospective house builders to submit their plans for the approval of the ground landlord who might also require the house itself to be of a specified cost and design. Few such model suburbs retained their strict building controls and leasehold tenure beyond their founding years. Australian suburbanites, it seems, did not care enough for the benefits of exclusiveness, at least to put up with the restrictions of leasehold. It was easier to maintain the character of a suburb by enacting and enforcing building regulations governing setbacks, minimum allotments and brick or timber construction than by the stricter, but more cumbersome, method of covenants or leasehold estates (McConville & Associates 1990, pp. 18–22). Only in Canberra, a city of public servants, ruled until recently by public servants, has leasehold been widely adopted as a form of land tenure, and then with results that deviate only marginally from Australian norms of suburban segregation or diversity.

One of the prime social goods that Australians have historically associated with suburbia is home-ownership. The connection, of course, is not a necessary one. You do not have to live in the suburbs to own your house; and you do not necessarily own your house if you do live in the suburbs. But the connection is certainly more than accidental. It derives from the link between the family life cycle and the cycle of urban development: the edge of the city is the only place where young couples have traditionally been able to afford to buy the amount and kind of accommodation that they have seen, rightly or wrongly, as necessary for child-rearing. One of the reasons that Australian suburbanites have generally resisted the introduction of leaseholds, building regulations, covenants and other planning devices is that they believed, correctly in many instances, that they would frustrate their democratic right to home ownership. From the 1850s onwards, working-class Australians tended to be strongly in favour of a regulated labour market, leading the world, for example, in the adoption of the Eight-hour Day; but they tended to be strongly opposed to a regulated housing market. One of the reasons that residents of Melbourne's inner suburbs resisted their incorporation into the City of Melbourne in the 1850s and 1860s was that they feared the imposition of higher rates and irksome building and sanitary regulations (Barrett 1979, pp. 116–21).

Many, perhaps most, working-class home-owners at any time until the 1960s acquired their homes by stages. First they put a deposit on a block of land. Then they paid it off in instalments. When they had done so, they borrowed enough to start building. Sometimes they did it themselves, or shared the job with friends or subcontractors. Often they began with only one or two rooms, then added others as they found the means to do so. When they arrived on the block, it was probably unserviced. The road was unmade, there was no gas or sewerage, possibly not even piped water. By their actions, the new suburbanites demonstrated that they put a higher value on the security of home-ownership and the opportunity to have their own bit of ground than they did upon health or natural surroundings.

Footscray, Melbourne's newest industrial suburb in the 1880s, was as famous for the size of its standard building allotments and its high level of owner-occupied houses as it was notorious for the stink of its noxious industries and its muddy, unmade streets. More than 60 per cent of householders owned or were buying their own homes, the highest level in the metropolis. A contemporary wondered whether 'there is another place in creation where the people as a whole are so comfortable, and so many of them freeholders' (Lack 1991, pp. 120–1). His conception of 'comfort' was obviously different from our standard definitions of 'liveabilty', for Footscray was also possibly the worst polluted suburb in the metropolis:

> Home-buyers [writes John Lack in his admirable recent local history] got nothing more than a house and the land it stood upon. Virtually none of the streets, footpaths or rights of way were formed, these tasks being left to municipal councils. By the late 1880s in Footscray only three of some 200 streets had been metalled to their full width, one third of the rights of way were unmade, and two-thirds of the street channels were earthen. Most of the house yards and sideways were neither paved nor properly levelled. Footscray's residential areas simply stank. (Lack 1991, p. 104)

Although the local council tried to clean up the mess and make the roads, the ratepayers were reluctant to pay for improvements. A local pressure group formed to bring the polluting industrialists under control, was denounced by working men as a threat to their livelihoods. 'If the swells found the stink too much for them let them go to St Kilda', they declared (Lack 1991, p. 100–2).

Footscray's experience was not unusual. From the first gold-rush suburbs, in Redfern and Collingwood, to the so-called 'heart-break' suburbs of northern Melbourne and western Sydney in the 1940s and 1950s, working-class Australians were prepared to give up much of the natural beauty and health that had inspired the creators of the romantic suburbs of the Victorian era. They were probably not careless of such matters, but their significance paled by comparison with the more fundamental desire for space and owner occupation. Working-class suburbanites in North America often made similar choices (Zunz 1982, ch. 6; Harris & Hamnett 1987, pp. 182–3). They had good reasons for doing so, for the owner-occupied house standing in its own ground was not only a way of acquiring a small property holding, and hence providing for one's old age, but it was also the source of economic, social and psychic benefits not found in a rented terrace in the inner city.

In the midst of our current debates about consolidation, urban infra-structure and the 'liveability' of our cities, it may be worth reminding ourselves of how many Australians have traditionally weighed the advantages of health and aesthetics, on the one hand, and space and ownership on the other. It goes hard against the professional judgment of the architects, planners and engineers to contemplate any relaxation of building and planning standards, but I suspect that if push came to shove, many Australians would prefer their cities to be a bit uglier, and even, perhaps, a little more dangerous, than to give up the prospect of owning their home, however humble, poorly serviced and unplanned it may be.

The suburbs: Living or only partly living?

Since the end of the nineteenth century, intellectuals have been eager to tell Australians what was missing in their suburban civilisation. Medical experts, aesthetes, social planners and political economists have all contributed some-thing to our changing understanding of 'liveability' in the suburbs. Their writings, it must be admitted, often tell us more about the preoccupations of the intellectuals than the day-to-day experience of the suburbanites. One of-ten comes away from reading them with an unpleasant sensation of having been patronised by experts who thought that they knew what was best for the average suburbanite.

Some critics reproached the Australian suburbs with failing to live up to the ideal. It was not spacious, private, natural or healthy enough. In the early twentieth century, sanitarians and planners, influenced by the Gar-den City ideals of Howard and Unwin, constructed a working definition of 'liveability' (a word, of course, they did not use) around the provision of adequate living space. While they were principally concerned with the physical health of the city-dweller, they shared the conviction of nine-teenth-century slum reformers that it was possible to live a virtuous and happy life only with plenty of room, outside and inside the home. The Royal Commission on the Housing of the People of the Metropolis which sat in Melbourne during the Great War focused its attention mainly on the problem of 'overcrowding'. In discussing a proposal to legislate a minimum size for suburban allotments, the commissioners articulated the tangled skein of reasoning—moral and social as well as scientific—behind contemporary planning theory:

> In a general view, it is regarded as insanitary, and otherwise undesirable practice, for two or more families to occupy at the same time a dwelling house of ordinary design and size, when evils due to overcrowding are to be looked for. So it is agreed amongst sanitarians that similar evils, on a larger scale, are to be expected where dwellings are built on allotments having dimensions so limited as to leave insufficient space for entrance of sunlight and fresh air around and into the house, or for privacy, or for adequate yard space, clothes drying ground, play area for young children,

or for fire breaks for the spread of fire from house to house, to say nothing of possible advantage presented by such open spaces in reducing risk from supposed aerial convection of infection. (Report of the Royal Commission 1917, pp. 25–6; see also Harris 1988)

In the mind of the physical determinists, such as the authors of this report, medical and moral influences were closely intertwined. It was this type of thinking, more than any other, that influenced the first generation of uniform building regulations, fire safety standards and local planning ordinances, and their influence is still with us today.

In the mid-twentieth century, these regulations became a favourite target of a second generation of planners and architects whose notions of suburban liveability were more aesthetic than sanitary. In 1953 a young Melbourne architect, Robin Boyd, visited the new Brisbane suburb of Serviceton, then growing up on the site of a former American army camp. What he found filled him with dread. The old army camp had consisted of nothing but Nissan huts, but they had been erected on sweeping roads that followed the contours of the land and took advantage of the natural shade of the big gum trees that dotted the site. But now the Queensland Housing Commission had arrived. The huts had been demolished, the trees cut down, and the curving army roads had been replaced by straight parallel streets. 'Serviceton', Boyd wrote,'now presents the bald, raw, sun-beaten drabness, which has become the salient feature of post-war Australian housing'.

> The Australian suburb [he continued] was originally a wonderful idea: the private castle for every man in place of the crowded gardenless urban terraces of Europe. We did not, of course, invent the idea, but we carried it further than most nations. The ironic thing is that its foundation was the late nineteenth century conception of a 'garden city'—a reaction to the overcrowded industrial town—a quiet, spacious residential parkland. Without the trees we are returning to something as depressing and forbidding as the brick jungle of the nineteenth-century industrial city, which first drove men out to seek the gardens of the suburbs. When we destroy greenery we destroy the justification for the suburb. (Boyd 1953a, see also Boyd 1953b, 1960)

Here, in embryo, was Boyd's famous attack on 'the Australian ugliness'. He invoked the values of the Garden City to condemn its unprepossessing Australian child. In spite of his patrician origins, and his insistence upon the high calling of the architect, Boyd's vision of the liveable Australian suburb in the 1940s and early 1950s was populist, if not exactly democratic. He was interested in the use of natural materials, like pise, as a means of lowering construction costs and in cooperative housing schemes. Above all, however, Boyd was a firm believer in the contribution of good design to happy living. His choice of adjectives for the unreconstructed postwar suburb—bald, raw, drab, depressing, forbidding—underlines the close link which he saw between aesthetics and liveability. Like other critics of his generation, Boyd too readily

assumed that an environment that looked uniform and boring from the outside must seem so to its inhabitants: that because (in the words of the famous
Pete Seeger song) 'they all lived in little boxes' they must all live, feel and
think the same. Whether the new residents of Serviceton found their environment as forbidding and depressing as Mr Boyd and Mr Seeger is, of course,
another matter.

Sanitarians and aesthetes invoked the suburban ideal to condemn its
products. A more forceful critique of suburbia, however, came from those
who contested the ideal itself. The suburb, I have suggested, was based on the
logic of avoidance, and its virtues, therefore, were essentially negative virtues.
In excluding everything that was dangerous and offensive, its critics alleged,
its creators had also banished everything that was stimulating and exciting.
In guaranteeing privacy, they had also guaranteed boredom and loneliness.
Suburbia, they implied, was too private, too exclusive, too leafy, too healthy,
and perhaps too virtuous (see Gilbert 1988, pp. 33–49). 'The only place outside a man's house where he could get to spend an evening was either a
public house or a prayer meeting' complained the newly arrived resident of
one Melbourne suburb in the 1880s.[4] In 1909 the socialist playwright Louis
Esson raged:

> The suburban home must be destroyed. It stands for all that is dull and
> cowardly and depressing in modern life. It endeavours to eliminate the
> element of danger in human affairs. But without danger there can be no
> joy, no ecstasy, no spiritual adventures. (Esson 1908, p. 99, compare Walker
> 1976, pp. 148–53)

In the early 1960s, Jeanne MacKenzie, a visiting English Fabian, asked a
young Czech migrant how she liked Australia: ' It is very nice', she replied,
'but there is something missing' (MacKenzie 1961, p. 127).

Every intellectual has a theory to explain what is missing. Socialists put
suburban dullness down to the practice of private ownership, which shackles
every householder to a mortgage and thus tamed the instinct to rebel. Social
democrats, like Hugh Stretton, associate monotony with social uniformity; if
only our suburbs were socially more mixed, he suggests, they would be more
lively as well (Stretton 1970, pp. 103–24). Feminists see the root of the problem in the bourgeois ideology of 'separate spheres' for men and women from
which the Romantic idea of the suburb, as a feminised zone of safety and
retreat, was first derived. In the early 1990s these several strands of criticism
have been invoked by the advocates of urban consolidation—more, one sus-
pects, as convenient props for policies that are driven rather by economics
than by social preference. They offer us the attractive prospect of denser cities
that will also be livelier, more equal, and friendlier, both socially and environmentally.

Meanwhile the suburbanites themselves display a disconcertingly high
level of satisfaction with their way of life. In doing so, they often register their
desire for values and conveniences that may not rate highly in the intellect-

ual's scale of proper urban virtues, but which have more utility, even in an environment of recession, than its alternatives. In spite of changing gender roles and work habits, rising mortgage payments and declining rates of capital accumulation, lengthening journeys to work and shrinking suburban allotments, the suburban house remains the goal to which most young Australians continue to aspire. It is a dream which the future may deny them, but which they seem unlikely to renounce of their own free will.

Notes

1   First published in *Australian Planner* (1993), vol. 31, no. 2, pp. 63–9, this chapter is reproduced with permission of the author.
2   *Age,* 20 November 1990. The reference is to a statistical analysis compiled by the Washington-based Population Crisis Committee. The ten basic indicators included food costs (per cent income spent on food), traffic flow (km/h in rush hour), public health (infant deaths per thousand births), living space (persons per room), public safety (murders per 100 000 people), services (per cent houses with water and electricity), education (per cent children in secondary schools), communications (telephones per 100 people) ambient noise, and air pollution. Sydney-siders, miffed that they finished only ninth in the world, complained that indices of climate and excitement were left out of the exercise.
3   Advertisement for land at Fivedock, 9 December 1836 as quoted in E. Russell (1971), *Drummoyne: A Western Suburbs History 1794–1871*, Municipality of Drummoyne, pp. 60–2.
4   *Boroondara Standard,* 2 March 1888 as quoted in G. Davison (1987), 'The Capital Cities', in G. Davison, J. W. McCarty & A. McLeary (eds), *Australians 1888*, Fairfax, Syme & Weldon, Sydney, p. 225.

References

Archer, J. (1988), 'Ideology and aspiration: Individualism, the middle class and the genesis of the Anglo-American suburb', *Journal of Urban History*, vol. 18, no. 2, pp. 214–53.
Arthur Phillip to Lord Sydney, 29 July 1788 (1892), *Historical Records of New South Wales*, vol.1, part 2, 1783–1792, Sydney, pp. 147–8.
Australian Population and Immigration Council (1976), *A Decade of Migrant Settlement: Report on the 1973 Immigration Survey*, AGPS, Canberra.
Ballantyne, J. (1871), *Homes and Homesteads in the Land of Plenty*, Mason, Firth & McCutcheon, Melbourne.
Barrett, B. (1979), *The Civic Frontier: The Origin of Local Communities and Local Government in Victoria*, Melbourne University Press, Melbourne.
Blackwell, E. (1889), 'Model suburbs I: Kensington, Sydney', *Centennial Magazine*, vol.2 , p.77.
Boyd, R. (1953a), 'The decline of the suburb', *Age*, 13 April.

Boyd, R. (1953b), 'Australian towns and cities', in W. V. Aughterson (ed.), *Taking Stock: Aspects of Mid-century Life in Australia*, F. W. Cheshire, Melbourne.

Boyd, R. (1960), *The Australian Ugliness*, F. W. Cheshire, Melbourne.

Broadbent, J. (1986), 'The push east: Woolloomooloo Hill, the first suburb', in M. Kelly (ed.), *Sydney: City of Suburbs*, University of New South Wales Press, Sydney, pp. 12–29.

Butlin, N. G. (1965), 'Long-run trends in Australian per capita consumption', in K. Hancock, *The National Income and Social Welfare*, F. W. Cheshire, Melbourne.

Davidoff, L. & Hall, C. (1987), *Family Fortunes: Men and Women of the English Middle Class, 1780–1850*, Hutchinson, London.

Davison, G., McCarty, J. W. & McLeary, A. (eds) (1987), *Australians 1988*, Fairfax, Syme & Weldon, Sydney.

Dyster, B. (1989), *Servant and Master: Building and Running the Grand Houses of Sydney 1788-1850*, University of New South Wales Press, Sydney.

Esson, L. (1908), 'Our institutions IV: The suburban home', *The Socialist*, quoted in *The Australian City*, Reader, Deakin University, Geelong, p. 99.

Fishman, R. (1987), *Bourgeois Utopias: The Rise and Fall of Suburbia*, Basic Books, New York.

Fricker, L.(1978), Some aspects of Melbourne's nineteenth-century urbanisation process, PhD thesis, University of Melbourne.

Frost, L. (1991), *The New Urban Frontier*, University of New South Wales Press, Sydney.

Gilbert, A. (1988), 'The roots of anti-suburbanism in Australia', in S. L. Goldberg & F. B. Smith (eds), *Australian Cultural History*, Cambridge University Press, Cambridge.

Green, J. (1889), 'Model suburbs II: Harcourt, Burwood', *Centennial Magazine*, vol. 2, pp. 150–4.

Harris, D. (1988), 'Not above politics: Housing reform in Melbourne 1910–29', in R. Howe (ed.), *New Houses for Old: Fifty Years of Public Housing in Victoria 1938–1988*, Ministry for Housing, Melbourne.

Harris, D. & Hamnett, C. (1987), 'The myth of the promised land: Social diffusion of home ownership in Britain and North America', *Annals of the Association of American Geographers*, vol. 77, no. 2, pp. 182–3.

Horne, D. (1964), *The Lucky Country: Australia in the Sixties*, Penguin, Ringwood.

Kerr, J. & Broadbent, J. (1980), *Gothick Taste in the Colony of New South Wales*, David Ell, Sydney.

Lack, J. (1991), *A History of Footscray*, Hargreen, Melbourne.

Loudon, J. C. (1982), *The Suburban Gardener and Villa Companion,* (first published 1838 by Longmans, London), reprinted, Garland Publishing, New York.

MacKenzie, J. (1961), *Australian Paradox*, F. W. Cheshire, Melbourne.

McConville, C. & Associates (1990), *Camberwell Conservation Study: Part One: An Environmental History of Camberwell*, City of Camberwell, Camberwell, Vic.

Morris, E. E. (ed.) (1888–9), *Picturesque Australasia*, Cassell, London.

National Trust, Victoria (1987), Grace Park, Hawthorn, unpublished report.

Report of the Royal Commission on the Housing of the People of the Metropolis (1917), *Victorian Parliamentary Papers*, vol. 1, no. 29, pp. 25–6.

Russell, E. (1971), *Drummoyne: A Western Suburbs History 1794–1871*, Municipality of Drummoyne, Sydney.

Stretton, H. (1970), *Ideas for Australian Cities*, Georgian House, Melbourne.

Trollope, A., Edward, P. D. & Joyce, B. (1967), *Australia* (first published 1873 in London), Queensland University Press, St Lucia.

Walker, D. (1976), *Dream and Disillusion: A Search for Australian Cultural Identity*, Australian National University Press, Canberra.

Zunz, O. (1982), *The Changing Face of Inequality: Urbanization, Industrial Development, and Immigrants in Detroit, 1880–1920*, University of Chicago Press, Chicago.

Chapter 8 | **Suburbia: Domestic dreaming**
Lyn Richards

> Urban fringe dwellers are not the isolated, socially disadvantaged families
> of popular myth, exiled to brick-veneer wastelands on the outskirts of our
> sprawling cities, but are happily keeping alive the great Australian dream,
> a major new study shows. (*Weekend Australian,* 17–18 July 1993, p. 1)

Suburbia has two faces, the dream achieved and the nightmare of dreary
living, deprivation and isolation. The dream is featured in the real estate
pages of any paper, the nightmare in the critical accounts of Australian
life, especially women's lives. 'The Australian suburban dream created at
one fell swoop the Australian housewife's nightmare' (Kingston 1975, p.2).
This chapter is about those two faces, the apparent contradiction of dream
and nightmare. It looks at recent studies of suburban dreams and the lives
they support, and argues that neither face alone presents a 'true' picture.

Suburbia, family, home

Both of the faces of suburbia, as the newspaper article quoted above makes
clear, are about family lives, in domestic spaces. And family life has many
faces in Australia. In popular and professional writing, family is functional for
society and oppressive for (at least some) people. Family is both a private
dream and a public problem. Family is an individual experience (often the
most intimate and important of all an individual's experience) as well as part
of a solid, dominating, constraining social structure. Family is an arena in
which we act out conflict and rapid change and also the site of consensus and
massive stability. Family is an experience that will be different for men and
women; her family will be different from his. The suburban dream of family
and home contains all these contradictions and contrasts. Why would we
expect that people with different resources, or at different stages of family
life, would have a common experience? Why would we expect a simple answer to the question: Dream or nightmare?

The major new study with which this newspaper story disposed of the nightmare did, indeed, portray the face of the dream. It was the Berwick Report, first area study report by the Australian Institute of Family Studies (AIFS) from its Family Living Standards Study (McDonald 1993). Part of a unique and very major study of Australian families, it was not designed to arbitrate on the suburban dream, but the data collected from outer-suburban areas certainly gave a significant portrait of the satisfaction of at least the adult members of the families there. From a series of detailed surveys of households with children in outer-suburban Berwick, near Melbourne, it reported very considerable satisfaction with the place and the way of life.

Contrast this account with the attack on what one writer has called 'the great Australian nightmare' (Kemeny 1983). The portrait of nightmare is not usually based on empirical data. The empirical studies of Australian suburban life have been few, and even fewer have listened carefully to the voices of women. In 1976, an action research project set out to address the needs of residents and make their voices heard (Wadsworth 1976). A year earlier, a ground-breaking study of women in Australia included a chapter on 'Suburban neurotics?' (Summers 1975). At the time of the Berwick report, the assumptions about suburban neurosis were well established, but few studies had explored, let alone tested them.

Indeed one of the interesting features of the debate about suburbia is that it is not about whether people get what they want, but about the prices paid for the dream. These are claimed to include the financial burden required to purchase a home, the necessity to go 'out' to the far suburbs in order to afford it, inadequacy of services and access to support and, above all, isolation, especially of women in the far-out homes on the flat, look-alike expanses of new 'communities' that lack any semblance of community.

Why would people pay such a price? There are two ways of looking at home ownership, too—hardly surprising, since it is about family. The 'family home' offers the image of a good life, peaceful, loving, the haven achieved. Home ownership, like motherhood, is almost always assumed in popular discourse to be a good thing. Despite changes in family options, in timing of family stages and in the economic realities of home purchase, studies (and experience) show that young adults still widely assume that they will have families and will live their family lives in private homes (Richards 1985a, 1994). It is hardly surprising, then, that Australia retains one of the highest rates of home ownership in the industrialised world, and is one of the slowest, among Western countries, to shift from traditional family structures. The 'great Australian dream' of the family in its own home contributes significantly to this stability.

Since the early days of suburban development, it has been widely agreed that this haven is about family life and should be 'manned', so to speak, by women. Home was, and is, presented as a 'place of rest and refreshment from the cares of the world' (Reiger 1991). Common parlance today still says so; women go 'out' to (paid) work; a home is a 'family home'. Whilst family life changes rapidly, there seems amazingly little change in the ways people link home to private family life, and the proper steps on the family ladder. In my interviews in the 1970s (Richards 1985b), the link between home and family was unquestioned. (A woman: 'I don't think a home is a home without children.' A man: 'We were both ready to have a child by then ... Getting the house was the main thing' [Richards 1990, p. 117].) At that stage, owner occupancy (owner or purchaser) accounted for over 70 per cent of households in Australia. It still accounted for 68 per cent of households as I began a five-year study of the growth of a new suburb I called 'Green Views'. A man:

> Oh yeah, there's a big stigma about renting... You never come across anybody who actually admits to just renting as a permanent structure. It's always, 'Just for the moment, until we can get enough money,' or whatever. But people tend to look down on the ones who haven't been able to save up enough for their deposit. And 'Fancy getting married and having kids if you don't have your own house!' sort of thing. (Richards 1990, p. 117)

In Green Views, 'Why do you want to own?' was sometimes answered (like 'Why did you get married?' in the earlier study), with, 'Everyone does'. 'The dream' was even cited, as the reason, especially by men:

> I don't know that I could give you a reason for wanting to. I suppose it's just like, as they say, the Great Australian Dream. It's just something you do. I couldn't rent for a long, long period. I mean, not on a permanent basis.

> I suppose it's the Great Australian Dream; we always expected to own a house, or own property, so we just bought... It's the done thing. I don't know, it would irk me, I think, to pay rent to someone else... It just sort of came naturally. The obvious thing is to buy a house and own it. (Richards 1990, pp. 117–18)

Satisfaction?

When home ownership is seen as so necessary for a good life, it will be hardly surprising if those who have achieved ownership tell interviewers that they got what they wanted. In Green Views, as in Berwick, people overwhelmingly said they had achieved what they came for.

The two areas, and the results of the two studies, are in some ways strikingly alike.[1] Both in Berwick and in Green Views, people were asked their reasons for moving to the suburb. The answers were very similar. In both studies, they wanted a house, with an environment for children. Women and men agreed the house was a necessary condition for family life. 'I couldn't have a baby in a flat', one woman said in Green Views—almost as though renting was a contraceptive.

The satisfaction expressed by large majorities, in Berwick or Green Views, is not restricted to women or men. And it is about privacy and family. In Berwick, the AIFS interviewed only in households with children, in Green Views we sampled from everyone who came, but found only two couples who did not intend to have children. Both studies were of people seeking and finding what the authors of the Berwick report called a 'child-centred life-style'. The parents of Berwick most often nominated child-related reasons for choosing Berwick (proximity to schools and safety for children to play), followed by a quiet neighbourhood and a large block of land and house. 'Those purchasing in Berwick were looking for a good place to bring up young children and they see themselves as having satisfied that aim' (Richards 1990, pp. 457–8). The young childless couples in Green Views were most likely to rank as important: owning the house, quietness, layout and atmosphere, style of house and a 'better area' and privacy; then came the child-related factors of open space, play areas, lawfulness, schools, playmates. Those who had children ranked the child-related factors more highly (Richards 1990, pp. 13–15).

And the price? This chapter is too brief to detail the results, but they can be fairly simply summarised: the two studies agree that the majority had suffered neither 'exile' to outer suburbia, nor 'isolation'. They had not been forced to the outer suburbs, and had not come 'out' merely to own a home. In its subsequent study of an older suburb, Box Hill, the AIFS established that the price of housing was very comparable with Berwick. Since Box Hill clearly offered better transport and services, there was no simple advantage to outer-suburban purchase in terms of amenities. The difference, crucial for Berwick residents as for those in Green Views, was the image of a *new* area, with new, clean houses, and a 'country atmosphere' in which to bring up children. To gain these, people were prepared to pay prices of distance and lack of facilities. In both areas, it appeared that people were not seeking just any house, and that cleanliness and newness mattered a lot, especially to young couples just 'starting out' on family, seeking an environment they saw as healthy and good for children, offering a 'country atmosphere'.

And 'isolation'? This has several dimensions, some about distance to travel (to work, facilities, friends) and some about networks, especially family networks. Again, the majority in both studies appeared to have considered and happily paid the price of commuting time and lack of facilities. And they had most certainly not been torn by great distance from their families. In both studies, almost all the households were nuclear families, almost all intact, and the majority were in easy distance and regular contact with extended family members.

Isolation can mean many things, some of which are highly desired. Historically, suburbanisation 'promoted more privatised households, less embedded within their communities', as housing was provided with spaces and 'people socialised more in their homes and gardens, and less on the street' (Gilding 1991, p. 46). Both in Green Views and in Berwick, open spaces and privacy were sought and achieved; in neither suburb did adults complain in large numbers of isolation from other residents. What then of the assumption of the critical literature that 'suburban residences tend to isolate women from involvement outside the home' (Saegert 1980, pp. 105–6).

It is very hard to assess the sense of community in Berwick because the questions asked about aspects of neighbourhood are largely about facilities such as traffic noise and television reception. But the data on contact with neighbours (McDonald 1993, pp. 275f.) gives intriguing pictures. Perhaps most startling is the difference between the more middle-class area of Berwick, (where 57 per cent said they knew a neighbour well enough to have a child minded regularly) and Doveton, where only 32 per cent said this. Intriguingly, one of the items listed under neighbourhood problems was 'isolation', but the results are not discussed in the relevant section (1993, p. 278) but shown in the tables (McDonald 1993, pp. 299–300). The proportion seeing this as a problem in their neighbourhood ranged from a low of 8 per cent in Doveton, to a high of 14 per cent in Endeavour Hills. But perhaps more significant was the proportion who did not know: from 63 per cent in Doveton, down to 46 per cent in Berwick. (Vandalism and graffiti are easy to see, isolation is much harder to identify.)

In both Green Views and Berwick, people were much more outspoken about the overt problems, in particular vandalism and, not unrelated, the lack of activities for teenagers (Richards 1990, ch. 3; McDonald 1993, pp. 255–9). Lack of activities for adults at home was less easy to discuss, since there was no overt evidence, and privacy was desired.

So is there, after all, no nightmare? Or, perhaps, was it a nightmare in previous decades, when suburbia housed women trapped without transport in the symbols of family life they were bound to maintain? In today's outer suburbs, the majority of households have two cars, and the majority of women are not there during the day.

Satisfaction and dreams: Issues of evidence

The Berwick Report raises the 'social justice' argument that suburban areas are 'isolating, lonely and lacking in neighbourliness, leading to psychological problems and dysfunction in various forms'. This argument, it concludes, 'receives very little support from our study'. Whilst 'there are many aspects of life in Berwick that can be improved... in the main, Berwick residents are satisfied with their circumstances' (McDonald 1993, p. 456). It was this overwhelming picture of satisfaction that prompted the claims that the report 'debunks urban myths'.

But does it? We need to ask several questions about this evidence of satisfaction. What is being measured, and how? What is the nature of the evidence? Is the evidence consistent with different interpretations? What is *not* being asked?

Firstly, what is being measured and how? In the detailed accounts of the results of the survey, the authors take care to point out the nature of the questions they asked and the variety of answers. Collecting ticks on lists of 'advantages' and 'disadvantages' of an area, or indications on a nine-point scale of satisfaction with nominated aspects of the area, gives a very simple picture of experience. So too does the method of reporting the data, topic by topic, often in terms of simple frequencies of answers to particular questions. It gives a broad-brush picture of responses on each topic, rather than showing how the separate aspects relate in the stories of individuals or communities, or identifying clusters of responses across the topics.

Secondly, what is the evidence like? Survey data is most reliable on issues of what people see as fact. To take a simple example, car ownership is a matter of fact. In both Berwick and Green Views we have clear reports in surveys of the numbers of cars in the household at a given time. (In both, the majority had at least two cars.) But once-off survey interviews tell little about process or interpretations of facts; in Green Views most couples came with one car, and during the next years the acquisition of a second car was sometimes desperately sought, the women often returning to paid work in order to afford it. The reliance on once-off survey data means the picture from Berwick is static, and lacks people's accounts of what matters to them, or how they interpret things. Most of the data on 'neighbourliness', for instance, (like that in most studies) is won by asking hypothetical questions. Do you know a neighbour well enough to help in a crisis? (Brownlee 1993). Most readers of this chapter would surely answer 'yes', especially if they have had no crisis lately, and it could be argued that most people would hope they had such possible crisis help. But the question cannot tap the subtlety of especially women's experiences of the tasks of what I have called 'network management', negotiating reciprocity, privacy and independence in a context of isolation and vulnerability. In the Green Views study, data from such questions responded to complex analysis with surprising results.

Different sorts of data access different aspects of the neighbouring experience (D'Abbs 1993). Qualitative data, from open-ended interviews or from participant observation, can give a very different picture if it is rigorously analysed.[2] Australian family studies have produced a strong strain of qualitative research (Richards 1985b), studies reporting the complexity and richness of people's accounts and daily lives. In the Green Views study, the qualitative data always expanded on the quantitative material, and sometimes directly challenged it. It was from this data, particularly from women's accounts of day-to-day life in the suburb, that evidence appeared that achievement of the desired house and area and the child-centred lifestyle clearly had a price:

> Everyone is working hard, weekends we go out ... I love this house, I love the area. I never see the neighbours. They're very busy, working ... nobody knows anybody. (Richards 1990, p. 164)

This Italian-born woman had minimal needs for community, but even these were not met. 'It's nice to be able to know who your next-door neighbour is and what their name is. I don't, because we've never even met' (Richards

1990, p. 164). But her survey responses showed her entirely satisfied with the choice to come to Green Views.

Similarly whilst a majority in Green Views (as in Berwick) rated the area well for 'community' and 'friendliness', the qualitative data in Green Views showed ambivalence in almost all the comments about local community—and not only from overloaded two-income households. A woman whose neighbours 'kept their heads down' was herself at home, but knew nobody 'past two doors' and was very sure people did not want to know each other. She had been employed until recently:

> Since I've had my child, I've got to know a few more people. It feels quite
> good. At one stage I was the only person home in the street out of seven-
> teen houses ... You feel as though you get watched quite often. Just talking
> to another few neighbours, they sort of feel that too. It's always someone
> looking out of curtains or something. (Richards 1990, p. 165)

Thirdly, is the evidence open to alternative readings? There are several problems with the happy assumption that majority satisfaction ratings indicate there is no problem with the dream of suburbia. The bland picture of suburban satisfaction hides the variety of responses; a majority that is satisfied can mean up to 49 per cent that is not. On some issues, the AIFS researchers report, 'for every group of parents who were positive about particular aspects of living in the area there was another group who gave negative comments' (McDonald 1993, p. 280). But the report offers few answers to the critical question, who is negative? The fact that a majority of people are satisfied tells us nothing about the experience of the often substantial minority who is not. It tells us merely that the majority had indeed achieved the sought home in the sought suburb. Any report relying on majority responses will be positive about suburbia, since the achievement of suburban life is likely to satisfy the needs of the majority of residents, namely, those who are usually not there. And any report relying on straight-forward questions about aspects, facilities etc. is unlikely to tap more private feelings and experiences.

Fourthly, and most importantly, what is *not* being asked? Can the results be seen differently from different theoretical positions? The critics of suburbia do not deny that the majority of residents of suburbia are satisfied by their achievement of home ownership; indeed they assert this, and worry about it. Their claim is that this achievement has a high price that people pay because the ideologically imposed goals of family and home ownership are all-important to them. Is this so in Berwick? Unfortunately, we cannot really tell. The AIFS researchers had not been given the task of asking if some people pay—and if so, who pays—a high price for achieving the dream. Such questions are not even raised; intriguingly hardly any of the references at the end of the present chapter are mentioned in that report.

The price of a dream

The price of dreams is extremely hard to research. There would be no inconsistency in a woman saying, for instance, that her first priority in choosing
Berwick was for a good place to bring up children, that she was very satisfied
with this aspect of it, even if she herself hated living there. Achievement of
that dream may be very consistent with loneliness and isolation, for at least
some. If a majority of people say they got what they wanted, this does not
mean it will give them the good life they expected.

Given workforce participation patterns, those daily absent will be almost all men, and a majority of women (mothers of school-age children). As
the Berwick Report puts it, with no hint of irony, 'in accordance with the
needs of children, labour force participation of mothers was related to the age
of the youngest child' (McDonald 1993, p. 36). The ideological assumption
that women will attend to those children's needs, by seeking part-time or
casual employment is presumably shared by those they interviewed. In accordance with the ideology of good family life, a small proportion of residents
are home to evaluate the daytime world of suburbia, and stitch together what
has been called the 'crazy quilts' of women's support networks. Clearly those
who commute will have very different needs and evaluations of the area from
those who are there in the daytime.

But that ideology is not unchanging. It is instructive to recall that the
suburban nightmare of the 1960s was a different one. More than thirty years
ago, a leading American sociologist set out to challenge 'the suburban myth'.
'If suburban life was as undesirable and unhealthy as the critics charged, the
suburbanites themselves were blissfully unaware of it; they were happy in
their new homes and communities, much happier than they had been in the
city' (Gans 1967, p. xvi). But what he challenged was an image of dreadful
conformity and facile socialising, the alleged costs of suburbia when its women
were at home:

> The critics charge that the suburbs are socially hyperactive and have made
> people so outgoing that they have little time or inclination for the devel-
> opment of personal autonomy. The pervasive homogeneity of the
> population has depressed the vitality of social life, and the absence of the
> more heterogeneous neighbours and friends has imposed a conformity
> which further reduces the suburbanite's individuality. (Gans 1967, p. 154)

Under this social activity, the critics alleged there was a 'suburban malaise' of loneliness. Gans found both boredom and loneliness rarely reported,
but that they overlapped, especially for those women who experienced loneliness from family as well as lack of friends. Gans concluded that 'if there is
malaise in Levittown, it is female but not suburban' (Gans 1967, p. 226).

Thirty years on, the achievement of suburban life for families whose
adults are more likely than not to be employed is a dream of privacy, not
community. The aspects of life in Berwick most clearly approved of by large
minorities were not about community. Green Views was sold as 'a family

community', but people's accounts made it clear that they did not seek community in the sociological sense. Close interaction, intimate neighbour relations and knowledge of each other was seen as dangerous, time consuming and often revealing of weakness. Good neighbours, like suburbia itself, have two faces. The most common definition offered in the Green Views data was 'There when you need them but not in your pocket'.[3] So there would be no inconsistency in a very lonely person saying she was satisfied with 'neighbourliness' in Berwick, if neighbourliness provided this desired privacy, albeit leaving her lonely.

After five years of detailed research in Green Views, we concluded that the nightmare of suburban isolation is not merely a 'popular myth', but a problem facing a small minority, some, not all, of those who are home in the suburb, and most constrained by the demands of privacy.

For the majority, isolation is a good thing. That helps explain serious puzzles in the data. For a long time in Green Views it appeared that suburban isolation was an invention of critical sociologists. As in Berwick, most people said they knew a lot of people. We rarely heard people talk of their own isolation. A lot of people told us how isolated *others* were (or must be). The conditions for such isolation are obvious. But women there rarely spoke of social isolation, and only awkwardly, apologetically, of personal loneliness.

Late in the project, we began to recognise that the pervasive themes were that this was a 'community' of people 'all in the same boat', where 'anyone can belong'. But neither 'community' nor 'belonging', in this context, implied close relationships or regular interaction. People saw the avoidance of community as a necessity—because 'everyone works' had the necessary result that 'nobody's home'. In all the material on women's employment, the most common assumption (after the assumption that children suffer) is that women's employment means loss of community. 'Most of them are working people' hence 'everyone just seems to keep their heads down'.

For many women, 'nobody's home' in Green Views was a self-fulfilling prophecy: women who stayed home were so lonely; they were thus more likely to return to paid work. This might help explain the puzzle described in the Berwick Report that women in the paid workforce persistently express more satisfaction with their work than men, even though they are in less well paid jobs (McDonald 1993, ch. 12). But it is usually only one reason for return to the workforce, and nobody in Green Views blamed isolation for workforce participation. Rather, throughout the data, women and men blamed the women; isolation was in one sense or another always their fault:

> All I did was stay home. We rarely went out, except perhaps to visit my mum or his mum. Once you don't go out, you lose it, you just don't know what to say to people ... The longer you stayed home the harder it was to get out to talk to anybody. And the odd times you did go out, you didn't know what to say to them, and you had a rotten time anyway. It was your own fault, but you just didn't know how to. (Richards 1990, p. 169)

'Your fault if you're lonely' suggests strongly that we need to understand not merely the conditions for isolation, but also the processes of the making and masking of women's isolation in suburbia. Like any other processes of blaming the victim, it distracts from the social construction of the problem.

In Green Views, where we had the data from five years of watching groups and activities, we found those not at home assumed it would be very easy to make friends if they were at home with children. (Having children gives people something in common. It also provides meeting places.) The most common assumption is that people are visible when they have young children—collecting them, chasing them:

> There's a few people that have retired into these houses. You hardly ever see them. They don't get out and about much. The young people, just married and with little kids and that, you see them all the time. (Richards 1990, p. 257)

We also discovered that the assumption was often wrong. Certainly for some women it was true that being home with little children made them not only visible but available. It provides common topics of conversation with other mothers and restricts movements away from them. But observation of the women's groups clearly indicated that lack of privacy can be a problem:

> Everybody knows what everybody else is doing ... everybody watches everybody else's ins and outs ... I would never live in a court again ... It is all borrow, borrow, and there is a lot of competition in the court, you know, about what have I got and you haven't. You know I'm mainly talking about women. (Richards 1990, p. 257–8)

And all the mothers have to be there, so workforce participation remains the enemy of community:

> I'd go out for a walk from the front to the letterbox and there was such a deathly silence, even if you were hanging out the washing at the back, you didn't hear children. There was no-one around, no neighbours around, 'cos you knew they were all at work. Really it was sort of a frightening thing sometimes 'cos you'd sense a noise, I'd sense someone walking up the side of the house or something.' (Richards 1990, p. 259)

Women who could not make contacts always considered returning to work:

> It's not exactly fun looking after two children, doing the same thing day in and day out. And it did get to the point where I was very bored and I constantly thought about going back to work. Just being able to get out. (Richards 1990, p. 259)

Unable to find childcare, this woman finally 'achieved' the second car, so she could get out, but now intended to use it to return to work. 'I think it might make me a bit more sane. I feel I'm going mad sometimes' (Richards 1990, p. 259).

Everybody needs a neighbour?

The evidence at Green Views was that near-neighbour friendships were frequently difficult. Those who achieved intimate local friendships usually did so away from near neighbours, by forcing themselves, sometimes almost literally, to 'join things':

> It is a case of having to, otherwise there is nothing. There is no social life in Green Views, there are no recreation facilities, it is designed so that you don't become too isolated in the street designs, no front fences, but you could very easily make the four walls of your house your front fence and it is a case of having to go outside the home to get involved. (Richards 1990, pp. 275–6)

For the women and men active in the groups, community was not guaranteed, conflict often was, and friendships seldom resulted from, sometimes, years of gruelling hard work. Throughout the stories of the groups, class differences divided, the life-stage wheel inexorably turned, and gender determined experience. The reasons given for assuming that people do not have to be lonely often proved unfounded. It was actually hard for those with children to meet, and if they did, there was no reason to expect children would cement relationships. If children are no guarantee of community, neither is a new area. In the early years, Green Views showed a 'flurry of activity' as people moved in, but that 'dropped off' quickly. People made it clear that they themselves put constraints on 'neighbouring' from the start. 'As time's gone on, naturally, everybody becomes a little bit more involved in their own problems and you don't seem to have as much time'. Some people never did welcome early-days neighbouring—especially those who had very busy lives outside:

> I usually like to stay very quiet when I'm home. I don't want neighbours coming in for cups of tea and all that sort of thing you see. I just like my friends that I can go and visit and they can come and visit me. (Richards 1990, p. 269)

A woman whose loneliness puzzled her said, 'I don't know why I haven't joined anything really. Probably because I don't know anyone'. She had lost touch with former friends, and not made new ones:

> I got up this morning and took the children to school. And because I didn't go to the market, I came home, read my paper and then went to bed for an hour. And after, I thought, look at me, I'm in perfect health. There's nothing wrong with me, and here I am laying in bed. And really because I was lost, I felt utterly lost. And isn't that ridiculous! Now I mean why did I go to bed? (Richards 1990, p. 270)

If you're lonely, it's your fault. There is certainly some truth in the assertion. In Green Views the evidence argued that the management of local social networks and negotiation with the ideology of family privacy is, for at least some people, a very active process over which they have considerable control:

I say 'hello' but I don't really know anybody. I suppose I'm too busy! That doesn't sound too good, does it! I don't know really. Everybody *works* here. This is one of the problems, I think. You know, everybody here *works*... I'm not really lonely for people. I've got my Mum, and I have a fairly busy life otherwise, you know. I've got aunts to visit and a sister to visit, and friends outside of Green Views. Green Views is not, I mean I don't feel that I'm trapped here, or anything like that. I don't think you need to be. (Richards 1990, p. 272)

Dream or nightmare?

The family was experienced as a little community, a self-contained unit which fulfilled the needs of its members for security, warmth, intimacy. People had higher expectations of domestic happiness based on marital compatibility and close relationships with their children. Home was a 'nest', the cherished possession, the place where you could express your 'real' self, the place where you chose to spend your time.

The relationship between this 'ideal' and the 'reality' is a complex one. As we have seen, the suburban dream does have a material base. But precisely because it is ideology, it offers only a partial account. Not only does it remain silent on the oppressive elements at the core of family life, but it has prevented these things from being spoken. (Game & Pringle 1984, p. 96)

Sociological studies, like ideologies, offer partial accounts (partly of course because sociologists, like all people, work within ideologies). To assess the evidence of a sociological study you need to ask about the version of reality it portrays. This usually involves asking sharp questions about theory and method. Why and how was this data gathered? By whom? What was asked? Of whom? Whose data is this, and what were the purposes of the study? Where did it start, theoretically, and does that tell us what assumptions were brought in and built into the analysis, and what further questions were or could be asked of the data?

Sociological studies also rarely offer such clear-cut conclusions as newspaper editors would wish. Certainly the Berwick Report is not nearly sufficient ammunition to destroy the critical attack on suburbia. That attack has never claimed people were not satisfied; as I argued at the start, the debate about suburbia is not about whether people get what they want, but about how those wants are imposed on them, and the prices they pay for their dreams. Nor has the critique of suburbia ever claimed everyone is disadvantaged by outer suburban living; rather that some, particularly those home during the day, and particularly those without resources and skills to find company and help, may be trapped in suburban homes. The Berwick Report offers nothing to contradict these claims, indeed ironically it could well support them, if the focus were on the minorities that are not content and those who are not supported. The picture it paints is, above all, of the majority not dependent on locality for social contacts, and the fact that it is so cheerful a picture is strong evidence that they have the numbers, given the changing nature of Australian family lives. If the problem of suburbia is after all a female problem, for those women who stay home, the frequency of occurrence of this problem is being reduced by attrition in their numbers. In outer suburbs increasingly those at home will say that nobody is at home. This increases their problem but decreases the numbers who share the problem. As the authors of the Berwick Report are quick to point out, this should not be allowed to support complacency—that all is well in suburbia.

Notes

1   There is no space in the present chapter for a detailed comparison. The Berwick study is reported by McDonald (1993), and Brownlee (1993) offers a focus on the neighbouring data in the AIFS study. The Green Views study is reported in Richards (1990) and its method in Richards and Richards (1994). For the purposes of the present argument, the important differences are in the variety of families covered by once-off surveys in the Berwick study, compared with the more homogeneous samples covered by five years of qualitative and quantitative data in Green Views. The municipality of Berwick itself is most like Green Views in occupational and class terms. The Berwick Report also covers more working-class areas and outer areas of semi-rural development. The Green Views housing estate was studied for five years from the first housing there, hence this study is different in several respects; all the residents were 'pioneers' in one identifiable 'family community', the majority were first-home owners, a high proportion was childless when they moved there, sharing the experience of 'getting set up' and 'starting a family'. Whilst many couples in Berwick had those experiences, the AIFS study also covers areas of long-established housing.

2   The requirements of the Green Views study for analytical techniques that permit rigorous indexing, sorting and exploration of textual material and thorough documentation of search procedures with large-scale qualitative data were the spur for design of the NUD•IST system for computer-assisted storage, indexing, retrieval and analysis, designed at La Trobe University by Tom Richards and myself (Richards & Richards 1994) and now marketed by Qualitative Solutions and Research, at the University's technology park.

3   Data reported here are from reinterviews in 1981 with 150 married residents, using a precoded schedule, but also taping. The Green Views study was funded by the Australian Research Grants Committee and La Trobe University. Details of the study and full report are in Richards (1990).

References

Brownlee, H. (1973), 'Who needs neighbours', *Family Matters*, no. 35, August, pp. 34–6.

D'Abbs, P. (1993), *Who Helps? Support Networks and Social Policy in Australia*, Australian Institute of Family Studies, Melbourne.

Gans, H. J. (1967), *The Levittowners: Ways of Life and Politics in a New Suburban Community*, Pantheon, New York.

Game, A. & Pringle, R. (1983), 'The making of the Australian family', in A. Burns et al. (eds), *The Family in the Modern World*, Allen & Unwin, Sydney.

Gilding, M. (1991), *The Making and Breaking of the Australian Family*, Allen & Unwin, Sydney.

Kemeny, J. (1983), *The Great Australian Nightmare*, Georgian House, Melbourne.

Kingston, B. (1975), *My Wife, My Daughter and Poor Mary-Ann*, Nelson, Melbourne.

McDonald, P. (ed.) (1993), *The Australian Living Standards Study, Berwick Report. Part 1: The Household Survey*, Australian Institute of Family Studies, Melbourne.

Reiger, K. (1991), *Family Economy*, McPhee & Gribble, Melbourne.

Richards, L. (1985a), *Having Families*, rev. edn, Penguin, Melbourne.

Richards, L. (1985b), 'Australian family studies', *Contemporary Sociology*, vol. 14.

Richards, L. (1990), *Nobody's Home: Dreams and Realities in a New Suburb*, Oxford University Press, Melbourne.

Richards, L. (1994), 'The ideology of the family: Women, family and ideology in three Australian contexts', in K. Pritchard Hughes (ed.), *Contemporary Australian Feminism*, Longman Cheshire, Melbourne.

Richards, L. & Richards, T. (1994), 'From filing cabinet to computer', in R. W. Burgess & A. Bryman (eds), *Analysing Qualitative Data*, Routledge, London.

Saegert, S. (1980), 'Masculine cities and feminine suburbs: Polarized ideas, contradictory realities', *Signs*, vol. 5, Spring, pp. S96–S111.

Saunders, P. (1990), *A Nation of Home Owners*, Unwin Hyman, London.

Summers, A. (1975), *Damned Whores and God's Police*, Penguin, Melbourne.

Wadsworth, Y. (1976), The Knox Project: A first annual assessment of the Knox Early Childhood Development Complex, duplicated, n. p.

Bibliography

Allport, C. (1986), 'Women and suburban housing', in J. B. McLoughlin & M. Huxley (eds), *Urban Planning in Australia: Critical Readings*, Longman Cheshire, Melbourne.

Baldock, C. & Cass, B. (eds) (1983), *Women, Social Welfare and the State*, Allen & Unwin, Sydney.

Balbo, L. (1987), 'Crazy Quilts: Rethinking the welfare state debate from a woman's point of view', in A. S. Sassoon (ed.), *Women and the State: The Shifting Boundaries of Public and Private*, Hutchinson, London.

Barrett, M. & McIntosh, M. (1982), *The Anti-Social Family*, Verso, London.

Broom, D. (1992), 'Review of "Nobody's Home"', *Australian and New Zealand Journal of Sociology*, vol. 28, no. 1.

Bryson, L. (1984), 'The Australian patriarchal family', in L. Bryson & S. Encel (eds), *Australian Society*, 4th edn, Cheshire, Melbourne.

Burke, T., Hancock, L. & Newton, P. (1984), *A Roof Over their Heads: Housing Issues and Families in Australia*, Institute of Family Studies, Melbourne.

Finch, J. & Groves, D. (eds) (1983), *A Labour of Love: Women, Work and Caring*, Routledge & Kegan Paul, London.

Gamarnikow, E. et al. (eds) (1983), *The Public and the Private*, Heinemann, London.

Gittins, D. (1985), *The Family in Question: Changing Households and Familiar Ideologies*, Macmillan, London.

Grieve, N. & Burns, A. (eds) (1986), *Australian Women: New Feminist Perspectives*, Oxford University Press, Melbourne.

Glezer, H. (1983), Changes in marriage and sex role attitudes among young married women: 1971–1982, Paper to the Australian Family Research Conference, Canberra.

Hall, S. (1983), 'Ideology in the modern world', *La Trobe Working Papers in Sociology*, La Trobe University, Bundoora.

Harman, E. (1983), 'Capitalism, patriarchy and the city', in C.V. Baldock & B. Cass (eds), *Women, Social Welfare and the State*, Allen & Unwin, Sydney.

Harper, J. & Richards, L. (1986), *Mothers and Working Mothers*, rev. edn, Penguin, Melbourne.

Kemeny, J. (1981), *The Myth of Home Ownership*, Routledge & Kegan Paul, London.

Reiger, K. (1985), *The Disenchantment of the Home*, Oxford University Press, Melbourne.

Seeley, J. & Sim, A. et al. (1956), *Crestwood Heights*, Basic Books, New York.

Stretton, H. (1970), *Ideas for Australian Cities*, Hugh Stretton, Melbourne.

Thorne, B. (1982), 'Feminist Rethinking of the Family', in B. Thorne & M. Yalom (eds), *Rethinking the Family*, Longman, New York.

Wearing, B. (1983), *The Ideology of Motherhood*, Allen & Unwin, Sydney.

Chapter 9 | I shop, therefore I am
Peter Spearritt

Every day of the week in urban, suburban and rural Australia, people are out shopping. Shops, from corner stores to grand shopping malls, are an integral part of our physical landscape. Shopping as a necessity or an activity of choice also looms large in the landscape of the mind. In our society it is hard to escape from the retailer, who reaches out on television, in newspapers and magazines and through the humble letter box. In a capitalistic society, where manufacturers, importers and retailers are tempted to cater for every whim which has a market, shopping is a serious business. For individuals, shopping may be a delight or a chore, depending on one's wants and needs and level of income.

Shopping reflects and to some extent creates the nature of production and consumption in our society. For much of this century it has been assumed that women had the primary responsibility for shopping. In 1969 the feminist broadcaster Julie Rigg wrote an article on 'The loneliness of the long distance housewife: Mrs Consumer', pointing out that women were responsible for at least two-thirds of family expenditure:

> The housewifely skills of today are less and less those of creation and improvisation, more and more those of selection. Decisions about purchases may well provide for Australian women a degree of autonomy and an affirmation of identity which many men find in their work. 'I buy, therefore I am'. (Rigg 1969, p. 143)

In the age of the supermarket, with a plethora of packaged goods, neither women nor men needed any longer to behead chickens for a roast or even collect eggs from the henhouse at the back of the garden. As late as the 1930s over one-third of all suburban households in Australia still kept chooks (chickens). Most women, in their socialisation and training for roles as housewives and mothers, were able to sew, cook, make jam and preserve fruit. In the postwar boom, with increased affluence and the coming of the supermarket, these skills became less necessary and also less valued, not least because of the increasing participation of women in the paid workforce (Pringle 1983; Reiger 1985; Whitwell 1989).

Shopping as economic activity

Shopping is something that most people do at least once a week and many people think about it much more often than that, especially when they enter the realm of desire for the acquisition of material goods, from engagement rings to cars. Retailing is at the heart of most economies, whatever the nominal economic system. Even in command economies, where conventional retailing and product range are often suppressed, retailing in the form of a black market may thrive.

The nature of retailing and the shopping experience now provides employment for market researchers around the world. Market segments and demands are studied from every imaginable angle. The key market variables: age, gender, household status (this used to be called 'marital status'), income and location are charted and mapped. Psychologists and market researchers devise strategies to pre-test products from the humble bread loaf to high-fashion clothes. Computerised bar codes now enable retailers to analyse the shopping preferences of their customers, including their reaction to 'specials' and the mix of products they buy.

Mainstream academic disciplines thrive in applied retailing studies. Sociologists advise on demographic patterns and questionnaire techniques. Psychologists construct small group-discussion sessions to assess the feel and market response for a new product. Geographers of retailing try to predict overall demand and travel patterns, while retail economists look at market mix and the question of core business plus add-ons.

The major financial institutions in our society—banks, insurance companies, corporate and union-owned superannuation schemes—'eye off' the major retailers as prospective investments. Retailers generate immediate cash flow, so they are attractive businesses to own, depending of course on the capital cost of buying in.

Four key factors influence whether greater diversity goes with size or not: the nature of the economic system, the balance of wealth and poverty in the economic system, the means with which people get to shops and the dominant politics of land use in a particular locality.

In command economies, like those of the former 'Eastern bloc' countries, retailing may be suppressed as an activity, usually because of central economic decisions about the range and nature of products that will be made and sold in an economy. Command economies often experience spectacular shortages of some products—from food to fashion—and their retailing is often satirised as one long queue. In economic systems characterised by extremes of wealth and poverty the very nature of retailing will vary from city to city and often within cities.

The means of getting to the retailing premises has an enormous influence on the nature and location of shopping. In cities where the road system and most of the physical infrastructure predates the age of the car the wealthy and the poor will often patronise markets or establishments in close proximity to each other. This can be seen in many of the world's great cities where the commercial areas in the city centres are highly constrained by geography and mass-transit systems. In Paris, London, New York and Melbourne the poor shoppers often rub shoulders with the rich, even if they usually visit different establishments. The same is true of capitalist Asian cities, such as Hong Kong, and command economy cities such as Beijing.

In cities or suburban areas which have developed in the age of the car it is much easier to separate middle-class customers from the underclass. It is no accident that the world's first drive-in shopping malls emerge in the most suburban and the most motorised societies—the United States, Canada and Australia.

Home delivery in the suburbs

When Barry Humphries's character Sandy Stone, of Gallipoli Crescent in the Melbourne suburb of Glen Iris, contemplates, from the grave, the prospect of his old house becoming part of a supermarket site, he reminisces about a nostalgic world of just-baked bread and home deliveries. In his 1993 production 'Look at me when I'm talking to you' Humphries opens the Sandy Stone segment with a supermarket set, a cornucopia of pre-packaged products in stylised aisles.

Most Australians over the age of sixty once lived in a society where bread was delivered by a local bakery, milk came in bottles—often from a nearby dairy—grocers happily delivered, as did butchers and other merchants on request. For more expensive purchases one usually went to 'town', meaning the city centre, to visit the grand emporia which offered electrical goods, furniture, soft furnishings, toys and, above all else, clothing—including high fashion.

This world has gradually fallen apart, although traces of it, and attempts to recreate aspects of it, do occur from time to time. The central elements in the demise of this regime—of home delivery, local shops, small strip-shopping centres and the grand city emporia—were first the rise of the cash-and-carry supermarket in the interwar years and the coming, with the great age of the car, of drive-in suburban shopping malls from the late 1950s.

Aspects of this world do reappear. Most nostalgic accounts of home delivery point to the baker and the smell of freshly baked bread on the doorstep, or they recall the age of ice delivery to keep the nation's ice chests functioning. Even in 1945, less than ten per cent of households had refrigerators. From the early 1950s hundreds of local suburban and country-town bakeries in Australia went out of business as large corporations—owning brands such as Tip Top—took over their activities and centralised them in fewer and fewer large plants. By 1970 the local baker in Australia was almost a thing of the past. With technological change and difficulties with the labour force in such large establishments, small baking plants that would fit into the size of an average suburban shop suddenly became economic. Little bakeries sprang up in suburbs all over the place and survive to this day. Some are in franchised chains, but most are in stand-alone businesses. They no longer home deliver but their clients go to them.

Corner stores and the shopping strip

The best way to imagine how retailing grows in a country town or a new suburb is to look at the hundreds of examples around Australia of towns founded between the 1850s and the 1880s that today have populations of around one thousand. The mix of businesses in the town will reflect the economic base of the town and its immediate hinterland. Gold towns and thriving ports often had a plethora of banks, while rural hinterland towns had stock and station agents. All towns had one or more basic grocery shops, a fruiterer, a blacksmith, a mercer, a newsagent (often owned by the local newspaper proprietor), a post office, at least one hotel (the gold towns with many more) and at least one bank. Most of these establishments sold goods, although some, like the post office and the banks, concentrated more on selling services.

With technological change, especially in transport, some establishments, like the blacksmith, disappeared entirely to be replaced by the modern equivalent, in this case the garage. Most of these shops had purpose-built structures: that is, the external facade made a statement about the products and services to be found within and the internal spaces were designed for the nature of the retailing business. Banks had grand facades and were invariably two-storey structures with the manager (and family) living above.Many stores provided accommodation above, both in the larger country towns and in the growing suburbs.

In smaller towns the ubiquitous 'general store' offered almost everything, from groceries and fruit to stationery and pots and pans. Suburban Australia, except in the most outlying parts, rarely had general stores, but it did have grocery establishments that offered a wide range of goods.

The cash-and-carry supermarkets

The first fully self-service supermarket appears to have opened in New Jersey in 1932. Cash-and-carry services came to Australia in the interwar years. Customers selected goods from tables, rather than from shopping gondolas or aisles, and took them to the counter to be wrapped. In 1933 Myers in Melbourne offered customers a counter, paper and string to wrap up their own parcels if they so wished. By refusing credit and lowering labour costs, cash-and-carry stores were able to undercut corner stores and even larger grocery establishments. The rise of grocery chains like Moran and Cato intimidated small grocers who found the specials of the chain stores, analogous to the 'loss leaders' of today, hard to compete with.

A complete self-service system did not become popular in Australia until the 1960s. Before then customers still relied on shop staff, not only to advise on what goods to purchase, but also to physically get the goods from the shelves. In 1958 only 9 per cent of food retail outlets in Australia were self-service. By 1968 this had risen to 27 per cent and by 1976 over half of such outlets had converted to or embraced self-service.

In the late 1950s the big variety-store chains, the Melbourne-based Coles and the Sydney-based Woolworths, entered the food business. Until that time, although they had built hundreds of variety stores in the suburbs and in country towns, they had avoided the food business, assuming that it was already well catered for. The coming of the supermarket, with its lower labour costs and cash-registered checkouts, enabled them to take on food as well. Coles purchased the J. C. Dickins chain in 1958 and opened its first New World supermarket in 1961 (Walker & Roberts 1988, ch. 11).

Drive-in shopping in the suburbs

Australia's first drive-in shopping centre opened in the Brisbane suburb of Chermside in May 1957. It promised to be 'a store dedicated to suburban family living, keyed to a casual way of life'. The advertisement carrying this text showed five smartly but casually dressed women, one wheeling a baby in a stroller.

Retailers in the centre were quick to point out that it offered all the goods and services to be had 'at the smarter end of Queen St' where Brisbane's grand emporia plied their trade. Chermside offered the same level of style and fashion to be found in the city but without the necessity, felt by most women, to 'dress-up' for the trip to town.

In a continuing series of advertisements, Allan and Stark, the largest retailer in the centre, depicted Chermside as 'an island of retailing in a lake of parking'. Patrons could come by car, bus or tram, but the ease of parking received the most attention. Women were reassured that they could park for as long as they liked and would no longer have to worry about getting tickets from male parking attendants. Drive-in shopping was also completely safe for children as 'traffic hazards are eliminated', with 'everything under the one roof' and completely air-conditioned to create 'the right atmosphere any time of the year' (Chermside Supplement, *Courier Mail*, 29 May 1957).

In its BBC store, Chermside offered a drive-in food market. Its opening specials included tins of Nestles reduced-cream, Letona diced peaches, kerosene ('4 gall tin'—the centre opened in winter), Tom Piper plum pudding and Rosella sweet corn, both in tins. The BBC advertisement showed a housewife wearing a casual, but smart, summer frock in command of a shopping trolley.

Almost all the retailers concentrated on women in their opening advertisements. Chandler's Appliance Store offered an 'expert Home Economist' to demonstrate 'how to prepare tastier meals for your family' while a representative from Hoover Washing Machines 'will show you how Monday's drudgery can become a day of leisure' (Chermside Supplement, *Courier Mail*, 29 May 1957).

Although Chermside was the first drive-in shopping centre in Australia, the big retailers in other cities, especially in Sydney and Melbourne, were cognisant of suburban growth and its possible implications. Grace Brothers, a large Sydney department store, found in the 1930s that its location of ten-minutes walk from Central Station was not ideal in a city where the centre of shopping action had moved near to the new underground railway stations of St. James and Town Hall. In the 1930s Grace Brothers established branch stores at Parramatta and Bondi. The suburban shops were designed as 'show-rooms' for its large emporium. They were to specialise in 'cash and carry' items and products not in stock would be secured from the central store in the city (Spearritt 1978, pp. 225–7).

The big emporia watched these developments with interest, but the Second World War delayed corporate decision making and it was not until Kenneth Myer visited the United States in 1949, and again in the 1950s, that the emporia started to take the challenge from the suburbs seriously. Chermside, backed by the Brisbane emporium of Allan Stark opened in 1957, with 700 car spaces, along with a smaller venture at Top Ryde, in Sydney. In the same year Grace Brothers built new stores at Bondi and Parramatta.

On one American trip Myer encountered Stonestown, San Francisco, a suburban development on a 40-acre site with parking for 2500 cars. An aerial photograph of this development, reproduced in the 1954 Melbourne plan, was approvingly captioned 'a large modern American suburban centre', re-plete with freeway and high-rise residential structures. The tiny market research industry in Australia pored over American magazines like *Chain Store Age'* (*Current Affairs Bulletin*, June 1967, p. 23).

Myer purchased 30 acres of land at Oakleigh, eight miles from the city, providing 2500 'free' parking spaces, just like Stonestown. The centre included the three-storey Myer Emporium, a Coles Dickins supermarket, 71 other shops, a child-minding centre for 60 children and 'kiddieland' with electric-car rides and a junior zoo. *Rydges Business Magazine* told its readers that in the new centres 'shopping should be fun! A store interior is like a stage. Its actors are the goods on display; the audience moves in and around the stage itself' (*Rydes Business Magazine*, 1 August 1960).

In December 1964 Patricia Rolfe explained to *Bulletin* readers that 'the flight' of retailers to the suburbs in Sydney was 'almost universal'. Being the yuletide season she pointed out that:

> Many children growing up in Australia now will never know the tradi-
> tion of a trip to town to see Father Christmas. You can grow sentimental
> over this if you like, remembering Christmases past, but Father Christmas
> is resilient. He now does just as good business as ever in the suburbs.
> (Rolfe 1964, p. 25)

Rolfe described company directors studying maps of Sydney and sub-urbs with 'the intensity of a Napoleon carving up Europe'. In describing the Grace Brothers' bid to build a centre in the Sydney suburb of Bankstown even bigger than Myer's at Chadstone she pointed to the demographic and travel statistics: 255 000 people within ten minutes' drive and 459 000 within twenty minutes drive. She outlined the reasoning behind selecting a site for a new centre:

> Entirely new areas are not sought after. Acres of fibro cottages may be filled with people who need furniture and appliances, but they are generally weighed down by mortgages and the expense of raising a family. Old suburbs generally have an old population, past their maximum earning and spending ... a good mixed area such as you see from the heights of Roselands, with a satisfying vista of tele-roofed, brick-veneer bungalows is what developers like to gaze on. (Rolfe 1964, p. 26)

Rolfe's reasoning is an impressive summary of what market researchers were saying at the time, including the description of 'tele-roofed' houses. In the first two decades after the introduction of television in Australia many suburban households needed tall aerials to get TV signals. These aerials were a dominant motif of consumption on the suburban landscape.

In the long run fibro suburbs, also within easy reach of Roselands, produced their share of cash flow as well, not least because of the spectacular increase of women in the paid workforce in the 1960s and 1970s. At a time of almost full employment more and more households had both husbands and wives in paid employment, and sometimes one or more offspring as well.

Shops and workers

Australia currently has over 170 000 shopfront, retailing outlets and over 35 000 motor vehicle retail and service centres. The makeup of this range of shops, supermarkets, cafes, take-away food outlets and garages is shown in the following table.

Table 9.1   Retail outlets in Australia, 1991–2

	Number	Persons employed
Supermarket and grocery stores	9486	180 826
Take-away food retailing	20 324	118 212
Other food retailing	23 466	
Department stores	459	87 148
Other clothing, footwear, fabrics	21 688	91 138
Furniture, floor covering, appliances	14 268	73 355
Recreational goods	12 913	60 071
Other personal and household goods	28 164	116 986
Household items repair	3238	9654
Cafes and restaurants	14 740	136 894
Hairdressing and beauty salons	15 628	51 945
Other personal services	8340	34 592
Motor vehicles/services	37 305	220 661

Source: Australian Bureau of Statistics (1993).

The 1.1 million people in these shopfront locations represent over 13 per cent of Australia's total employment. The number of locations has increased by 18 per cent since 1980 while the number of people employed has increased by 48 per cent, from 720 000 in 1980. Employment is growing faster than the number of outlets, reflecting the growth of take-away food outlets such as McDonalds and Kentucky Fried Chicken and the trend for petrol stations to be combined with supermarket functions. Although there are fewer than 500 department stores they account for 8 per cent of employment and 10 per cent of turnover.

Of the 1.1 million people employed in shopfront retailing, 54 per cent work full time and the remainder work part time. Of those working part time 70 per cent are female. Variations in patterns of employment are shown in Table 9.2.

Table 9.2 Employment patterns for selected retail groups, 1991–2

	Full time		Part time	
	Male	Female	Male	Female
Supermarket and grocery	34 000	39 000	34 000	75 000
Meat, fish, poultry	18 000	5000	2000	3000
Take-away food	26 000	27 000	25 000	40 000
Department stores	8000	20 000	13 000	46 000
Cafes and restaurants	32 000	24 000	29 000	51 000
Car retailing	44 000	9000	1000	2000
Fuel retailing	23 000	9000	12 000	9000

Source: Australian Bureau of Statistics (1993).

These figures show spectacular differences from industry to industry, reflecting a long history of gender-specific work practices in Australia and the influence of strong trade unions in some areas of employment. Meat, fish and poultry retailing remains a predominantly male domain, characterised by individual shops rather than chain stores. The predominantly male workforce in butchers' shops is well unionised and has successfully fought off attempts to bring in more part-time workers, although the latter are much more common within the meat areas of supermarkets.

Females outnumber males as both full-time and part-time workers in supermarkets and grocery stores, in take-away food, and in department stores. Males continue to dominate in car retailing, including managerial and sales positions, with most of the females in this sector in secretarial jobs. With a striking decrease in the number of petrol stations and an increase in their size and sales volume, females have been hired in both full-time and part-time jobs on the check-out style counters that are now ubiquitous in the larger outlets.

A critique of the shopping mall

In the last twenty years the self-appointed defenders and promoters of urban culture in Australia—the cafe society devotees to be found in the inner suburbs of all the major cities—have condemned the spread of the car-based shopping mall. Their attack is similar to the disdain with which intellectuals greeted suburbia in the 1960s, so well displayed in Sydney's journalist Allan Ashbolt's attack on the 'Australian man of today' in 1966. Ashbolt wrote of a privatised world of 'a block of land, a brick veneer' where on Sundays the 'high decibel drone of the motor mower called the faithfull to worship' (Ashbolt 1966, p. 373).

When the sociologist John Carroll analysed what he called 'shopping worlds' in 1979 he subtitled his article 'An afternoon in the palace of modern consumption'. Like many analysts of the grand malls that emerged in the 1970s, often as extensions of 1960s establishments, he remarked on their similarity to cathedrals, especially their grand central hall space, usually 'skirted by an upper balcony'. Shops open on to this space and people 'wander in and out of them as a diversion from the central parade'. Without citing any evidence Carroll states that 'well over eighty per cent of the people buying at Shopping World are suburban wives'. On the basis of a modicum of observation he notes that it seems common:

> ... to proceed on arrival to the Supermarket section and speedily purchase the week's groceries ... Her duty done she can throw herself with a good conscience into the pure pleasure of Shopping World... Ladies can pretend to themselves that their motive for coming here is to do something useful, even necessary ... Once they have done their serious shopping and thereby absolved their utilitarian guilt they can relax, having successfully rationalised an hour or two at leisure in the fair. Moreover there are no clocks here to remind them of duties that await elsewhere. (Carroll 1979, p. 14)

Even though he was writing over fifteen years ago, Carroll's characterisation of 80 per cent of shoppers as suburban wives represents a grand misunderstanding of the shopping public, especially in a society with, at that time, a rapid increase of female participation in the paid workforce.

In analysing shoppers and their habits today, market researchers point to demographic and locational trends. One-fifth of Australia's 5.6 million households have only one person in them, while another quarter are couples (of any age) without resident children. Half of the households are occupied by one family and, of these, almost one-fifth are single-parent households. The nearest Australia ever got to 'suburban wives' dominating shopping was a brief period in the 1950s. In the 1990s 'suburban wives' jostle with teenagers, single men and women of all ages, along with currently married and divorced men in the palaces of modern consumption. This mix represents people in full-time or part-time work, along with age pensioners and the unemployed. The buying power of the modern shopper, bolstered by the age of the credit card, can vary from almost nothing to almost anything. The most prestigious credit cards boast that they have no pre-set spending limits.

Suburban councils throughout Australia are proud of their suburbs and their facilities, including their grand shopping malls. The annual reports of councils are full of booster prose about new malls or councils' efforts at creating malls in existing shopping centres by restricting traffic and creating a themed atmosphere, as the Fairfield Council has done in the western Sydney suburb of Cabramatta. 'Cosmopolitan Cabramatta', a major centre for Asian and especially Vietnamese settlement in the 1980s, sells itself as the 'multicultural capital of Australia'. In 1989 the Council imposed a Development Control Plan to 'preserve the uniquely Asian identity of the centre', insisting on oriental facades to all new buildings (Powell 1993, pp. 138–9). This is not unlike the aesthetic edicts issued by managers of freestanding shopping malls.

Cultural critics are alive to the imposed nature of many of these developments, but they often have difficulty in coming to grips with certain realities in our society, not least the primacy of the motor car. Even the casual visitor to Carlton, Glebe, or Subiaco will soon deduce that a fair proportion of the cafe society is motorised. Nonetheless, many intellectuals writing about Australian suburbia retain their distaste for the car. John Carroll characterised Australia's malls in 1979 as 'set in the middle of a plateau of asphalt covered with rows of parked cars' (Carroll 1979, p. 11). Lynne Strahan, the official historian for the middle-class, middle-ring Melbourne suburb of Malvern, describes the car as 'rocketing citywards'. Chadstone, fifteen kilometres southeast of Melbourne, is to Strahan, a 'bitumenised expanse ... released for worship of the private car' (Strahan 1989, p. 241). Susan Parham, a town planner from South Australia, told a Women and Planning Conference in Melbourne in 1993 that: 'In order to consume, most people now drive to regional centres, set in a sea of car parks'. She went on to point out that drive-in food chains, unlike food courts in the big shopping centres, 'tend to deny even the need for some intensity of human activity as a context for their operation' (Parham 1993, p. 48).

When Meaghan Morris analyses the shopping centre she approaches it in terms of architectural meanings, its impact on its varied publics, especially women, and its range of meanings. She argues that the big centres are 'monolithically present' because they are large and 'indisputably on the landscape, and in our lives', while simultaneously providing a variety of responses, because centres may involve interactions with crowds or on other occasions be relatively empty. She points out that marketing philosophies embrace diversity and market segmentation (Morris 1988, pp. 195, 204).

These features can be seen in most Australian malls and in the world's largest mall, at West Edmonton in Canada. It boasts over 800 shops, 11 department stores, 110 restaurants and 20 cinemas.

One of its developers claimed that the mall brought together New York, Paris, Disneyland and Hawaii. Despite these claims, the mall's mixture of

American and Canadian chains, with a few local specialty stores, rigorously repeats the range of products offered at every other shopping mall. Nonetheless, the mall is enormously successful and 70 per cent of its customers come from outside the state of Alberta.

In her article 'The world in a shopping mall' Crawford argues that malls repackage the city 'in a safe, clean and controlled form', that malls can serve as 'the hub of suburban public life' providing 'a common consumer focus for the amorphous suburbs'. In such commentary we find again the critique predicated on the assumption or conviction that the suburbs are amorphous and that only in real cities can urban life be fulfilling. Crawford acknowledged that in real American cities urban life can be dangerous, so that downtown malls that have been developed in some American city centres provide shoppers with protection 'from the dangerous and messy streets outside' (Crawford 1992, pp. 23–4).

There is no doubt that shopping malls are here to stay. Their attraction to shoppers is obvious: they are safe pedestrian environments, especially for people shopping with children. They provide some degree of choice, depending on the size of the mall and the nature of franchising and ground rents within it, and they offer a kind of one-stop shopping that had not been possible before.

Critics of the malls, fearing that the world of cultural interpretation in the form of museums is being merged with the more elaborate malls, where atriums often encase remnant historic structures, should notice that many retailing shopping strips defy 'mallification'. Australia's most famous shopping strips—Chapel St, Prahran in Melbourne or Double Bay in Sydney—retain a rich mix of shops and cafes. This mix is based on a large and relatively well-off clientele and a varied pattern of ownership, although even here franchise outlets for food and clothes are common. Nonetheless there is no mall manager overseeing the entire operation, monitoring storeholders' cashflow and conducting market research to see which stores should survive and which should not (Spearritt 1994).

There is certainly a sameness, even a blandness about many of our biggest shopping malls, not least because franchised operations dominate so many of their retail offerings, from jewellery to clothes to food to specialty goods. Malls have been slow to offer child care, although some now do, albeit at high hourly rates. In Australian society regular shopping trips are a way of life for the bulk of the population. Electronic shopping is not yet a reality and the apparent popularity of new themed, shopping experiences—Southbank in Brisbane (the old Expo site), Darling Harbour in Sydney and Southgate in Melbourne—suggests that the promenade element in shopping is on the rise. To ensure their commercial viability the biggest suburban malls are creating their own promenades with larger and larger atriums.

In the midst of the grand suburban malls one can find traces of resistance or at least the creation of alternatives. The most notable instance of this has been the rapid growth, in the last decade, of suburban markets, usually half-day affairs on a Saturday or Sunday. In an ironic twist, these markets are often located in the deserted car parks of supermarkets or malls, outside their normal opening hours. Instead of franchises and big stores we find hundreds of small operators plying their wares in the time-honoured tradition of the marketplace where rich and poor, young and old, shop together; some out of necessity, most out of curiosity, although the prospect of acquiring something is never far away.

In a society in which many people spend up to six hours a week in retail outlets—from food and groceries, to clothing, home renovations and antiques—the art and the practice of shopping will continue to be central to our self-image as consumers. In the shop, unlike many other settings in our lives, we are offered at least the illusion of choice.

References

Ashbolt, A. (1966), 'Myth and Reality', *Meanjin*, vol. 25, no. 4, pp. 373–83.

Australian Bureau of Statistics (1993), *Retailing in Australia 1991–1992*, AGPS, Canberra.

Carroll, J. (1979), 'Shopping Worlds', *Quadrant*, August, pp. 11–15.

Crawford, M. (1992) 'The world in a shopping mall', in M. Sorkin (ed.), *Variations on a Theme Park: The New American City and the End of Public Space*, Noonday, New York.

Current Affairs Bulletin (1967), 'Shopping centres', vol. 40, no. 2, pp. 1–32.

Morris, M. (1988), 'Things to do with shopping centres', in S. Sheridan (ed.), *Grafts: Feminist Cultural Criticism*, Verso, London.

Parham, S. (1993), 'How has women's involvement in urban planning changed our cities?', *Urban Futures Journal*, vol. 3, no. 3.

Powell, D. (1993), *Out West: Perceptions of Sydney's Western Suburbs*, Allen & Unwin, Sydney.

Pringle, R. (1983), 'Women and Consumer Capitalism', in C.V. Baldock & B. Cass (eds), *Women, Social Welfare and the State in Australia*, Allen & Unwin, Sydney.

Reiger, K. M. (1985), *The Disenchantment of the Home: Modernizing the Australian Family 1880–1940*, Oxford University Press, Melbourne.

Rigg, J. (ed.) (1969), *In Her Own Right: Women of Australia*, Thomas Nelson, Melbourne.

Rolfe, P. (1964), 'Revolution in the suburbs', *The Bulletin*, 19 December, pp. 25–7.

Spearritt, P. (1978), *Sydney Since the Twenties*, Hale & Iremonger, Sydney.

Spearritt, P. (1994), 'Suburban cathedrals: The rise of the drive-in shopping centre', in G. Davison & A. Dingle (eds), *The Cream Brick Frontier*, Melbourne University Press, Melbourne.

Strahan, L. (1989), *Private and Public Memory: A History of the City of Malvern*, Hargreen Publishing, North Melbourne.

Walker, R. & Roberts, D. (1988), *From Scarcity to Surfeit: A History of Food and Nutrition in New South Wales*, University of New South Wales Press, Sydney.

Whitwell, G. (1989), *Making the Market: The Rise of Consumer Society*, McPhee Gribble, Melbourne.

Chapter 10 | **Inner suburbs: From slums to gentrification**
Renate Howe

Australia pioneered suburban living in the great urban expansion of the late nineteenth century and the suburb has dominated analysis of the Australian city. The focus of study has generally been the 'new' residential suburbs of 1880–1914 or the automobile suburbs of the postwar period, a focus that has distracted attention from the inner-city areas of capital cities, especially Sydney and Melbourne, where for over a century (c. 1850–1950) most Australians lived. In terms of their number of residents, their economic importance in the metropolis and their political significance, the inner areas have been central to the history of the Australian city.

The study of Australian inner areas has been complicated by comparisons with other countries. Few cities shared the urban form of Australian cities, especially the large land area they covered and the dominance of single-storey detached dwellings. Comparisons have also been complicated by the difference in population size. Sydney and Melbourne, with populations around half a million, were 'world' cities by the turn of the century but the other capital cities were smaller; Brisbane, for example, was around 120 000 in 1901. Differences in size and form have implications for the comparisons often made between Australian inner-city areas and the poverty and tenement housing of the East End of London and the 'urban jungle' images of American inner cities.

Comparisons also often fail to account for different systems of urban government. In Britain, inner-city local government is a confused picture with many institutions dating back to medieval times—guilds, the City, the parish. However, by the end of the nineteenth century the units of urban local government were far larger and more powerful than in Australian cities. Amalgamations of municipalities, for example the formation of the Greater London Council, fostered a metropolitan approach to city government although much of the suburban development adjacent to large cities was governed by parish councils. This juxtaposition of metropolitan government and smaller units of suburban government was also the pattern in America where city hall was responsible for a defined metropolitan area while outside the city limits was the territory of self-governing suburbs. These systems of city government have meant there has always been a marked political distinction in American and British cities between city and suburb.

In Australia, where most of the nation's population has been concentrated in capital cities, state governments have had major responsibilities for cities. Metropolitan city councils have been largely confined to the central commercial area (referred to in this chapter as City areas) with some abutting inner-city areas annexed to their boundaries. The exception has been the Brisbane City Council which was established in 1925 to replace smaller units of urban local government. Otherwise in Australia, local government has remained small-scale—the inner city sharing the same model of suburban government with the outer suburbs. This lack of distinction between metropolitan and suburban government in Australia reflected a different relationship between inner city and suburbs. Although there was more social differentiation and poverty in cities than Australians have cared to admit, the distinction between city and suburb was never as definitive and inner-city areas were never the alien territory of American or British cities.

This chapter will examine the complex relations between slum and suburb, firstly through looking at the different ways in which the role and function of inner areas in cities have been interpreted. These conceptual frameworks will be further explored in relation to the changes in Australian inner-city areas between 1890 and 1914, when the 'slum' problem was first identified and the emergence of a new 'gentrified' image in the 1970s following the slum abolition movement of the postwar period. Through these changing representations, the inner city was and remains a challenge to the dominant suburban ethos of Australian cities.

Conceptualising the inner city

Despite the distinctive nature of Australian cities, explanations of poverty and social division in the larger cities of Sydney and Melbourne have drawn on British and American traditions of urban social analysis. One of the most influential of these traditions came from Chicago, the city of diverse immigrant neighbourhoods. In the early twentieth century, the 'Chicago School' of urban sociology focused on the role of the city in the reception and acculturation of immigrants and on the study of 'urban pathologies' associated with the condition of the uprooted (Kilmartin, Thorns & Burke 1978). One of the most influential models of analysis of inner-city areas to come out of the Chicago School was Ernest Burgess's (Figure 10.1) concentric zone theory, which represented the inner city as a zone of transition, a phase in the movement outwards to the suburbs. Although Burgess later modified his model, it remained an influential image in American scholarship and, in the 1960s, urban historian Samuel Hays portrayed the city as 'a giant escalator', the move from the inner city to the suburbs being associated with social mobility.

Such concentric zones can be identified in E. C. Buley's description of a train journey to the City of Melbourne in 1905:

Next to his own suburb is one of detached villas, each with its own garden, then comes the region of wooden cottages, all neat and comfortable; and finally, stucco terraces, rather dingy and crowded, and many of them with cards in the window proclaiming that 'board and residence' may be obtained within. Suddenly a corner is turned and the city area is reached. (Buley, quoted in McCalman 1984, p. 7)

Geographic patterns of concentric zones and sectors have been applied to Australian metropolitan areas. Adelaide historian Susan Marsden has described the shape of the metropolitan area as 'essentially circular':

The older inner suburbs clustered around the parkland perimeters of the city proper, coalescing at their outer edges with other suburbs which had grown in their turn about once-independent villages a few miles from the city. (Marsden 1986, p. 146)

Ronald Lawson has used the Burgess model in his study of Brisbane in the 1890s in an interesting and creative way (Lawson 1973) and in his book *The Inner Suburbs* Bernard Barrett applies geographic models of concentric zones and sectors to the cities of Sydney and Melbourne. Barrett concludes that, while it is easy to find a prima facie case for both patterns in the development of Melbourne, in the end the approach is superficial without detailed studies of particular suburbs (Barrett 1971, pp. 2–3).

Another influential approach has flowed from Friedrich Engels's analysis of British industrial cities, published in 1848, which related industrial change to class divisions and the emergence of poor and overcrowded living conditions. Contemporary radical urban sociologists such as David Harvey have focused on the way in which the city as a centre of consumption (housing, employment, education, transport, culture etc.) controls and distributes development and services. Inner-city areas in this interpretation are areas of deprivation, the outcome of the powerlessness of the residents. Analysis of the capitalist nature of Australian urban expansion by geographers, sociologists and economists has especially drawn on this approach, with Harvey's early book, *Social Justice and the City* (1973) being an important influence on Australian academic analysis (see Berry, Chapter 3 of this book).

The third approach argues that poor neighbourhoods and their inhabitants are constructions of the city's middle-class guardians—philanthropists, the police, church missionaries, school teachers—who define 'slums' and poor neighbourhoods and label the deviant and outcast. Historians Michel Foucault (1973) and Jacques Donzelot (1979) have emphasised the importance of delving beyond 'representations' in the study of the city and their approach is especially relevant to analysis of the inner city where communities have been labelled 'slums' and 'bad neighbourhoods' for much of their history.

More recent writing has stressed the marginalisation of gender, ethnicity and race in urban analysis. The influence of postmodernist analysis which argues that 'economic and social relations are culturally mediated and seek to discover the multiple narratives and discourses of everyday life, refusing to privilege one cultural discourse over another' (Duncan & Ley 1993), has encouraged an interest in the diversity of experience in inner-city areas and the process of creating community identities within the context of urban power relations.

Figure 10.1   The growth of the city

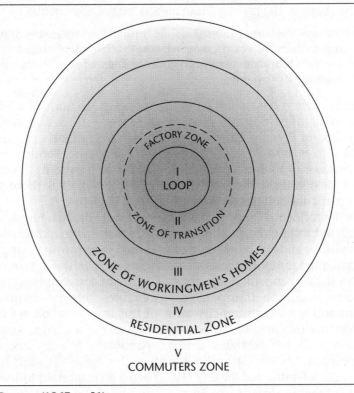

Source: Burgess (1967, p. 51)

All these ways of analysis have at some time been applied to the Australian inner city; Australian urban history is nothing if not eclectic in its interpretative approach (Davison, Dunstan & McConville 1985, p. 5). Because urban historians usually write on one suburb or city, the lack of a comparative approach has led to a limited understanding of the distinctive nature of Australian urbanisation, especially the complexity of the relationship between the inner-city areas and the suburbs (Frost 1992).

Constructing 'slums' at the turn of the century

The period of prosperity 1870 to 1890 was a period of growth and suburban expansion and the the cities echoed with the rhetoric of progress. Between 1881 and 1891, Melbourne almost doubled its population and Sydney grew almost as fast, while the population of Brisbane trebled. The areas of spectacular growth were in new suburbs opened up by the building or extension of public transport systems.

Yet this time of suburban progress was also the period in which social divisions and tensions emerged, epitomised in the built environment in the contrast between the villa suburbs and the inner suburbs. From the 1870s, parts of the inner areas of Sydney and Melbourne were increasingly identified as 'slums'; by the 1890s the wonders of suburban expansion in the two cities were eclipsed by the poverty and suffering of the depression and class confrontation during the Maritime Strike (Davison 1978; Fitzgerald 1987).

The word 'slum' is an evaluative, not an empirical, term and is usually carelessly applied to mean overcrowded urban areas, unhealthy environments, disorderly behaviour, moral and physical pollution. British historian, H. J. Dyos believes the term 'has no fixity':

> ... like poverty itself, slums have always been ... relative things, both in terms of neighbouring affluence and in terms of what is intolerable or accepted by those living in or near them ... It is not now possible to invent a satisfactory definition of a slum in the nineteenth century. (Dyos 1967, p. 44)

In Melbourne and Sydney the term was applied to 'slum pockets' in older parts of the central city and inner-city areas. Typical were the west wards of the City of Sydney (Gipps, Brisbane, Denison and Phillip) which in the 1870s housed almost half the city's population in a small area:

> Behind the squalid structures and fevered bustle of the wharves of the coastal shipping companies, rows of cramped terraces and crooked streets came into view, jammed between factories, flour mills and the gasometers of the Australia Gas Light Company. This area contained some of the worst slums of Sydney, many of them old, ill drained, badly ventilated and overcrowded. (Fitzgerald 1987, p. 23)

In Melbourne, the term was first used in the early 1880s for the 'back slums' area which was centred in the eastern ends of Little Bourke Street and Little Lonsdale Street, the City of Melbourne's red-light and Chinese area. *The Outcasts of Melbourne* has shown the emotive representations of the area as 'vile', filled with 'dens of iniquity' and the centre for 'the white slave traffic', and the way such representations drew on the imagery of British 'slummers' (Davison, Dunstan & McConville 1985). The area attracted the 'rescue' missions of the evangelicals and the benevolent, but more unusually was also something of a spectacle, a tourist attraction, in 'Marvellous Melbourne':

> Because it was a 'world apart', Little Bourke Street did not tarnish Melbourne's self respect. By furnishing a textbook example of the hideous consequences of poverty, overcrowding and vice, it may even have reinforced the city's dominant ethos of suburban respectability. By highlighting this one sink of depravity it also diverted public attention from the many other hidden pockets of poverty and vice throughout the metropolis. (Davison, Dunstan & McConville 1985, p. 2)

Indeed, there was little contemporary discussion of the emergence of the pockets of poverty in the inner areas of Melbourne and Sydney. Dazzled by 'Marvellous Melbourne', the 'Queen City of the South', few noticed the social and economic impacts of metropolitan expansion on the inner areas. R. E. N. Twopeny, for instance, in 1883 could not see 'any sign of poverty or anything at all resembling Stepney or the lower parts of a European city' (Twopeny 1973 [1883], p. 92). Yet, as Dyos has remarked, poverty is relative and if Melbourne did not have slums the city had 'embryo slums'; the clustering of the destitute in overcrowded living conditions, characteristic of European and American cities, was being reproduced in the Antipodes, albeit on a smaller scale. In Sydney, perceptions of such areas:

> ... became increasingly an outsider's image during the course of the nineteenth century. It was a vision produced and sustained by suburbia, and in particular by middle-class suburbia. Glimpsed only fleetingly by commuters during the morning and afternoon rush between work and home, the residential districts of the western city especially became known by the all-embracing label, 'the slums of the city'... an alien and vaguely disquieting presence in Sydney. (Mayne 1982, p. 17)

The reluctance to acknowledge such areas was related also to the ethos of New World cities, which had aspired to avoid the poverty and rigid class distinctions of the Old World. Sydney historian Shirley Fitzgerald believes that Sydney slums challenged two firmly held assumptions about Australian society—that the society was wealthy and that it was egalitarian:

> The notion that anyone could make a comfortable living was often recast into the more dangerous idea that everyone did make a comfortable living and that therefore there was no cause to regulate social behaviour or make provision for a non-existent poor. Even the most cautious observers, who admitted that poverty did exist in Sydney, were agreed that it was a temporary state ... It was generally acknowledged that conditions in Australian cities were better than in British ones, and that Australian workers enjoyed conditions of urban living to be envied, although the hard evidence for these claims was often inadequate. (Fitzgerald 1987, p. 7)

Assumptions about the high standard of living of the colonial worker were often based on aggregate figures which too easily hid the pockets of poverty in Sydney and Melbourne (Kelly 1987, p. 67). Because the distinctive pattern of poverty in Australian cities was that of hidden slum pockets, detailed studies of the different economies and social structures of inner-city communities are necessary for an evaluation of the extent of poverty and poor living conditions.

To understand the quality of life in inner areas, as distinct from the deteriorated housing in some of the City wards of Sydney and Melbourne , it is necessary to understand the different urban development of the capital cities. Although all the cities grew from a central City area, the inner-city areas of each capital city have had distinctive histories. Lionel Frost has identified two contrasting types of city in nineteenth century Australia.

> Sydney, Brisbane, and Hobart were compact, land-intensive cities which more closely resembled those of Britain, Europe, and eastern North America, than they did the other Australian cities. Melbourne, Adelaide, and Perth were of far lower density with sprawling suburbs like those of the American West. (Frost 1992, p. 191)

Thus employment, especially casual employment related to port and waterfront, has been very important in Sydney, Brisbane and Hobart—Sydney and Hobart maintained residential populations close to the City, port and harbour until well into the twentieth century. The lack of linking transport routes between City and suburban areas in Sydney before 1906 further encouraged a dense residential population with many living within walking distance of their employment.

Melbourne, Adelaide and Perth had port areas (Port Melbourne, Port Adelaide and Fremantle) linked by railway to the City, although the docks on Melbourne's Yarra River employed a resident workforce in North and West Melbourne. Victoria's policy of fostering a manufacturing industry through protective tariffs meant that the character of Melbourne's inner-city communities was influenced by the type of employment—engineering establishments in South and North Melbourne, clothing factories, printing and other small food and furniture manufacturing works in the City of Melbourne, Carlton, Fitzroy and Richmond and the concentration of the footwear industry and tanneries in Collingwood (Howe 1992).

The transport links by train and tram between the suburbs and inner areas meant that more of Melbourne's population could more easily separate their work in the City and inner city from their residence in the new suburbs. There were push and pull factors in the move to the suburbs, and the accepted view, that those who could afford it moved to the new 'dormitory' suburbs, leaving behind the working-classes who could neither afford to move nor afford to live far from their place of work, needs some modification. As Barrett points out in comparing the inner-Melbourne suburbs of Collingwood and Fitzroy, not all inner suburbs experienced the same changes in the 1880s. Some suburbs like Collingwood had been working class from the start, while others (Fitzroy) had been mixed suburbs with a strong middle class who moved out especially in the boom years of the 1880s (Barrett 1971). Middle and working-class residents moved because of 'push ' factors—high rents, overcrowding and the location of housing in low-lying areas near sewers and drains—as well as for the 'pull' of the suburban lifestyle. By the 1890s the Yarra River had become the social dividing line of Melbourne with the poorest and most industrialised suburbs forming a ring around the City—North Melbourne, Carlton, Fitzroy, Collingwood, Richmond, South Melbourne and Port Melbourne. In Melbourne 'the poorer majority of its people were clustered within a three-mile inner ring, the affluent minority dispersed through a wide arc of semi-rural south-eastern suburbs' (Davison 1978, p. 152). In Sydney the pattern of social division was more complex—the inner industrial suburbs located on an arc to the south of the City—Erskinville, Alexandria, Ultimo, Waterloo, Pyrmont, Wolloomooloo, Surry Hills and Redfern—while the 'posh' suburbs were those in attractive scenic locations to the south and east.

Despite the movement to the suburbs, the inner areas increased their population in this period. According to Fitzgerald (1987, p. 41), almost 60 per cent of the population increase in Sydney between 1871 and 1891 was in the City and the older suburbs with the continuing subdivision of areas like Newtown and Redfern. In Melbourne there were extensive developments of jerry-built timber cottages in the inner city although the tram and train lines also made possible the subdivision and development of more middle-class terrace house areas such as North Carlton, North Fitzroy and Albert Park. The historian of Subiaco, in Perth, points out that social mobility was catered for by moves *within* the suburb to a bigger house as well as by moves to other areas of the city (Spillman 1985, p. 115).

By 1891 there were three identifiable sectors in Melbourne—the inner suburbs, the new working-class suburbs to the north and west, mostly developed with detached timber housing, and the villa suburbs to the south and east. Although the most spectacular population increases between 1881 and 1891 had been in the new villa and working-class suburbs, most of Melbourne's population still lived in the inner areas where the population had increased by 30 per cent over the decade (see Table 10.1).

Table 10.1 Population of Melbourne, 1861–1911

Groups of suburbs	1861		1881		1891		1901		1911	
	000	%	000	%	000	%	000	%	000	%
City of Melbourne	37	30	66	25	73	15	69	14	71	12
Inner suburbs	55	44	122	45	182	39	173	36	188	32
South and east	23	18	51	19	120	25	131	28	163	27
North and west	10	8	29	11	98	21	105	22	140	24
Other areas	–	–	–	–	–	–	–	–	31	5
Total	125	100	268	100	473	100	478	100	593	100

Source: McCarty (1947, p. 27)

These divisions were not as evident in the more complex social geography of Sydney, but the same pattern is there. Sydney's new working-class suburbs were not developed with the timber homes of Melbourne's Footscray, Brunswick or Northcote, but with brick terraces in the suburbs adjoining the older inner areas, such as Balmain, Leichhardt and Paddington. Putting these new suburbs and the inner areas together, Lionel Frost concludes that 'for almost all of nineteenth-century Sydney's inhabitants, "home" was a terrace house not too far from Sydney Cove' (Frost 1992, p. 193).

What was the distinguishing feature of the slums?

The slum was defined by the suburb; the label was freely applied to those areas which did not meet the criteria of the suburban ethos as it was defined in the later part of the nineteenth century. Davison has written that the achievement of the suburban ideal depended on fulfilment of a number of material conditions 'notably a reasonably spacious dwelling, access to the natural refreshment of a secluded garden setting, the security of home ownership and an income sufficient to support a family with some degree of comfort and leisure' (Davison 1978, p. 140). This was especially difficult to achieve in the older parts of the inner areas of Melbourne and Sydney, where for those not able to move to the newer suburbs or to the new developments within the inner city, the two alternatives were poorly built new housing on small allotments or crowding into existing housing. Whereas before the 1880s, the 'slum pocket'—low-grade houses fronting a right-of-way or lane with lack of adequate light or drainage—was the focus of attention, new housing problems emerged in the changing cities. A study of Melbourne's inner areas in the 1930s found other problem housing areas as well as the slum pocket:

- *the congested area*—houses built on narrow allotments and exceeding forty to the acre;
- *the blighted area*—mixture of housing on small allotments and factories; and
- *the decadent area*—districts with large once-fashionable houses now apartment houses or boarding houses (Victoria, Housing Investigation and Slum Abolition Board 1937).

The inner areas of other capital cities shared these housing characteristics to greater or lesser degrees. In Adelaide, such conditions were mainly concentrated in the City of Adelaide and in neighbouring Hindmarsh where row houses were common (Marsden 1986, p. 11). In Brisbane and Perth, perceived as small provincial towns not requiring planning, a significant proportion of the housing stock was poorly located and of makeshift construction. In Brisbane, demolition of housing to make way for factories and railway lines in the 1890s contributed to overcrowding although not on the scale of the other eastern capital cities (Lawson 1973, p. 108).

In all the capitals, the tenement houses of British and European inner cities were unknown. Densities were very low in the smaller capital cities (around 10 persons per acre). In Melbourne, Fitzroy with 37 persons per acre had the highest density of the inner areas, although parts of the City of Melbourne would have exceeded this figure as aggregate population figures for municipalities disguised the extent of overcrowding. Some parts of inner-city Sydney had 79 persons per acre, the highest density in an Australian city at this time (Frost 1992, p. 195). Royal Commissions and investigations into housing tabulated appalling housing conditions and overcrowding; the Victorian Housing Investigation and Slum Abolition Board Report (1937) found many examples of appalling overcrowding in inner-city Melbourne, such as thirteen occupants (two families) living in a small three-room house in North Melbourne.

The poor in Australian cities were dependent on the private housing market as there were few philanthropic or municipal housing projects. Most were renters rather than owner-occupiers. The depression of the 1890s increased the number of tenants in the inner city as buyers were unable to repay instalments to banks and building societies. In a study of owner-occupancy in Melbourne, the highest tenancy rate was 75 per cent in the Barkly Ward (which covered one of the older areas of Collingwood) (Davison 1978, p. 181). In Sydney, a study of owner-occupation found tenancy rates as high as 90 per cent in inner areas (Fitzgerald 1987, p. 41). In parts of the inner areas of Melbourne, and especially Sydney, it was the culture of the landlord and rent day that dominated—not the suburban ideal of owner-occupation.

A major distinction between the inner areas and suburbs was the deterioration of the urban environment as increased population and industrial development strained the ramshackle infrastructure of the colonial capital cities. All the Australian capital cities were slow to plan and build water and sewerage systems partly because of the confused responsibilities of state and local government. Fitzgerald argues that not only the inner areas of Sydney but the new working-class suburbs also suffered from a degraded environment in this period, while John Lack's study of the new but industrial working-class suburb of Footscray reaches a similar conclusion (Fitzgerald 1987, pp. 69–100). Although Lionel Frost argues that the public health impact of the lack of sewerage systems in Australian cities has been exaggerated, the huge open drains carrying industrial as well as domestic waste impacted especially on inner-city areas. In Melbourne, where a sewerage system was gradually introduced after the turn of the century, the 10-feet-deep and 15-feet-wide bluestone-lined Reilly Street drain ran through Carlton, Fitzroy and Collingwood carrying stormwater, household drainage and effluent from factories and slaughterhouses to the Yarra River. In Brisbane, open drains ran through Spring Hill, Fortitude Valley and South Brisbane until the 1890s— the inappropriately named Breakfast Creek was a polluted stream (Lawson 1973, p. 100). Sydney's epidemic of rat-borne bubonic plague in 1900 stimulated the resumption by the State of virtually all the buildings in inner-city Miller's Point (Fitzgerald & Keating 1991). Such conditions contributed to the persistently high infant death rates in the inner-city areas compared with the suburbs. The *Victorian Year Book* of 1907–08 listed Fitzroy (12.86 per cent of births) and Collingwood (10.39 per cent) as having the highest infant death rates in the city, compared with the deaths of only 3.99 per cent of babies born in suburban Kew.

A major difference between inner-city areas and suburbs was the proximity of work and residence. The villa suburbs were residential suburbs while in the inner areas factories and houses were intermixed, or workers lived close to their jobs on the waterfront. Inner Melbourne was especially affected by the growth of manufacturing industry, encouraged by the protectionist policies of the Victorian government. The inner areas of the 1890s were in a state of economic transition from an immature industrial structure based on sweating and small workshops to a modern factory-based industrial system. The resulting restructuring of the workforce created more jobs, especially for women and juveniles, but as Davison points out, it also resulted in substantial deskilling and more regulated impersonal work practices (Davison 1987). In port areas, workers were forced to live in proximity to wharves because of the 'pick-up system' used by stevedores in selecting labourers at the wharf gate. A study of Miller's Point in Sydney stresses the hardship of this system which 'pitted each man against the other and gave enormous power to the employers' (Fitzgerald & Keating 1991).

The ability to afford or participate in the suburban lifestyle was therefore influenced by the employment structures of inner-city areas where casual and unskilled jobs predominated. The suburban ideal presupposed the separation of residence and work as well as a gender division of work—males in the paid workforce and women undertaking unpaid domestic work at home. Neither was possible in inner-city areas where the nature of work required workers to live near their employment and where low wages resulted in high participation in the paid workforce by women (Fitzgerald 1987, p. 112–14).

Underemployment and unemployment, especially following the devastating depression of the 1890s, meant poverty and destitution. The poor could no longer be portrayed as an exotic outcast group confined to the back slums, nor were they portrayed as the victims of poverty and industrial change. The Royal Commission on Charitable Institutions, after hearing evidence from clergy and social reformers in Melbourne in 1890–91, concluded that the chief factors causing poverty were:

- industrial conditions, such as intermittent employment, insufficient remuneration, and sweating;
- moral infirmity, such as intemperance and improvidence; and
- physical infirmity, such as sickness and premature and senile decay (Royal Commission on Charitable Institutions 1891, p. vi).

However, explanations of poverty in the inner city emphasised moral infirmity more than poverty. The Reverend Charles Neville, Superintendent of the Presbyterian Mission in Fitzroy, told the Royal Commission inquiring into Melbourne's inner-city housing in 1914 that:

> ... there is no inducement in such surroundings given to the people to overcome temptation, but the tendency is to make them liable to yield to drink, gambling and licentiousness. Intemperance is as much an effect as a cause of bad and overcrowded houses. (Neville, quoted in McCalman 1984, p. 47)

These views were reinforced by the street life of the inner suburbs. Larrikin 'pushes', made up of groups of young factory workers bent on acts of defiance and destruction, roamed the streets of inner Melbourne and Sydney and the City areas. Chris McConville has traced the relationship between 'pushes' and depressed areas of the inner-city of Melbourne such as the Bouverie 40s and the Cardigan Street mob from South Carlton (Davison, Dunstan & McConville 1985, pp. 72–6). The large number of hotels in inner-city areas and the disproportionate number of drunk and disorderly convictions did not go unnoticed in suburbia; in Melbourne some of the eastern suburbs passed local by-laws forbidding the sale of alcohol.

Differences in attitude to alcohol consumption reflected the religious differences between the inner areas and the suburbs. The Irish-born made up a high proportion of the unskilled workforce in the inner areas; they and their children were 25–30 per cent of the population in some Sydney and Melbourne suburbs, their Roman Catholic churches and schools as visible a part of the inner-city landscape as the red-brick suburban Protestant churches and Sunday schools were of the suburbs (Fitzgerald 1978, pp. 43–9). These religious differences were ultimately reflected in political differences when, after the turn of the century, the Australian Labor Party drew support from the Irish networks of inner-city Melbourne and Sydney (McCalman 1984).

The slums were portrayed as a political, moral and environmental threat to society, and their residents were often lost sight of in the furore which followed this discovery. As the *Collingwood Observer* noted, 'if a crime is committed anywhere, the offender must be a Collingwood larrikin. If an epidemic breaks out, it must have its source in Collingwood'. However, Barrett writes that 'although housing and sanitation were bad, it would be a mistake to speak of Collingwood as a 'slum'... it is probably wiser to think of Collingwood as an area of low-cost housing rather than a slum' (Barrett 1971, p. 12). As well as the areas of destitution and crime around Vere and Wellington Streets, Collingwood had many steady workers living in modest cottages while respectable artisans lived in the Clifton Hill area. Janet McCalman has argued that the undifferentiated slum image applied to inner-city areas has meant that the great and most significant divide in Richmond life 'between the "respectable" and "rough" the casually employed and those in regular employment has been overlooked' (McCalman 1984, pp. 20–9).

The voices and opinions of the people themselves are difficult to find in the nineteenth century—the historian is reliant on official sources such as statistics or interpretations mediated through the middle class. Benevolent organisations and missions working in the inner city were one source of information, although, as in the case of the Reverend Charles Neville quoted earlier, this was often a view influenced by class and culture. Later, oral evidence from residents themselves can be used, for example, in Janet McCalman's history of Richmond, *Struggletown* (McCalman 1984). In Shirley Fitzgerald's and Christopher Keating's studies of the Sydney inner-city communities of Chippendale, Surry Hills and Miller's Point there is a huge gap (especially in relation to Surry Hills) between the views expressed by the well-to-do residents of more salubrious suburbs and the self-perceptions of the residents. In Chippendale, residents 'often remember life in these parts with affection and pride. They talk of a sense of community, of neighbourliness and caring which their less fortunate suburban counterparts missed out on' (Fitzgerald 1991, p. 72). The historian of Subiaco in inner-city Perth writes that:

> Subiaco was and would long remain a 'working-class suburb', but in the early days that label did not hang heavily upon those residing in the area. In their own perception they were 'ordinary' people, 'real' people, with fewer airs than their wealthier neighbours in West Perth but with every bit as much grace. If by comparison with other suburbs Subiaco was a poor area, not even the poorest of its residents seemed to feel in any way imprisoned by their poverty. (Spillman 1985, p. 115)

The detached house with garden in the suburbs symbolised the good life in Australia and this suburban ideal was widely shared across the social spectrum. Real-estate agents and land developers promoting the ideals of *rus in urbe* contrasted the villa suburbs with the degraded environment of the inner areas. In Sydney, 'literature advertising the garden suburbs appealed directly to class snobbery deprecating the older suburbs' (Fitzgerald 1987, p. 42). From the 1890s, Sydney's ubiquitous terrace houses were seen as 'an inherently bad form of housing that fostered slum attitudes, crime and immorality' (Fitzgerald & Keating 1991, p. 80), a reminder of the rift between suburban dreams and urban reality.

This rift was never so wide that the inner areas of Sydney and Melbourne became alien territory as, for example, the immigrant areas of American cities or the East End of London. The differences in size, diversity of population and intensity of industrial development are a large part of the explanation but there was also a more substantial and continuing middle-class presence in the inner areas of both the Australian cities, especially in Melbourne. In that city the reforming middle class maintained a strong presence in the inner areas through churches, kindergartens, schools and missions. Recent research has suggested that inner-city residents themselves were not without power while the middle class was reminded of inner-suburban reality (Davison, Duncan & McConville 1985, see chapters by Shurlee Swain and Roslyn Otzen).

Apart from the University of Sydney Settlement House in nearby Newtown, the bridge-building settlement houses so numerous in British and American cities, were not established in Australian cities. When the Reverend E. S. Hughes suggested at the opening of the Mission of the Holy Redeemer, in inner-city Fitzroy, that young men from Toorak might bridge classes by living at the Mission and spending a fortnight amongst the poor, 'there went up from the audience ... a loud unbelieving laugh ...Were they ignorant of what had been done in England and Scotland and the United States? Have they never heard of Toynbee Hall—of the various universities' settlements?' (Hughes, quoted in Howe 1972, p. 90).

There have been differing interpretations among Australian historians of the extent of urban social differentiation in the nineteenth century. Graeme Davison, in his study of Melbourne in the 1880s and 1890s, has argued that the main distinction was one of scale, that the sharing of the suburban life style was widespread and that the only distinction was the size of house that could be afforded. 'Most workingmen had little gardens attached to their homes, and even the back-street slums of Collingwood had potted ferns at the windows' (Davison 1978, p. 140). Lionel Frost agrees with Davison, arguing that Melbourne had 'only minor slum districts', that the suburbs were accessible and that most were able to take up the suburban ideal (Frost 1992, p. 196). However, Frost believes that poor living conditions were more widespread in Sydney and the suburbs less accessible, hence the contrast between interpretations of Australian urban life in the two major histories of each city—Shirley Fitzgerald's *Rising Damp* ... (1987) and Graeme Davison's ... *Marvellous Melbourne* (1978)—a difference reflected in their titles. There were substantial differences between the cities in terms of class divisions and urban differentiation but the historians of Melbourne have, like contemporary observers, been dazzled by the villa suburbs. The extent of the 'slum pockets' and the horror of their living conditions has not been seriously studied, nor has the political and social significance of the 'proletariatisation' of the inner suburbs been fully explored. The forces which created the residential suburb also required the maintenance of a poorly paid and insecure workforce; despite the potted plants in the Collingwood windows, the divisions between inner and villa suburbs were the expression of structural division, not just a question of scale.

The deconstruction of slums

Writing now, a century on from the depression of the 1890s which revealed the extent of poverty and industrialisation in inner areas, it is interesting to reflect on the changed image and role of the inner city. The Burgess zones are difficult to apply to the complex mixture of social classes, the range of ethnic backgrounds and the changed economic base of the inner areas of Melbourne and Sydney today. The images of 'bad neighbourhoods' and 'slums' hardly linger in the popular consciousness. Today's dominant inner-city images are cosmopolitan and 'trendy', of cafe society and urbanity, while slum housing is now the much sought-after 'heritage' housing. The suburbs, hugely expanded in the postwar period, are now not only residential but also commercial and employment centres making their core image of retreat and escape from urban life more difficult to sustain. However, although the relationship between the suburb and the inner city has changed, it remains as important as ever and certainly as complex and difficult to conceptualise.

Hal Kendig, in a study of postwar urban and social change in the inner suburbs of Sydney, Melbourne and Adelaide, identifies the major changes to include:

> ... non-residential incursion, the building of flats and, most importantly, the improvement and changing occupancy of the existing stock of housing. At the same time, there have been large population losses, and stable working-class communities have evolved into diverse mixes of population which also include, relatively, more old people, non-British migrant families and affluent young adults. (Kendig 1979, p. 1)

Behind this bland description lies a history of contested space and structural economic change. In Sydney and Melbourne, the 1960s and 1970s was a period of conflict between residents, state infrastructure authorities and private developers over destruction and redevelopment of inner areas. In the same period, traditional employment closed or moved to new locations, especially the manufacturing industry in Melbourne and waterfront employment in Sydney. Commercial employment expanded in the City areas, while retailing and small manufacturing establishments declined. These structural shifts encouraged a rapid change in the population groups living in inner areas. Ethnic groups, who from the 1950s had been the chief buyers of inner-city housing, were especially affected. By 1961, for example, almost a quarter of the houses in Paddington was owned by non-English-speaking background migrants, mostly Italians, while a similar proportion of mostly Greek migrants owned houses in Redfern (Kendig 1979, p. 113). In Melbourne, around a third of Fitzroy's houses was owned by ethnic groups, especially Macedonians and Italians (Howe 1989). These ethnic-background owners had rescued the reputation of the terrace house as a place to live as well as restored its fabric, albeit with a 'Mediterranean finish'.

The number of ethnic-background residents in inner areas declined during the 1960s. Consistent with the invasion/succession of the Burgess zonal model, many migrants, having established themselves in a new country, moved to suburban housing. Others moved because of changed employment opportunities in the inner areas and yet others were displaced by competition from young middle-class Australians wanting to combine residence and work in the inner city. In Sydney between 1966 and 1971, 'the percentage of professionals and other higher-status, white-collar workers rose by 5 per cent metropolitan-wide, but by 7 per cent in Paddington, 6 per cent in Balmain, 5 per cent in Glebe and 3 per cent in Chippendale' (Kendig 1979, p. 125). In

Melbourne young professionals moved into areas such as Carlton, South Melbourne and Fitzroy. This movement of the so-called 'yuppies' and 'trendies' into working-class communities has been one of the most significant developments in the recent history of the inner suburbs.

The so-called 'gentrification' of the inner areas was a global phenomenon not confined to Australian cities:

> The details will vary according to local conditions. In one place there will be 'whitepainting'; in another, 'brownstones' are renovated: elsewhere, warehouses are converted to residential use, or old buildings demolished and replaced as high-rent apartments or condominiums. But whatever the details, commentators agree that there has been a widespread transformation of landscapes in many of the inner cities of the advanced industrial nations. (Mills 1993, p. 150)

There have been three broad explanations of gentrification:
- changing consumption-oriented lifestyles and changing career patterns:
- production-side explanations pointing to the influence of government and financial institutions on a national and international scale—especially the switching of investment back into inner-city areas: and
- the restructuring of class and gender relations consequent upon changes in the organisation of work and the domestic sphere.

A study by W. S. Logan of the gentrification of inner-city Melbourne concluded that 'city structural change (demographic, ageing, industrial relocation and attendant shifts in workforce residence) and lifestyle motives are most important' (Logan 1985, p. 298). Although identifying structural change and lifestyle issues as more important than investment decisions by financial institutions (as does Kendig) in the changing inner city, Logan does not explore the influence of gender, for example, the increased workforce participation of women and changing patterns of family formation. The gentrification of inner areas was associated with a rejection of suburban values. Hugh Stretton's best-selling book, *Ideas for Australian Cities*, (1970); was, in part, a response to criticisms of the Australian suburb by 'urban intellectuals' and city planners. Stretton was critical of the stereotype of suburban 'vegetation' in the performances of actor Barry Humphries or the critiques of architect Robin Boyd:

> The accusers themselves are quite inconsistent in thinking it's the monotony that matters ... The similarity of tastes and choices is all right if they are good tastes and choices. Even if not, the similarity is often and above all a sign of *freedom*; more and more people are at last getting what all of them have always freely, independently, identically wanted. Before we got the same houses, the contrasts of mansion and slum did not signify individual differences of desire, nor a tenth of the free choices we have now. (Stretton 1970, pp. 10–11)

To Stretton's chagrin, the inner-city metaphor was reinforced with patterns of urban life elsewhere such as the cosmopolitan cafe society of European capitals, or London mews. For the first time the 'dysfunctions' of the inner city, the mixture of uses, the variety of housing and the varied background and age of residents, were seen as advantages while the community identity of inner-city neighbourhoods was contrasted with the anonymity of the suburbs.

One-dimensional depictions of the new residents as motivated by economic greed through their investment in undervalued inner-city housing underestimate their important role in forming coalitions to protect inner-suburban areas from development by investors and state authorities. The dominant images of inner areas as slums, reinforced in the 1930s and 1940s by slum abolition movements and the establishment of state housing authorities to redevelop inner-city areas, did not easily adjust to the changed social and economic conditions of the inner suburbs. The influential Victorian Housing Investigation and Slum Abolition Board Report (1937), researched and written under the supervision of Methodist layman and economist, F. Oswald Barnett, cast its shadow on Melbourne in the 1960s. Although Barnett identified the problem of unemployment and casual employment as basic to deteriorated housing conditions in the inner city, in publicising his report and mobilising public opinion on the issue, he emphasised traditional representations of slum residents as a threat to the stability of society. The solution advocated by the Victorian Housing Investigation and Slum Abolition Board Report (1937) was 'to rescue families through their deliverance into a new environment' by the demolition of slum pockets and the provision by the state of 'proper housing for the lower paid worker' (Tibbits 1988, p. 125). Christopher Keating, in his study of Surry Hills, writes that the crimes of the Surry Hills residents were taken as proof 'that the success of the slum clearance movement was predicated on the portrayal of Surry Hills as a decaying anachronism that threatened "normal" society' (Keating 1991, p. 12).

In Melbourne, images of the inner city as an unruly, unhealthy place gave power to the statutory authorities: the Housing Commission, the Melbourne Metropolitan Board of Works and the Country Roads Board. In the 1960s and 1970s, the Housing Commission implemented the slum abolition program advocated in the 1930s, building a ring of high-rise public-housing flats around the City, despite increasing hostile and aggressive community opposition to comprehensive clearance schemes. In Sydney, violence erupted when private developments and freeway construction were opposed by residents supported by the Building Workers' Industrial Union's 'green bans'. These battles reflected the intensity of the pressure for destruction of the old inner-city areas. They also marked the eclipse (although not total eclipse) of the long-standing inner-city 'slum' image.

Despite these conflicts, 'the postwar redevelopment of Australia's inner suburbs has been, in many respects, a success story' (Kendig 1979, p. 173). There has not been the dramatic decline of the American inner city or the neglect of British inner-city areas. Although the fears of a 'doughnut' city and of the emergence of an underclass constantly surface, such fears are exaggerated in the Australian situation. True, the inner city has lost population and is no longer the main source of the city's employment, but it remains a popular residential location and is still a significant locus for jobs. In a nation of suburbs, the inner city has survived the social and economic changes of a century as well as the destructive images of the past.

References

Barrett, B. (1971), *The Inner Suburbs: The Evolution of an Industrial Area*, Melbourne University Press, Melbourne.

Burgess, E. W. (1967), 'The growth of the city: An introduction to a research project', in R. E. Park, E. W. Burgess & R. D. McKenzie, *The City*, (first published in 1925), University of Chicago Press, Chicago.

Davison, G. (1978), *The Rise and Fall of Marvellous Melbourne*, Melbourne University Press, Melbourne.

Davison, G., Dunstan, D. & McConville, C. (1985), *The Outcasts of Melbourne: Essays in Social History*, Allen & Unwin, Sydney.

Donzelot, J. (1979), *The Policing of Families*, Pantheon, New York.

Duncan, J. & Ley, D. (1993), *Place/Culture/Representation*, Routledge, New York.

Dyos, H. J. (1967), 'The slums of Victorian London', *Victorian Studies*, vol. 10, no. 1.

Fitzgerald, S. (1987), *Rising Damp: Sydney 1870–90*, Oxford University Press, Melbourne.

Fitzgerald, S. (1991), *Chippendale: Beneath the Factory Wall*, Hale & Iremonger, Sydney.

Fitzgerald, S. & Keating, C. (1991), *Millers Point: The Urban Village*, Hale & Iremonger, Sydney.

Foucault, M. (1973), *The Order of Things: An Archaeology of the Human Sciences*, Vintage Books, New York.

Frost, L. (1992), 'Suburbia and inner cities', in A. Rutherford (ed.), *Populous Places: Australian Cities and Towns*, Dangaroo Press, Sydney.

Harvey, D. (1973), *Social Justice and the City*, Edward Arnold, London.

Howe, R. (1972), Protestant churches' response to urbanisation, PhD thesis, University of Melbourne.

Howe, R. (1989), 'Together but different', in *Fitzroy: Melbourne's First Suburb*, Hyland House, Melbourne.

Howe, R. (1992), 'Far from a worker's paradise: Social and economic change in Melbourne's inner suburbs, 1890s–1940s', in A. Rutherford (ed.), *Populous Places: Australian Cities and Towns*, Dangaroo Press, Sydney.

Keating, C. (1991), *Surry Hills: The City's Backyard*, Hale & Iremonger, Sydney.

Kelly, M. (1987), *Nineteenth-Century Sydney: Essays in Urban History*, Sydney University Press, Sydney.

Kendig, H. (1979), *New Life for Old Suburbs: Post-war Land Use and Housing in the Australian City*, Allen & Unwin, Sydney.

Kilmartin, L., Thorns, D. & Burke, T. (1978), *Social Theory and the Australian City*, Allen & Unwin, Sydney.

Lawson, R. (1973), *Brisbane in the 1890s: A Study of an Australian Urban Society*, University of Queensland Press, Brisbane.

Logan, W. S. (1985), *The Gentrification of Inner Melbourne*, University of Queensland Press, Brisbane.

McCalman, J. (1984), *Struggletown: Public and Private Life in Richmond, 1900–1965*, Melbourne University Press, Melbourne.

Marsden, S. (1986), *Business Charity and Sentiment: The South Australian Housing Trust, 1936–1986*, Wakefield Press, Adelaide.

Mayne, A. J. C. (1982), *Fever, Squalor and Vice: Sanitation and Social Policy in Victorian Sydney*, University of Queensland Press, Brisbane.

McCarty, J. W. (1947), 'Australian capital cities in the nineteenth century', in C. B. Schevdin & J. W. McCarty (eds), *Urbanisation in Australia: The Nineteenth Century*, Sydney University Press, Sydney.

Mills, C. (1993), 'Myths and meanings of gentrification', in J. Duncan & D. Ley, *Place/Culture/Representation*, Routledge, New York.

Royal Commission on Charitable Institutions, 1890–91 (1891), *Votes and Proceedings*, vol. 3, Victorian Legislative Assembly, Melbourne.

Spillman, K. (1985), *Identity Prized: A History of Subiaco*, University of Western Australia Press, Perth.

Stretton, H. (1970), *Ideas for Australian Cities*, Georgian House, Melbourne.

Tibbits, G. (1988), 'The enemy within our gates: Slum clearance and high-rise flats', in R. Howe (ed.), *New Houses for Old: Fifty Years of Public Housing in Victoria, 1938–1988*, Ministry of Housing and Construction, Melbourne.

Twopeny, R. E. N. (1973), *Town Life in Australia*, facsimile edn, (first published 1883 in London), Sydney University Press, Sydney.

Victoria, Housing Investigation and Slum Abolition Board, 1936–37 (1937), First (Progress) Report, Melbourne.

Bibliography

Greenwood, G. & Laverty, J. (1959), *Brisbane, 1859–1959*, City of Brisbane, Queensland.

Howe, R. (1988), *New Houses for Old: Fifty Years of Public Housing in Victoria*, Ministry of Housing and Construction, Melbourne.

Kelly, M. (1987), *Sydney: City of Suburbs*, University of New South Wales Press, Sydney.

Chapter 11 | 'Mythologising spaces': Representing the city in Australian literature

Frances Devlin Glass

Many readers, both sophisticated and unsophisticated, believe the illusion that literature, especially realist literature, represents reality. It is the source of much of the power of this mode of discourse. My intention in this chapter is, however, to interrogate the basis of the power we accord to narratives and to demonstrate that the mimetic (mirroring, reflecting) function of literature is of minor significance compared with its role in articulating ideology. We shall observe how narratives about the Australian city have been used not so much to mirror our cities, but rather have been enlisted in the service of a wide range of ideologically driven debates about Australian identity, about the repression of desire and difference, about ecology and multiculturalism. Cities are not only places where we live and work: but in their very formed shapes at the macro and micro-levels (city design being an instance of the former, and the design and decoration of rooms within houses, an example of the latter), they are sites for the negotiation and contestation of cultural, social and personal meanings (Fiske, Hodge & Turner 1987).

I have chosen to look at clusters of texts which concern themselves with cities at three key moments in Australian history:

1 texts produced in the period often designated as the hey-day of bush nationalism, the 1890s and the decade after federation; such texts acquired powerful symbolic status in the hands of the social-realists and socialist critics in the period 1930–70;

2 texts produced in the two decades after 1945, often by expatriates who professed a despair-filled love of Australia and a hatred of suburban constraints; and

3 some texts which represent the postmodern city of the 1980s and 1990s and a radically de-centred view of the individual.

It is a crucial assumption of my argument and methodology that even if these texts announce themselves as the individualistic effusions of unique, often tormented, artistic minds, each of them is, in fact, implicitly (and occasionally explicitly) intertextual, by which I mean that each implicitly refers to pre-existing texts (not necessarily literary ones) and each takes up ideological positions in relation to pre-existing discourses and debates. How these discourses change over time, and what makes particular discourses dominant and others subdominant, are fascinating studies in themselves, but beyond the scope of this essay.

1 Bush nationalism and the 1890s

The first moment, the 1890s, I shall deal with briefly since its lineaments have been extensively documented and critiqued (for useful summaries and critiques of bush nationalism see Cantrell 1977; White 1981; Carroll 1982; Whitlock & Carter 1992) and its broad brushstrokes are familiar to most culturally literate Australians. I refer to the cultural invention of the nationalist significance of a particular decade, that of the 1890s. The literature of this period was deemed to exemplify *the* Australian ethos (assumed to be unitary), and the decade (arbitrarily detached from its literary ancestry) was reified as the point at which the nation became self-conscious, self-confident and self-defining in two phases by two generations of cultural analysts:

- between the wars by writers (like Miles Franklin) and promoters of Australian culture (Vance and Nettie Palmer in particular); and

- later in the 1950s and 1960s when Australian literature and history were first being institutionalised in universities (mainly by historians and literary critics of a sociological bent).

Such commentators celebrated the emergence of a national 'type': that of the battler (always male), a mate (who is a necessary defence against the hardships of loneliness and the physical rigours of the outback—women, every bit as exposed, were rarely depicted as mates, unless ironically by, for example, Barbara Baynton), a democrat every bit as good as his boss, an outdoors man of prodigious physical prowess, a laconic fatalist, a misogynist who casts women in the role of 'nay-sayer' to male pleasures, a believer in 'a fair go' but one who is contradictorily a racist with a horror of Asiatics and a misplaced conviction that the Aboriginal race was doomed to extinction. The masculinist/misogynist bias of the myth has, of course, been exposed by feminists (see Baynton 1902; Sheridan 1985; Schaffer 1988; Magarey, Rowley & Sheridan 1993) and its racism has been noted; there are those, too, who read the corpus of bush literature not in affirmative and nationalist terms but see the bush as a site of dehumanisation and horror (Cantrell 1977, pp. xx–xxi). And yet the myth continues to have symbolic power as a source of nationalist identity in advertising, tourism, films and artefacts metonymically connected to it like Akubras and beer.

A standard procedure in constructing an argument in fiction (and in many other discourses) is to set up a simplifying (and therefore distorting) opposition, a binary opposition, in which one pole is deemed to oppose the other. In polemics, and in ideological debates, one pole is never the equivalent of the other, never equal and opposite. An important component of the myth of the 'nineties was the privileging of the bush over the city. The Australian stereotype in this narrative was a bushman with a hatred of the city. Ironically, many of the perpetrators of the myth, among them Henry Lawson, were city bohemians who had fled the bush and for whom pro-bush rhetorical poetry and short stories were a (difficult) living at six pence a line for staged 'debates' in the columns of the popular press, especially *The Bulletin*.

The city was the anti-type against which the bush could be valorised. The distinction is as old as the pastoral convention, said to have been invented in the third-century BC by a court poet, Theocritus, yearning for the bucolic Sicily he had left to become upwardly mobile in Alexandria (Preminger et al. 1965, p. 603). By the late nineteenth century, the discourses for the negative pole of the binary opposition, the one in which the city is imaged as an industrial and impersonal hell, already existed in the literature commonly being read in Britain and Australia: writing in 1982, Graeme Davison identified the key texts in these anti-city discourses as the novels of Charles Dickens, the journalism and light verses of George Robert Sims, and James Thomson's long poem 'The City of Dreadful Night' which was revived in the late nineteenth century (Davidson 1992). Images of 'the dirty, dusty city' with its cramped 'dingy offices' feebly lit by 'stingy/Ray(s)' were available for 'Banjo' Paterson to import into 'Clancy of the Overflow' (Paterson 1992) as the negative pole in a debate in which 'the vision splendid of the sunlit plain extended' with its promise of autonomy, healthy lifestyle, freedom from routine and drudgery, freedom to wander (with its implied release from boss, wife and children) was to be foregrounded.

Many valued features of city life are omitted from such representations of the colonial Australian city: what had been the pride of the previous generation of city-dwellers in the 1840s and 1850s in Sydney, and a little later, in the 1860s and 1870s in Melbourne, was the proliferation of Mechanics' Institutes, libraries and galleries set up to educate the working man, which led to the designation of Sydney as 'the Athens of the south' (Stewart 1988).The large cities also played host to touring theatrical companies featuring the controversial Ibsen, while vaudeville and melodrama catered for their defined class-marked market sector. The change in representation of the city between the 1850s, when it was a locus of high culture, and the 1890s may also have been the result of a change in literary taste (a preference for gritty grainy realism in the last two decades of the century), or perhaps a response to the deep economic depression after the excesses of the boom of the 1880s, especially in Melbourne, or it may have been that the writers came from a different class with different political affiliations from the earlier generation's. Another aspect of Australian cities, their literal location, was rarely exploited except by Chris Brennan in *Poems 1913* (Brennan 1960). It was the postwar generation that celebrated beaches in writing, though Impressionist painters had done so much earlier. In 1929, Jean Curlewis, daughter of Ethel Turner and literary sister to one of the surfing movement's stars, Sir Adrian Curlewis, was to write a superb essay celebrating how Sydneysiders used the beach (Curlewis in Goodwin & Lawson 1991, p. 248–9), and the next decade would see the novels of Christina Stead, Henry Handel Richardson and Eleanor Dark celebrate Sydney's harbour and beaches (see 'A Haven and a Paradise: Images of the Beach' in Falkiner 1992).

Brennan, although in no sense a pro-bush rhetorician (his concerns were metaphysical and philosophical—they were with the notion of man as spiritual questor and with the inadequacy of cultural definitions and systems of knowledge), finds potent images of the city to express a sense of being expelled from Eden (symbolised in Arcadian terms) which is made to represent a paradisal sense of freedom and innocence (see 'Towards the Source', *Poems 1913*, in Brennan 1960). His Sydney—with its skies of 'uncreated mud', its cramped 'unmysterious homes' that trap would-be wanderers and adventurers—is a symbolic soul-scape rather than a mimetic (mirror-like) representation and a metaphor for the limitations of philosophical systems in the Modernist period. The point to be made here is that Brennan, while not party to the city–bush debate and while having his own intellectual agendas quite separate from those of the Sydney bohemians (he was a university man), nonetheless images the city in ways that would have been familiar to those reading the anti-city discourses of the turn of the century.

In a similar manoeuvre, but one which one reads naturalistically at one's peril, the proponents of bush were engaging in debates which had more to do with national identity than with the bush per se. The subtextual concern with the 'coming Australian', his bodytype, temperament and politics, was congruent with the scientific concerns of the time, and participated in the discourses of ethnology and medicine. It is explicit in Furphy's *Such is Life*, 1903 (see Devlin Glass et al. 1991, pp. 467–70), though other writers of the period tended to engage with the debate more obliquely. As has often been pointed out, the bush writers were essentially an urban intelligentsia (Furphy was a rare exception), prosecuting a socialist politics and seeking to differentiate a 'new race' from the more hierarchical and feudal politics of the Old World. The city–bush debate constituted a useful populist shorthand, but far more germane to the literary and ideological debates being waged in the period was the subtextual obsession with defining, and scientifically categorising, the 'coming Australian'.

Apart from ethnological concerns, what, then, were the ideologies which sustained the anti-urban sentiments that were expressed in the city–bush debate? The economic imperatives of empire demanded that all the colonies, not Australia alone, be producers of raw materials to feed the industrial mills of the 'mother country', so this was a powerful impetus to represent the newly colonised land as Arcadian. Urbanisation, then, was an affront to Arcady (Lansbury 1970). Rural Arcadia was also a useful image to encourage migration to a territory where fears of under-population and Asian invasion were rampant. What was new and had to be invented (though not entirely from scratch, as cognate imperial discourses, such as the biblical story of the

Promised Land, the nationalist discourses of Ireland in which land tenure was a key issue, and such works as the short stories of Kipling provided models) was a semiotic of the bush and bushmen.

Even if the city–bush debate can be seen to have been supplanted by other ways of construing national identity even as early as the 1920s (White 1981), it continues to have resonances in our own time in Australian iconography. One might think of the *Crocodile Dundee* phenomenon, known to be a fantasy by most Australians, but able to be taken as realistic and representative by those not familiar with the country.

2 'Cultural deserts'

> Sprawl is really classless, though ...
> An image of my country ...
> (Murray 1983, pp. 28–9)

> God created the city, but secular men the suburbs: they are his secret
> hope of heaven.
> (Shuster cited in Dawe 1978, p. 23)

In the period between 1920 and 1940, ethnology having been institutionally coopted in the service of racism (to devalue the Irish as much as the Asiatic and the Aborigine) had been sufficiently discredited by its uses and abuses by Nazis (White 1981, p. 157) as to warrant a subtle shift in the 'national conversation'. This affected how suburbia was represented. Richard White in *Inventing Australia* tracks a shift from rural to urban iconography through a series of phases. He identifies a change in terminology in the postwar period, with 'race' being supplanted by the phrase that became the catch-cry of the Menzies era, 'the Australian way of life' and attempts to define it. (White 1981, p. 158). Suburbia, a house on a quarter-acre block, came to be seen as a central signifier of this 'good' in political and domestic discourses, but it was construed differently in literature.

In Australia, a recurrent anxiety among post-Second-World-War writers—and even in earlier fiction, for example, the work of Eleanor Dark and Norman Lindsay (1930, 1933, 1947)—was the homogenising tendencies of urban and rural-town suburbia, the stifling of creativity and fear of difference. What is not familiar (whether by belonging to a different culture, or by not conforming to normative codes of behaviour or ethics) is cast as 'other', not as simply different but is perceived as remote, alien, and threatening to all that is solid, substantial and worthwhile in the culture. Bruce Bennett observed:

> Metonymic use of 'suburban' for ignorant, conformist, mechanical behaviour was common among Australian intellectuals in the inter-war and early post-war years. (Bennett 1984, p. 42)

Barry Humphries's 'Days of the week', one of the Sandy Stone monologues, was devised for theatre in 1958, and has since been televised and recorded. What is added to language by performance, in particular, where Humphries places emphases, the pace and pitch of delivery, the function of pauses, his use of facial and hand gestures and body language, the whistle (he affects) through false teeth, is critical to the meaning constructed. Humphries's costume of striped flannelette pyjamas, checked woollen dressing-gown and brown slippers, and his moth-eaten Genoa velvet armchair under a dim standard lamp, constructed the archetypal *homo suburbiensis* (Humphries 1990, pp. 1–2).

On the surface, this narrative is as sparse as a narrative can be: it simply lists the events of a week as experienced by the speaker and his wife. The events are located in post-Second World War, suburban Glen Iris, complete with Foodorama. Having outlined the 'plot?' details, the reading–reception problems proliferate: the listener–reader is exposed to a double narrative. Sandy's narrative can be and will be read on its own terms as a simple contented man's account of the suburban round. More likely, though, and it is constructed for this audience, it will be read ironically as a satire on the dreariness and emptiness of life in the suburbs. In other words, its simple realistic surface will be seen to be a distorting mirror rather than a reflection of life in Glen Iris. What such a reader will probably pay attention to is the ironic voice (in narratological terminology, the voice of the implied author), which implies (and never states) that his evening entertainments, far from being utterly satisfactory, constitute a kind of treadmill of sameness which masquerades as variety. To find Humphries's monologue not comic, is to position yourself either as an unsophisticated reader who has missed the irony (this positioning would then be unwitting), or a sophisticated one who resists the lure of complicity to laugh at Sandy in company with the author. The reader who cannot laugh at Humphries's monologue may find the satire too cruel: satire normally exposes power structures rather than the victims of them. If Sandy is a victim, what forces victimise or disempower him?

This theatre monologue can be said to offer a recognisable account of life in the suburbs of Melbourne, as lived by a particular kind of man at a particular point in time (not long after the Second World War). Sandy's pleasures are ones that many would share with him: pride in his suburban villa in Gallipoli Crescent complete with burgundy Axminster 'wall-to-wall' (carpet), the opportunity to drink at his club with acquaintances, to share in the 'educational' benefits of his friends' tourism, to go to movies (cheerful ones only) and newsreels (which reinforce the sense of one's good fortune to live in middle-Australia), card games, footy matches, looking after the rhododendrons in his garden. These ordinary suburban avocations are not in themselves laughable. It is Humphries's discourse which makes them so.

Sandy's definition of 'strife', what makes suburban life difficult, invites scrutiny: the major challenges posed are those of parking at the Junction and the football, eggs on the carpet, and invitations to social events which might tempt him to stay out too late. He does not complain of too many invitations, and seems to relish social opportunities and the various 'excitements' his life offers. So, on any objective measure, 'strife' (Sandy's word for everyday difficulties) would seem an overstatement, and reading realistically (rather than through the intended ironic frame) Sandy's life could be construed, by one not familiar with the negative discourses about suburbia in Australian cultural life, as quite idyllic.

Figure 11.1   Sketch of Sandy Stone by Barry Humphries

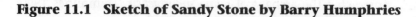

Source: Humphries (1990)

An hypothesis about the ideal reader of Humphries's text can be constructed: one who believes that Australia is deficient in cosmopolitan Culture (note capitalisation), and one whose horizons culturally, socially, educationally and intellectually extend beyond the home and a small group of family and friends and, perhaps most controversially, one who might have remained within that restricted circle and is happy to laugh at a class considered to be unfortunate to have 'got stuck' in suburbia. Humphries's text is similar ideologically to many written in the 1950s and 1960s by an expatriate generation of writers who frequently found it necessary to leave Australia in order to be able to write about it. Among them were Alister Kershaw, Patrick White (whose novels, plays and essay, 'The prodigal son', secured much attention), A. D.

Hope, George Johnston and Robin Boyd, architect and author of *The Australian Ugliness*. Their arguments frequently exhibit the 'cultural cringe'. A common complaint is that Australia lacks history and culture and must look to Europe to supply it. Suburbia was often a symbolic focus of their sense of dislocation from history and culture.

It must be said too that even the critics of suburbia have often qualified their contempt and defended suburbia (Boyd 1960; Horne 1971; McGregor 1972; Stretton 1970) as a site whose diversity and vitality may not always be acknowledged. To be pro- and anti-suburbia may seem a trivial issue, but in fact it tends to be an index of deeper ideological issues (Gerster 1990) and is probably implicated in the justifications individuals would offer for their choice of lifestyle, or for the kind of lifestyle to which they might aspire. Images of imprisonment may signify intellectual or professional stagnation (Gwen Harwood), or a revolt against the nuclear family by those who feel trapped in it by children or mortgages (Anderson 1978; Harwood 1990). Anti-suburban discourses may constitute a protest against restrictive moral or social codes (Bail, White, Anderson, Johnston), or signal conflicts between black and white (Davis, Gilbert, Langford, Mudrooroo Narogin), or ethnic–dominant ways of life (Brett, Gunew), or frustration at the difficulties of the suburbanite being politically engaged (Sylvia Lawson), or a protest at how suburbanisation distorts and subjugates nature (Hanrahan, Malouf), or swallows up desirable rural land. Alternatively, they may represent dissatisfactions with real lived-in cities as against the hoped-for ideal city of the imagination (Modjeska 1989, p.1). Posed against suburbia, in another false binary opposition, inner-city life is often designated as a site for different, more experimental lifestyles such as those of the counter-culture in Garner's Carlton (Garner 1978), or of anti-nuclear family collectives as in Modjeska's (1989) or Langford's (1988) inner Sydney, or of the university push of Moorehouse's Balmain (see Bennett 1984, p. 53). Gerster (1990, p. 574) argues that the restriction of suburbia's representations to satire and ridicule and the compensatory glamorisation of the inner city (the positive pole in this particular binary opposition) have resulted in many distortions of suburban life, arguably false claims about its uniformity (Halkett & Brooke 1976; Gregory 1990) and have had the effect of disenfranchising its constituency (most Australians).

When one becomes aware of the wider cultural debates in which Humphries's theatrical text participates, one realises that storytelling is not innocent; it has 'the power to change human situations', either by reinforcing them, reversing them or, in the case of Humphries's satire, by subverting them, but probably only for those inclined to agree with the ideology encoded in the text (a point to which I shall return later). Chambers argues that:

> ... narrative is most appropriately described as a transactional phenomenon. Transactional in that it mediates *exchanges* that produce historical change, it is transactional, too, in that this functioning is itself dependent on an initial *contract*, an understanding between the participants in the exchange as to the purposes served by the narrative function, its 'point'.
> (Chambers 1984, p. 9)

The study of narrative as transaction and exchange (see also Reid 1992) discloses the ideological and cultural assumptions of these enabling stories that are constitutive of culture. Humphries not only exposes in his text what he sees as the lethal emptiness of and lack of intellectual scope in the suburban round, in the process he exposes himself as an elitist. Paradoxically and unwittingly, given the range of cultural phenomena which need to be explained to a non-Australian reader—RSL (the Returned Services League), Gallipoli Crescent, the propaganda purposes of the Movietone newsreel—Humphries lays bare the vivid variety in the rituals of the suburban round of which he is so critical. His probings of the dream of home ownership in the Menzies and post-Menzies eras in Australia was the more audacious when one considers who his original commercial audiences were—middle-class suburbanites, people perhaps whose lives were more like than unlike Sandy's.

A literary article which was written several decades after that of Humphries, but which is more explicit about what is repressed in suburbia, is Murray Bail's 'Home Ownership' (1980). In the opening section, the narrator mimics the discourses of feature-writing journalism, detailing two separate lives (ironically those of a husband and wife). The story functions as a kind of 'case study' of the emotional costs, very much steeper than the financial costs, of home ownership in the suburbs. The narrative method is more poetic than realist, relying on a central extended metaphor whereby the front that the house shows to the street is systematically compared to the face of Parker, the man who owns it, and the furbishments of the house to the agent of them, his wife, Joyce.

The impersonal narrative voice makes a series of statements about life in Brisbane: there is reference to the felt need to 'impose order on the harsh elements', to its 'humid emptiness', its tendency to drive the sane to drink, and its 'slow-moving days'. Joyce's dalliance with the 'lizard-eyed' traveller is perhaps an ex-centric adaptation to suburban Brisbane: her capacity for laughter, fondness for lipstick and her firm-breastedness are juxtaposed with her husband's Methodism. Some key turning points in this narrative are treated obliquely: the point at which Joyce first engages in adultery, and her death. The reasons for either event are not explicit, or not presented as 'causes', one event leading to the other. It is worth considering, for instance, whether the outbreak of war is coincidental with her adultery or causes it. Another darker reading is that Joyce's 'transgression' is socially constructed by the conditions of life in suburbia: although her liaison with the salesman was essentially innocent, nuclear families in suburbia are subject to the kind of moral control and monitoring not essentially different from those applied in more coercive institutions (Foucault 1979). A feminist reading whereby suburbia becomes a key tool in the maintenance of patriarchy is easily arrived at. At the point where the couple emerge from the cool underhouse space, the reader is positioned among those in the Parkers' street who might gossip and speculate, but not finally know about her 'guilt' or otherwise. From this point onwards, the house is represented as in decay.

Patrick White, arguably the most esteemed and articulate of the critics of suburbia, reserved his most acid satire for the uncultivated, materialistic inmates of suburbia who are almost always excluded from spiritual illumination, or the capacity to be creative. Len and Myrtle Hogben in 'Down at the Dump' (White 1964) and Girlie Pogson in *Season at Sarsparilla* (White 1965) construct tombstones for their desire in the shape of suburban villas, while Daise Morrow, the *illuminata*, opens her heart and legs to those in need, and is imaged in terms of the natural world. Those who yearn to create are forced to leave. Despite his romanticisation of certain kinds of fleshy lower-class consciousness (valued because of the indifference of this class to bourgeois consumerism), White's vision is manifestly elitist, misanthropic and self-serving: his method of enlisting high-art recruits is to require complicity in sniggering at middle-class ways of living.

3 Some postmodern readings of the city

> ... light me bright me match me cigarette me bright city turn on be loud tell everybody switch yes sing red pencil tick me to on centre mid town go go glow sky lit lines wire buzz me to see ring on me in neon on heady excite me thrill me hold me to tight rush rush be big loud go right through now... ('Neons', Walwicz 1989, p. 247)

In the postmodern period, significant changes in literary representation have occurred, and been theorised. The national conversation has mutated, and a different set of binary oppositions has been constructed around the notions of monocultural and multicultural identity. Additionally there has been a significant paradigm shift concerning the relationship of the individual to environment and society. This is most obvious in the literary texts created for children which are often at the cutting edge of literary experimentation and interventions in social formation (see also Harlen 1992; Horniman 1992; Marchetta 1992; McCarthy 1992). A representation (loosely based on St Peters, Sydney) of what is now an inner-city neighbourhood, *My Place*, by Nadia Wheatley (writer) and Donna Rawlins (illustrator) was produced for the bicentennial (Wheatley & Rawlins1988). Its narrative method is simple but allows for as much complexity or simplicity in its reading as the reader can bring to its text and visuals: it tracks backwards at ten-year intervals the inhabitants of a particular hut–tenant-farmer's cottage–terrace house from 1988 to 1788, and sees in the passage of time evidence of successive waves of migration—Kooris, supplanted in turn by London-born convicts, free settlers, American gold-diggers, German tradespersons, English builders and professional families, Irish blue-collar workers, Greek migrants, and a Koori extended family. Beginning and ending with Kooris who inhabit the site, under very different conditions in 1988 and 1788, it maps the changes in housing and land use. The only enduring features of the landscape are a vast Moreton Bay fig-tree and a creek which flows into the ocean at some distance from the house.

Each decade has its child-narrator, though none is any more important than the other—a device which is rare in fiction of any kind. The choice of children as narrators is significant: although first person juvenile narrators are a familiar fictional convention, they are rendered voiceless by the culture as historians or commentators on city design (school exercises excepted, and these are deemed to be low-status discourses in the self-privileging adult world). They are more than marginalised in the culture, so this text's fictive conferring on them of a voice is subversive. One of the most important subtextual analyses we are offered is of how the children use their house and the space around it to recreate. Of central significance in each of the twenty childhoods is the tree which is variously used for escape, imaginative games, swings, treehouses and surveying the territory and the skies. The creek, the other enduring physical feature, begins to be polluted by 1828 and is deemed unswimmable after the dam is constructed between 1828 and 1848; the loss of this amenity is lamented thereafter. Apart from the tree, the pleasures the children detail are either those enjoyed in one's imagination, or social (clannish). Food, represented as abundant and a ritual partaken, often interestingly, outdoors, is a key element in their sense of well-being. Choosing as narrators children whose interpellation into adult culture is incomplete has other ideological advantages: they read history against the grain according to their own experience rather than in terms of the political rhetoric their hapless elders have had to endorse to be socialised: Col knows by age eleven that the resistance offered to the bailiffs by his evicted Irish neighbours is hollow and token; and Bertie, nine in 1918, thinks that Gallipoli heroics 'stink'; Barangaroo's conviction, handed down traditionally, that 'We've always belonged to this place … For ever and ever' is the crowning poignant irony of the history which is offered. The resistance these children offer in small inoffensive ways to the official version of history and its normalising discourses is a clever strategy by Wheatley. It serves to dramatise possible interrogations of seemingly beneficent forms of thought and social control that typically operate in all cultures, of the sort that postmodern analysts of power, like Foucault (1969), theorise. It has the effect of inviting the reader to see history as a set of discourses which function to unify and totalise, and mobilise support for the insupportable. Another effect of this angle of narration is that on questions of race, the children are remarkably free of prejudice, or if they mouth the words of their elders, as Minna does (speaking of Wong Ga Leck, the Chinese market-gardener in 1868, she says, 'I'd quite like to be a savage'), they use adult language in ways that transgress its usual meanings. What emerges is an account of the multicultural city where difference is neutralised by contiguity and where class is more divisive than race. Wheatley on this account might be criticised for a totalising narrative of a Marxist or Pollyanna-ish sort, but individual instances of interchange across ethnic differences are both plausible and morally defensible in terms of the intended audience, and are ones finally dictated by space, by contiguity in the suburb based on St Peters, in inner Sydney. This text works to suggest that 'social relations are constructed spatially' (Watson 1989, p. 7).

Wheatley's book implicitly participates in the post-Saussurean debates of post-structuralism, challenging, as it does, the Western cult of individualism. It is an unusual fiction in that it does not have a single emotional focus. Characters are sidelined, perceived as figures in a landscape and a history: if anything, the house and the tree are the key 'characters', and beyond this the central focus is the nature of space and time and how successive groups of people adapt to it. Each family experiences the same physical reality of place, but they understand it in terms of the mental structures and meanings their different cultures have imposed on it. This is to demonstrate a key notion expounded by poststructuralists: each individual is socially constructed through the series of discourses in which they are interpellated: legal, economic, political, familial, literary, culinary and so on. These discourses actively construct ideology which is manifest in even the most minor aspects of daily life—from how and why we play games, the pets we have, what we wear, to how we construe work and leisure, and bury our dead. Tarzan can inhabit Michaelis's tree in 1958 because of the advent of television, whereas Anna's world sports dragons (Chinese ones), courtesy of her exciting market-gardening neighbours. The ideological basis of much of what we do is invisible to us because it seems natural, rather than socially constructed, and often cultural and ideological difference only manifests itself when cultural differences cause friction (as in the class-based fig-pelting games so common in the tree at different points in its history). Whatever the class or nationality of the child, or the terms in which it is variously imagined, the tree is a good, as is having a place and a neighbourhood.

David Malouf, in texts of a very different complexion—*Johnno* (1975), *12 Edmonstone Street* (1985), *The Great World* (1990a) and in a lecture entitled 'A first place: The mapping of a world', similarly challenges the primacy of the individual and sees cities and houses as actively and dialogically constructing minds. He describes his topo-biographical enterprise as seeking to explain:

> ... not facts, or not only facts, but a description of how the elements of a place and our inner lives cross and illuminate one another, how we interpret space, and in so doing make our first maps of reality, how we mythologise spaces and through that mythology (a good deal of it inherited) find our way into a culture. (Malouf 1990b, p. 298)

His key idea is that topography (whether on a macro- or micro-scale, whether of the hills and river, or the architecture of houses on stilts) maps minds: the proliferation of hills in Brisbane teaches 'restlessness, and variety and possibility', the serpentine river requires the imposition of a conceptual grid in the shape of a tramline system, which in no sense corresponds with quantifiable distances, in order to make the city comprehensible. Or, to put it another way, it is socially constructed in response to topography. Similarly, domestic spaces perform the same function, interacting with mind, creating social codes and conventions:

> You learn in [timber] houses to listen. You build up a map of the house in sound, that allows you to know exactly where everyone is and to predict approaches. You also learn what not to hear, what is not-to-be-heard, because it is a condition of such houses that everything can be heard. Strict conventions exist about what should be listened to and these soon become habits of not-listening, not-hearing. So too, habits grow of not-seeing.
>
> Wooden houses in Brisbane are open. That is, they often have no doors, and one of the conventions of the place (how it came about might be a study in itself) is that doors, for the most part, are not closed. Maybe it is a result of the weather. Maybe it has something to do with the insistence that life as it is lived up here has no secrets—or should have none. Though it does of course.
>
> … How different from life as it is lived in solid brick houses, with solid walls and solid doors and the need to keep them sealed against the air. Brisbane houses are unsealable. Openness to the air, to the elements, is one of the conditions of their being—and you get used to that too. (Malouf 1990b, p. 300)

Malouf's reading of how the 'Queenslander' (house on stilts) in which he spent his earliest years shaped his psyche is self-consciously written within a Freudian frame (see also the essay by David Malouf, 'Enslaved to Freud', *The Age, Extra,* 31 July 1993), with the underhouse section of a house on stilts corresponding directly with repressions—personal, social and cultural.

Barbara Hanrahan similarly uses a psychoanalytic frame but applies it to different ends in her descriptions of Adelaide. She uses it as an analytic tool for exploring historical (rather than individual) repression. In a short story and essays, she examines not the personal repressed but an historical set of homogenising discourses of respectability which have, in her view, bred 'weirdness' and extremism:

> In Adelaide, anybody can jump out at you and cut you up and put you in a glad bag … A kid goes to the loo and disappears—in such a quiet little place, so many folk disappear … They say there are more topless waitresses in Adelaide for its size than any other city in the world. Adelaide is a lovely place to bring up a family … It's full of pickled Old Girls who still put on their best clothes for going to town …
>
> Everyone has their own feelings about Adelaide, and they tend to be extreme. It's either Garden City of the South (where flourish the arts and sciences, and all those things which spell the culture of twentieth-century civilisation), or that ideal setting for a horror movie of Salman Rushdie's infamous *Tatler* piece (exorcisms, omens, shingings, poltergeists, things that go bump in the night). (Hanrahan 1989, p. 73)

In this disturbing, somewhat gothic version of an Australian city, one must penetrate the veneer of ordered, civilised 'toy town' with its 'right-angled streets and squares' to arrive at the unnaturalness. She locates the disjunction in two phenomena: first, the displacement and denial of libidinous energies by even the most eminent of the founding fathers, and secondly, the imposition of cultural practices on an environment antithetical to them:

> Scone trays, cake dishes, pillow-shams, doilies, tea-cosies, blue-beaded milk-jug covers, English china tea-sets with artistic pink rose sprays. The weirdness of suburbia becomes weirder when it's set in an exotic landscape. Bearded bottlebrush, woolly tea-tree, spider orchid, bidgee-widgee. The gum trees rising up, tier upon tier, freaked-out blue of the sky. But at night, five stars in the form of the Saviour's cross. (Hanrahan 1989, p. 76)

Hanrahan's rhetorical method is that of metonymy and the parts she selects to bear symbolic weight are politically toned. For her, what is most absurd are the pretensions of upper-class styles of living in a space which is flea-infested and inhospitable to the forms of living imposed on it, and what she finds regrettable about the changes she has perceived in the cityscape of her personal past is the loss of its working-class 'untrendy' ephemera which she finds 'beautiful': the Rosella Sauce parakeet on a grocery wall, the old gasometer on the corner of Maria Street and the Daisy Dell milkbar on the Beach Road.

Implicitly both Malouf and Hanrahan in their essays and fictions acknowledge the regional differences which make Adelaide and Brisbane different kinds of cities from Sydney or Melbourne. This has been an increasing tendency in the literature of our own times with writers with strong regional identities emerging with, for example, Elizabeth Jolley, Jack Davis and Mudrooroo Narogin marking out the specific features of life in Perth, Thea Astley creating the regional peculiarities of town life in far north Queensland, and Hal Porter detailing life in a provincial centre (Bairnsdale).

In many texts of the last two decades, what makes the representation of the contemporary Australian city differ from its 1950s and 1960s progenitors seems to be the celebration of diverse multicultural ways of living in the city and, more recently, suburbia where they occupy the urban spaces and homes formerly the habitats of the dominant culture. Just how differently migrant families occupy suburban villas is dramatised in Lily Brett's 'Our House':

> In
> our
> shiny
> square house
>
> with rose bushes
> and
> fig trees
>
> and
> handmade
> up to date
> tables
> and couches

you
were
never alone
a bedraggled
pack
of
scrappy
people
lived
with
us
they
were joined
sometimes
by
people
you hardly remembered
and
I'd
never seen
at
celebrations
they sang
and danced
when
things went wrong
they jostled
to push
their point of view
on
anniversaries
of bad memories
they wept
and wailed
nothing
passed
their
comment
they
were
delighted
by technology
hadn't
lived
to see
everywhere telephones
and television
and
the food
the food
was riveting

> it
> was hard
> to invite
> people
> home
>
> to
> such
> a
> crowded
> house.
> (Brett 1986, pp. 111–12)

Whereas Lily Brett's narrative voice is acutely aware of the differences between ethnic and dominant culture inhabitation of space, and has made what she sees as an irrevocable choice in moving across the migrant–dominant culture divide, thereby forgoing experiences which she will regret, Malouf is more sanguine that the choice is not an either/or one. Aware of the role of genealogies in constructing culture because of his Lebanese–English Jewish parents' ethnic origins, his father's rejection of his migrant background and his own upbringing as a middle-class Australian who claims the privilege of living in both Tuscany and Sydney, Malouf explores the ways in which such definitions of identity are historically contingent rather than eternally necessary forces. If made, they can be unmade, so long as the maker is aware of the constructed nature of the phenomenon. The relevance of this for those aspects of city living which are traditionally used to express Australians' diverse forms of cultural inheritance is far-reaching: it amounts to an argument against cultural fixity, against definitions: it is to live in 'multinational hyperspace', to have difference without opposition (Lather 1991, p. 33). It is to question false binary oppositions.

Postmodernist texts about the city challenge the reader in another way. The old certainties about texts being read in a linear progression from A to Z has been critiqued, especially by feminists: Nadia Wheatley's *My Place* (Wheatley & Rawlins 1988) can be read from 1988 to 1788 as published, but will be enriched by a 1788 to 1988 reading. Either way, a subtly different text is experienced. Additionally, Donna Rawlins's maps require as much interpretive attention as the written text, implicitly depriviliging the written form, and they may be read in conjunction with the text for the plethora of subtextual stories they tell about neighbours and their fortunes. Furthermore, there are the urban dramas that are quite unacknowledged in the text, for instance, the changes in land use along the high street.

Just how powerful the reader and the reader's interpretive strategies are, and how beyond the control of the author, are well demonstrated by another picture book for younger children about an encroaching city: *Window* by Jeannie Baker (1991). A collage text using mainly natural materials, it details from the same window, at two-yearly intervals, the transformation of an idyllic bush block into a suburban one, and ends with the city child repeating the process with his own son twenty-four years later, but further out on the periphery of the city. The lovingly constructed collages are idyllic when they depict the bushland. Increasing urbanisation is accompanied by images of violence: gumtrees turned into forts, birds shanghaied, frogs removed from the environment by twelve-year-old Sam, windows broken and evidence of increasing litter and visual degradation. Although the ideology of the text would seem clear and the author's endnote makes it quite explicit, this text can be misread by city children, especially, in my experience, by those under seven, who have not been interpellated into green discourses. It may be that the ingenuity of the collages of cityscapes, their familiarity and their busyness, compared with the ones depicting the pastoral, are attractive to such readers. It is wise then to keep in mind what postmodern reader response theorists, like Culler (1978), Fish (1980), Holland (1975) and Iser (1978), are aware of—that texts become powerful at the point where their readers construct them. Reading is an exchange, and writers, while powerful in articulating ideology, do not have total control over how their texts are read.

Conclusion

The admittedly selective survey of literary constructions of the city from 1890 to 1994 offered here indicates the need for readers to be alert to the extent to which even the most avowedly realist–naturalist account of the city partakes, not in the mimetic act of reflecting the city, but in discourses which enact ideology. What is most simplifying about literary discourses is their tendency to construct false binary oppositions, whether they be city–bush, inner city–suburbs, Australian suburban conformity–cosmopolitan pluralism. The reality is that cities and houses are where we (mainly) live in Australia and about which we dream, and on which we spend a large proportion of our incomes. Insofar as we live in either, they are, like everything in nature, subject to violent flux, destruction and reconstruction–all aspects of the cycle being imbricated in signifying systems and ideological webs. In Bachelard's terms, and it constitutes a more general truth:

> A house that has been experienced is not an inert box. Inhabited space transcends geometrical space. (Bachelard 1989 [1964], p. 278)

References

Anderson, J. (1978), *Tirra Lirra by the River*, Penguin, Ringwood.

Bachelard, G. (1989 [1964]), *The Poetics of Space*, cited in D. Modjeska (ed.), *Inner Cities: Australian Women's Memory of Place*, Penguin, Ringwood.

Bail, M. (1980), 'Home Ownership', *Quadrant*, vol. 24, January–February, pp. 95–7.

Baker, J. (1991), *Window*, Julia MacRae Books, London.

Baynton, B. (1902), 'Squeaker's mate', *Bush Studies*, Angus & Robertson, Sydney.

Bennett, B. (1984), *Place, Region and Community*, James Cook University of North Queensland, Townsville.

Boyd, R. (1960), *The Australian Ugliness*, Penguin, Ringwood.

Brennan, C. (1960), *Poems 1913*, reproduced in A. R. Chisholm & J. J. Quinn (eds), *The Verse of Christopher Brennan*, Angus & Robertson, Sydney.

Brett, L. (1986), 'Our house', *The Auschwitz Poems*, Scribe, Melbourne.

Cantrell, L. (1977), *The 1890s: Stories, Verse and Essays*, University of Queensland Press, St Lucia.

Carroll, J. (1982), *Intruders in the Bush: The Australian Quest for Identity*, Oxford University Press, Melbourne.

Chambers, R. (1984), *Story and Situation, Narrative Seduction and the Power of Fiction*, University of Minnesota Press, Minneapolis.

Culler, J. (1975), *Structuralist Poetics*, Routledge & Kegan Paul, London.

Dark, E. (1985), *The Little Company*, Virago, London.

Davison G. (1992), 'Sydney and the bush: An urban context for the Australian legend', in G. Whitlock & D. Carter (eds), *Images of Australia: An Introductory Reader in Australian Studies*, University of Queensland Press, St Lucia.

Dawe, B. (1978), *Sometimes Gladness, Collected Poems 1954–1978*, Longman Cheshire, Melbourne.

Devlin Glass, F. (1991), 'Furphy and the land: The feminine as a metaphor for landscape', *Westerly*, vol. 36, no. 4, pp. 39–44.

Falkiner, S. (1992), *The Writers' Landscape: Wilderness*, Simon & Schuster, East Roseville.

Fish, S. (1980), *Is there a Text in this Class? The Authority of Interpretive Communities*, Harvard University Press, Harvard.

Fiske, J., Hodge, B. & Turner, G. (1987), *Myths of Oz: Reading Australian Popular Culture*, Allen & Unwin, Sydney.

Foucault, M. (1969), *The Archaeology of Knowledge*, trans. A. M. Sheridan, Tavistock Publications, London, 1972.

Foucault, M. (1979), *Discipline and Punish*, Vintage, New York.

Garner, H. (1978), *Monkey Grip*, Penguin, Ringwood.

Gerster, R. (1990), 'Gerrymander: The place of suburbia in Australian fiction', *Meanjin*, no. 3, pp. 565–75.

Goodwin, K. & Lawson, A. (eds) (1990), *The Macmillan Anthology of Australian Literature*, Macmillan, South Melbourne.

Gregory, J. (1990), 'Imagining suburbia: The role of the real estate agent', *Westerly*, vol. 35, no. 4, pp. 85–90.

Halkett, I. & Brooke, P. (1976), *The Quarter-Acre Block: The Use of Suburban Gardens*, Australian Institute of Urban Studies, Canberra.

Hanrahan, B. (1989), 'Weird Adelaide', in G. Whitlock (ed.), *Eight Voices of the Eighties: Stories, Journalism and Criticism by Australian Women Writers*, University of Queensland Press, St Lucia.

Harlen, J. (1992), *The Lion and the Lamb*, Hodder & Stoughton, Rydalmere.

Harwood, G. (1990), *Selected Poems*, Angus & Robertson/Harper Collins, Pymble.

Holland, N. (1975), *The Dynamics of Literacy Response*, Norton, New York.

Horne, D. (1971), *The Lucky Country*, Penguin, Ringwood.

Horniman, J. (1992), *Sand Monkeys*, Omnibus, Norwood.

Humphries, B. (1990), *The Life and Death of Sandy Stone*, introduced and edited by C. O'Brien, Pan Macmillan, Sydney.

Iser, W. (1978), *The Act of Reading: A Theory of Aesthetic Response*, Routledge & Kegan Paul, London.

Kershaw, A. (1992), 'Far from the old folks who aren't at home', *Australian Book Review*, December/January, no.137, pp. 17–18.

Langford, R. (1988), *Don't Take Your Love to Town*, Penguin, Ringwood.

Lansbury, C. (1970), *Arcady in Australia: The Evocation of Australia in Nineteenth-century English Literature*, Melbourne University Press, Carlton.

Lather, P. (1991), 'Charting Postmodernism', *Feminist Research in Education: Within/Against*, Deakin University Press, Geelong.

Lawson, S. (1989), 'La Citoyenne 1967', in D. Modjeska (ed.), *Inner Cities: Australian Women's Memory of Place*, Penguin, Ringwood.

Lindsay, N. (1930[1959]), *Redheap*, Ure Smith, Sydney.

Lindsay, N. (1933[1961]), *Saturdee*, Ure Smith Sydney.

Lindsay, N. (1947), *Halfway to Anywhere*, Angus & Robinson, Sydney.

Magarey, S., Rowley, S. & Sheridan, S. (eds) (1993), *Debutante Nation: Feminism Contests the 1890s*, Allen & Unwin, St. Leonards, NSW.

Malouf, D. (1975), *Johnno*, Penguin, Ringwood.

Malouf, D. (1985), *12 Edmonstone Street*, Penguin, Ringwood.

Malouf, D. (1990a), *The Great World*, Chatto & Windus, London.

Malouf, D. (1990b), 'A first place: The mapping of a world', in K. Goodwin & A. Lawson (eds), *The Macmillan Anthology of Australian Literature*, Macmillan, South Melbourne.

Marchetta, M. (1992), *Looking for Allibrandi*, Puffin, Ringwood.

McCarthy, M. (1992), *Ganglands*, Puffin, Ringwood.

McGregor, C. (1972), *The Australian People*, Hodder Stoughton, Sydney.

Modjeska, D. (ed.) (1989), *Inner Cities: Australian Women's Memory of Place*, Penguin, Ringwood.

Murray, L. (1983), 'The quality of sprawl', in *The People's Otherworld*, Angus & Robertson, North Ryde.

Paterson, A. B. (1992), 'Clancy of the Overflow', in selection by L. Murray, *A. B. Paterson: Selected Poems*, Collins/Angus & Robertson, Sydney.

Preminger, A. et al. (ed.) (1965), *Encyclopaedia of Poetry and Poetics*, Princeton, Englewood Cliffs, NJ.

Reid, I. (1992), *Narrative Exchanges*, Routledge, London.

Schaffer, K. (1988), *Women and the Bush: Forces of Desire in the Australian Cultural Tradition*, Cambridge University Press, Cambridge.

Sheridan, S. (1985), '"Temper romantic: Bias, offensively feminine": Australian women writers and literary nationalism', *Kunapipi*, vol. 7, nos 2–3, pp. 49–58.

Stewart, K. (1988), 'Journalism and the world of the writer: The production of Australian literature, 1855–1915', in L. Herghenham (ed.), *The Penguin New Literary History of Australia*, Penguin, Ringwood.

Stretton, H. (1970), *Ideas for Australian Cities*, rev. edn, Georgian House, Melbourne.

Walwicz, A. (1989), *Boat*, Angus & Robertson, North Ryde.

Watson, S. (1989), 'Social spatial connections', in D. Modjeska (ed.), *Inner Cities: Australian Women's Memory of Place*, Penguin, Ringwood.

Wheatley, N. & Rawlins, D. (1988), *My Place*, Collins Dove, Blackburn.

White, P. (1958), 'The Prodigal Son', *Australian Letters*, vol.1, no.3, pp. 37–40.

White, P. (1961), *Riders in the Chariot*, Penguin, Harmondsworth & Ringwood.

White, P. (1964), 'Down at the Dump', *The Burnt Ones*, Penguin, Harmondsworth & Ringwood.

White, P. (1965), 'Season at Sarsaparilla', *Four Plays by Patrick White*, Sun, Melbourne.

White, R. (1981), *Inventing Australia: Images and Identity 1688–1980*, Allen & Unwin, Sydney.

Whitlock, G. (ed.) (1989), *Eight Voices of the Eighties: Stories, Journalism and Criticism by Australian Women Writers*, University of Queensland Press, St Lucia.

Whitlock, G. & Carter, D. (eds) (1992), *Images of Australia, An Introductory Reader in Australian Studies*, University of Queensland Press, St Lucia.

Bibliography

Bliss, C. (1988), 'Dialectic of many and one: City and outback in Patrick White's fiction', in A. Cromwell (ed.), *From Outback to City: Changing Preoccupations in Australian Literature of the Twentieth Century. Four Essays*, American Association of Australian Literary Studies, New York.

Boyd, R. (1968), *Australia's Home: Its Origins, Builders and Occupiers*, 2nd edn, Penguin, Ringwood.

Buckley, V. (1976), *The Golden Builders and Other Poems*, Angus & Robertson, Sydney.

Davis, J. (1981), *Kullark (Home): The Dreamers*, Currency Press, Sydney.

Davis, J. (1985), *No Sugar*, Currency Press, Sydney.

Davis, J. (1988), *Barungin, Smell the Wind*, Currency Press, Sydney.

Devlin Glass, F., Eaden, R., Hoffmann, L. & Turner, G. (eds) (1991), *The Annotated Such is Life*, Oxford University Press, Melbourne.

Falkiner, S. (1992), *The Writer's Landscape: Settlement,* Simon & Schuster, Sydney.

Gare, N. (1961), *The Fringe Dwellers,* Sun Books, Melbourne.

Gilbert, K. (1990), *The Blackslide: People are Legends and Other Poems,* Hyland House, South Yarra.

Gunew, S. (1989), 'Memory crop', in D. Modjeska (ed.), *Inner Cities: Australian Women's Memory of Place,* Penguin, Ringwood.

Hope, A. D. (1972), *Collected Poems,* Angus & Robertson, Sydney.

Mudrooroo Narogin (formerly C. Johnson) (1986), *The Song of Jacky and Selected Poems,* Hyland House, Melbourne.

Mudrooroo Narogin (formerly C. Johnson) (1965), *Wild Cat Falling,* Angus & Robinson, Sydney, 1979.

Walker, D. (1976), *Dream and Disillusion: A Search for Australian Cultural Identity,* Australian National University Press, Canberra.

Wheatley, N. (1982), *Five Times Dizzy,* Oxford University Press, Melbourne.

Wheatley, N. (1985), *The House that was Eureka,* Puffin, Ringwood.

Chapter 12 | Space, knowledge, power and gender

Margo Huxley

> The built environment, once constructed, forecloses possibilities for change by virtue of its existence. It is massively real, undeniable and reminds one in its apparent autonomy and coerciveness of a Durkheimian social fact. (Kilmartin & Thorns 1978, p. 160)

> ... the things which seem most evident to us... reside on a base of human practice and history; and ... since these things have been made, they can be unmade, as long as we know how it was they were made. (Foucault, quoted in Smart 1985, p. 141)

There has been a tendency in feminist analyses of the built environment, and of the home in particular, to 'read off' the physical form of the building from the relations of power under patriarchal capitalism. That is, some critiques tend to assume that there is only one possible use to be made of designed/socially-produced spaces and it is the use dictated by the male 'architect–hero', builder or planner, or by the underlying social and economic structures of capital accumulation and patriarchal domination. This has created a parallel tendency to imply that non-sexist, non-capitalist cities will have to be designed and built anew, either by moving to new sites removed from existing cities, or by 'bulldozing the lot' and starting again.

I suggest that these drastic implications are derived from the too-narrowly deterministic starting points of the analyses. Alternative interpretations of the built environment might indicate polymorphous points of production and more creative uses for existing space.

Feminist critiques of the form of contemporary urbanisation have shown how masculinist, dichotomised assumptions or ideologies about the proper place of domestic life in the suburbs and public world of work in the city (Saegert 1981,1985) have meshed with the interests of capital accumulation to advantage the sphere of production and paid work over the sphere of consumption, reproduction and daily life (Pringle 1988; Wajcman 1991). More than a decade ago, in 1983, Liz Harman traced the development of the capitalist, patriarchal city in Australia and showed how inadequate the assumptions about women's place being 'in' the home were for understanding the every-day life of household management (Harman 1988). In fact, household work requires extensive daily travel and logistical time-budgeting in order to nego-tiate the barriers presented by the built environment. Yet, work done in the domestic sphere is still seen as unproblematic by policy-makers, planners and designers, despite increasing pressures to create conditions more favourable to carrying it out (Fincher 1991). Women are not only still disadvantaged by the form of urban areas, but attempts to give women greater access to hous-ing and mortgage finance have not had marked effects on women's abilities to provide their own housing independently (Gartner 1986; Watson 1988).

Feminist critiques have also been directed at the design and production of the built environment. The practices of design, architecture, planning and building have all come under scrutiny for failing to encourage women's in-volvement in these professions and for actively devaluing alternative ways of working that depart from the model of the 'architect-hero'; and for failing to produce houses, shops, workplaces or neighbourhoods that serve the diverse needs of people who actually inhabit and use these spaces and places (Franck 1985; Matrix 1984; Stimpson et al. 1981; *Transition* 1988; Wekerle, Petersen & Morley 1980. For a fuller discussion of feminist work in the field of urban studies and the built environment, see Fincher 1990, Huxley 1993 and Johnson 1989).

The two aspects of these critiques I would like to take up are:

- the implicit idea that capitalist, patriarchal cities would have to be rede-signed and built again from the ground up in order to create more responsive, convivial, diverse urban spaces; and
- the notion that there is a direct correlation between what architects assume or intend in their designs and what actually takes place in a building.

These two aspects are centrally related to any strategies for change that see social relations and spatial structures as integral to each other.

Jos Boys, of the English women's architectural collective Matrix, poses the following questions in relation to critiques of conventional architecture:

> ... to what extent does architecture actually reflect social relations (that is, can literally be taken as a *map* of any society) when people obviously use any building in many different ways both at one time and throughout its history? What is the relation between architectural intention in making the building and the reality of its use? How is social 'meaning' in architec-ture transmitted and how interpreted? To what extent can buildings offer conflicting symbolic or spatial information? (Boys 1984, p. 26)

In partial answer to some of these questions, I take an approach to the problem which begins with the works of Foucault (especially 1979, 1980 and 1986), and the archaeologists, Shanks and Tilley (1987). Rather than rely on prior knowledge of the social relations through which the contemporary built environment has been produced, we can suspend this knowledge in order to look at cities and buildings as archaeological artefacts of an unknown but material culture for which a variety of social relations could be suggested. This kind of interpretation tries to uncover the potentialities of power possible in a given built form. It suggests that there are multiple ways of using the same space and multiple meanings that attach to it: although much is 'given' in built form, much more is possible.

Thus, 'non-sexist cities' could be created from the already existing built environment (Hayden 1981a), provided we understand the conditions under which it was made and can re-envision possibilities for its use.

Interpreting material culture

How do archaeologists proceed from describing traces, artefacts, structures or decorative patterns to interpreting these as evidence of the particular social relations that produced them? Shanks and Tilley (1987), while barely mentioning gender, provide a critique of traditional archaeology's focus on dating and classifying material remains. The methodology is empiricist and positivist, seeking to establish regularities or discontinuities in the occurrence, shape and decoration of types of artefacts over space and time and, on the basis of quantified data, constructing hypothesised patterns from which to reconstruct the societies in which individuals manufactured given artefacts.

Shanks and Tilley reject this individualist epistemology and propose that artefacts studied as discrete, isolated instances of regularly occurring patterns foreclose other possible interpretations of the relations of power in pre-literate societies. To make such leaps of faith is like placing a brick in the middle of London and analysing in detail its composition, shape, size and colour as a method of understanding the social relations of the whole city (Shanks & Tilley 1987, pp. 94–8).

Rather, they propose that any artefact is a product of a polysemous web of signifieds and signifiers that cannot be understood in isolation from the whole culture in which it was produced. For Shanks and Tilley, archaeology must take clues from every possible manifestation of that culture and create plausible stories about their interlocking meanings:

> ... material culture can be considered to be an articulated and structured silent material discourse forming a channel of reified expression and being linked and bound up with social practices and social strategies involving power, interests and ideology. (Shanks & Tilley 1987, p. 102)

Thus, what is important is not the correct interpretation of, say, decorative patterns as being of increasing 'accuracy' or complexity, either evolving or degenerating over time and space; not whether marks resembling two concentric ovals are 'really macrozamia' (macadamia) nuts or vulvas (Davidson & Noble 1989, p. 136); but that these patterns form a series of references to other aspects of the material and social culture. Material culture as embodied in individual artefacts 'does not provide a window which we can see through and read off past social reality' (Shanks & Tilley 1987, p. 210).

Particularly, I would add, material cultural artefacts do not necessarily indicate specific gender relations in terms of ritual performance, cooking, gathering, pot-making, hunting, weaving or child-rearing. These relations remain problematic in the absence of further cross-referential evidence (see, for example, Bleier 1984 and Eichler 1980 for critiques of the gendered assumptions made in biological science and anthropology). Similarly, in relation to the remains of buildings—and contrary to what some feminist architects have implied about the universality of essential feminine attributes in design, for instance, that women build low, round structures (Kennedy 1981)—it is not possible to adduce simply from their shape or placement who constructed them or how they were used.

This approach to understanding artefacts and buildings allows the possibility that existing buildings need not be, and indeed almost never are, used in the way an individual architect might have intended. Existing cities offer innumerable possibilities for interpretation and re-interpretation, use and re-use, small-scale additions and subtractions, which attest to the flexibility, rather than the permanence of built form.

Built form and the micro-politics of power

The open-ended nature of the possibilities of built form are integral to an understanding of the micro-politics of power which Foucault sees in prisons, asylums, hospitals, schools and factories. For Foucault, built form, like gender, is not a fixed 'Durkheimian fact,' but open to alternative interpretations, meanings and practices (Foucault 1986, pp. 239–56).

I will quote at length from an interview with Foucault by Paul Rabinow, titled 'Space, knowledge and power', since it seems to me to sum up the essence of an understanding of different interpretations of the built environment:

> Let me bring up another example: the Familistere of Jean-Baptiste Godin at Guise [1859]. The architecture of Godin was clearly intended for the freedom of people. Here was something that manifested the power of ordinary workers to participate in the exercise of their trade. It was a rather important sign and instrument of autonomy for a group of workers. Yet no one could enter or leave the place without being seen by everyone — an aspect of the architecture that could be totally oppressive. But it could only be oppressive if people were prepared to use their own presence in order to watch over others ...
>
> Men [sic] have dreamed of liberating machines. But there are no machines of freedom, by definition. This is not to say that the exercise of freedom is completely indifferent to spatial distribution, but it can only function when there is a certain convergence; in the case of divergence or distortion, it immediately becomes the opposite of that which had been intended. The panoptic qualities of Guise could perfectly well have allowed it to be used as a prison. Nothing could be simpler. It is clear that, in fact, the Familistere may well have served as an instrument for discipline and a rather unbearable group pressure. (Foucault 1986, pp. 246–7)

The physical configuration of the building only constrains or enhances certain practices: it does not of itself create those practices. Neither do these practices necessarily accord with the intentions of the designers. Elsewhere in the interview, Foucault talks about architecture as an element of support for disciplinary functions, 'to ensure a certain allocation of people in space, a *canalisation* of their circulation, as well as the coding of their reciprocal relations' (Foucault 1986, p. 253), but this architectural framework does not *determine* the social relations of the use of space.

Similarly, the intentions of the designers and the interpretations of symbolic meanings are not always transparently inscribed in built form. Foucault (1986, p. 255) gives the exceptional example of the military camp as a physical inscribing of space with instantly readable social hierarchies, but otherwise he indicates that architects are less important in the fields of power relations than doctors or prison warders:

> After all, the architect has no power over me. If I want to tear down or change a house he [sic] built for me, put up new partitions, add a chimney, the architect has no control. (Foucault 1986, p. 247–8)

While it is certainly the case that the intentions of the architect are less powerful than the power relations embodying the uses to which buildings are actually put, what Foucault ignores here is his own power to effect changes to the building, predicated on knowledge, the ownership of property and the command of resources. Prisoners, asylum inmates, rental housing tenants may have fewer means of resistance to the architect's control over the 'canalisation of their circulation'. The way in which architects and designers have designed public housing to educate and improve the working classes is a case in point (Reiger 1985; Roberts 1991).

But resistance to the power relations embodied in built form is ever-present, and can be seen in various descriptions by despairing architects and philanthropists complaining of the inability of the working class to understand the 'correct' use of domestic spaces:

> The architects ... sought to provide a functional separation of cooking, eating, and living, but this conflicted with the habits of the people being re-housed. Consequently, people ate at the draining boards by the sink because they thought the kitchen was the place for meals, even though it was too narrow for a table. (Gardner 1978, p. 3)

This was in Britain in 1944. Almost twenty years later, the Parker-Morris Report on housing standards admitted defeat:

> We have heard it said on more than one occasion that the kitchen should be planned so that it is impossible to take meals in it, with a view to raising the social and living standards of the occupiers. We believe that this is an unsuitable motive on which to choose a plan; and even if it were not it would be necessary now, after ten or fifteen years of trying it out, to recognise that it is misconceived. (Parker-Morris Report 1961, quoted in Matrix 1984, p. 76)

Despite years of designing postwar British Council housing with small kitchens and separate dining rooms, the architects still could not persuade the occupants of the 'undesirability' of eating in the kitchen. (There is an apocryphal story, from the 1960s in Victoria, of Housing Commission Tenancy Officers finding a family keeping a horse in a fourteenth-floor flat — in the 'spare' room.)

Women's use of the built environment: Oppression, resistance and change

Dolores Hayden (1981b) in her book *The Grand Domestic Revolution* details the many experiments carried out by American women over the last one hundred years, in attempts to create built environments that would allow women equal participation in the worlds of paid work and the home. Many proposals, such as those by Charlotte Perkins Gilman and Melusina Fay Pierce (Hayden 1981b) at the end of the last century, included the idea of the socialisation of cooking: designs for kitchenless houses or communal cooking arrangements attempted to free (middle-class) women from the endless round of domestic work that kept them from entering the public sphere.

Sadly, few of these feminist utopian social arrangements succeeded, in part because they were contrary to working-class and middle-class beliefs about home and hearth. The powerful images of the kitchen as the heart of family life in workers' homes (compare the Parker-Morris Report) and of the home as haven and retreat for the middle-class male, were too firmly entrenched to allow the potentialities of alternative arrangements to emerge. In part also, the experiments in designing new social relations failed because they directly threatened, at one and the same time, patriarchal domestic power relations and capitalist property relations.

Women are still disadvantaged by the physical arrangement of houses and in the dispositions of social interactions across space. The form of the Australian city is particularly unsuitable for carrying out home and non-residential domestic tasks (Harman 1988), with large suburban lots and car-based transport creating severe space–time constraints faced by women in their daily battle to chauffeur children, shop, find paid employment and run a household (Ferrier 1983; Sarkissian 1978; Wajcman 1991).

What a reading of the existing built environment shows is that women — or anyone charged with management of the household — have been rendered invisible and virtually incapable of carrying out the expectations of the job. The conjunctures of technology (such as the car and roads), ideology (such as the ideal of the 'home' embodied in the detached dwelling), and health and safety assumptions (such as land-use zoning and building regulations) reinforce masculinist separations of 'home' from 'work' and the capitalist devaluation of unpaid labour. Thus, for most women, every act of daily existence in the city can be seen as a costly and heroic act of resistance to underlying power relations.

In the same way, the detached house has been analysed and criticised for no longer reflecting — if it ever did — the needs of changing household composition, the realities of everyday life for households with adult members in the paid workforce and for rendering invisible the work that is performed to keep the houshold running (Matrix 1984; Roberts 1991; Thompson 1992; Wajcman 1991). The detached house on its suburban lot with its profligate use of land, materials, goods and energy is also a postwar consumption palace of the 1960s that the 1990s can no longer afford.

The Australian government is currently attempting to curb 'urban sprawl' and promote higher density housing, but these measures are unlikely to either change the overall pattern of development or bring house prices down. Therefore, they are unlikely to be of much benefit to women. Indeed, it may be the case that large suburban houses on large suburban lots can be used in more communal and creative ways and we should think twice before building over the backyard (see Huxley 1985).

Dolores Hayden (1981a) has suggested ways in which ordinary residential blocks can be altered at minimum cost to provide shared vegetable gardens, shared play areas, appliance, tool and car pooling, childcare and cooperative food buying (see Figure 12.1).

Some of these ideas are not new and have been promoted by environmentalists for some time (Cock 1979; White et al. 1978), but usually the gender dimension has been neglected, so that being environmentally sound ends up meaning 'more work for mother'. Hayden is explicitly proposing that these new uses for existing spaces must entail new relations of domestic and non-domestic work — all work must be shared equally between the residents. This cannot be drawn on the plan, and once again illustrates the limitations of trying to design a new city, or a new society, into existence. Nevertheless, her ideas allow us to glimpse some of the possibilities lying latent within the constraints of the built environment.

The same suspension of the 'social facts' of the built environment can be exercised to reinterpret the suburban house:

> What is ... offered [in the display home] is a set of socio-spatial relations between members of the household which reaffirms, but does not preclude their challenge and change ... It confirms, but also allows, the subversion of dominant social relations. (Johnson 1992, p. 46)

So, the larger the detached house, the more people can live in it and, in times when it takes more than one income to buy a house, pool resources to afford it. Two or three bathrooms, large bedrooms, playrooms, family rooms and large gardens can be reinterpreted as resources for communal occupation. We can interpret the 'family' home in ways that stand conventional 'canalisations' of activity on their heads: family rooms used for collective productive purposes; all children sleeping in the 'master bedroom' with en suite bathroom; adults distributed through other rooms according to relations which have no necessary connections with gender, age, parenthood, property-ownership or domination (see Figure 12.2).

Figure 12.1

A. Suburban neighbourhood block plan
B. Same suburban block with new common space and facilities

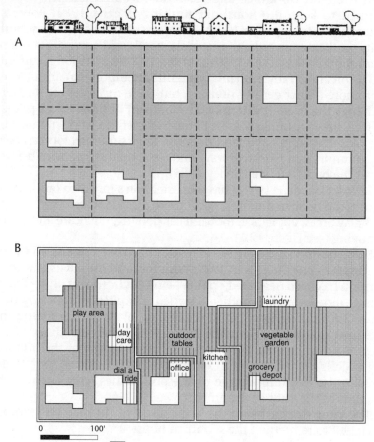

Source: Hayden (1981a, p. 181)

These fictional variations on the theme of suitable shelter, household composition and the meaning of home, are no more dramatic than the changes in use and social relations undergone in the average inner-suburban terrace house since its construction. Over the last hundred years, the basic configuration of rooms may have housed up to ten people — a middle-class family and servants; been a boarding house or sweatshop; and now, house one or two highly paid executives cohabiting in any of a number of possible sexual and financial arrangements; or four or five students. Such changes in domestic relations would have been unimaginable to the original builders of the terrace.

Figure 12.2   Floorplan of the 'Regency' and other possibilities

With all but the most obvious and basic room designations removed, it is possible to imagine any number of different uses for the spaces provided in a typical suburban home.

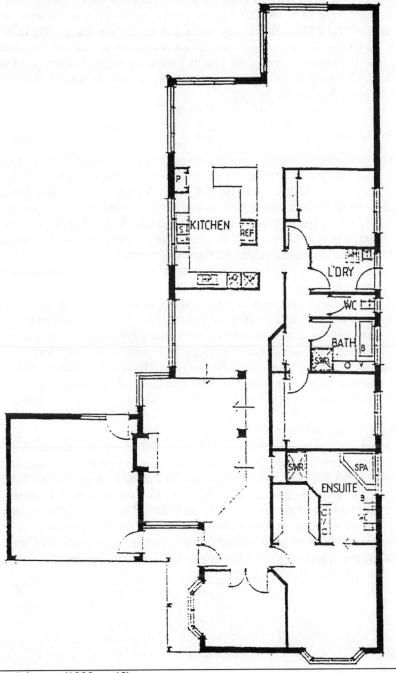

Source: Johnson (1992, p. 45)

But counterpoised against the demographic and social changes that become accepted practice, there are a host of mundane government regulations backed up by conventional expectations and dominant ideologies that can prevent the creative uses of existing spaces (Huxley 1985; Johnson 1992). This is often why 'non-standard' or utopian communities must set up anew, outside existing cities, where they can more easily live alternative lives, but where, at the same time, they are unlikely to challenge dominant modes of existence. Changing the uses we make of the existing built environment requires challenging the systems of domination and circuits of power that produce everyday life in the city.

Conclusion

Cities are massively constraining because of the physicality of their presence, and it is unlikely that purpose-built new cities will be created overnight — unless they are 'multifunction polises', into the creation of which neither feminist designers nor women users are likely to have much input. In any case, the idea of a feminist blueprint for the ideal city is not an appealing one, since it implies the existence of an omniscient designer with universalised intentions and unlimited power to carry them out.

What feminist designers, architects and planners can contribute to strategies of transformation is the small-scale creation of new built forms and ideas for the creative use of existing forms which include enabling communities and groups to undertake their own designs and constructions (see Matrix 1984). Designers and planners can join with local communities in attempting to change local land-use, transport and community facilities to more balanced, accessible (and energy-efficient) distributions (see White et al. 1978). These feminist forms of practice are still 'marginal and powerless in the social hierarchy of ... societies which they seek to transform' (Weedon 1987, p. 40), but can constitute powerful avenues of active and potentially transformative critique that should not be neglected.

The built environment is indeed fixed, but not as fixed as all that, and persists long after the intentions of its creators are forgotten — if indeed they were ever known. But it does not have the 'reality of a Durkheimian fact': it is open to multiple interpretations, and is imbued with multiple meanings; buildings and spaces are used and reused, added to, subtracted from; creatively destroyed and communally redeployed. The fluctuation of form, meaning and use over time and across space opens up possibilities for feminist practice in the design and the use of the built environment.

References

Boys, J. (1984), 'Is there a feminist analysis of architecture?', *Built Environment,* vol. 10, no. 1, pp. 25–34.

Bleier, R. (1984), *Science and Gender: A Critique of Biology and its Theories on Women,* Pergamon Press, New York.

Cock, P. (1979), *Alternative Australia,* Quartet Books, Melbourne.

Davidson, I. & Noble, W. (1989), 'The archeology of perception: Traces of depiction and language', *Current Anthropology,* vol. 30, no. 2, pp. 125–53.

Eichler, M. (1980), *The Double Standard: A Feminist Critique of Feminist Social Sciences,* Croom Helm, London.

Ferrier, M. (1983), 'Sexism in Australian cities: Barriers to employment opportunities', *Women's Studies International Forum,* vol. 6, no. 1, pp. 73–84.

Fincher, R. (1990), 'Women in the city', *Australian Geographical Studies,* vol. 28, no. 1, pp. 29–37.

Fincher, R. (1991), 'Caring for workers' dependents: Gender, class and local state practice in Melbourne', *Political Geography Quarterly,* vol. 10, no. 4, pp. 356–81.

Foucault, M. (1979), *Discipline and Punish: The Birth of the Prison,* Vintage Books, New York.

Foucault, M. (1980), 'Questions on geography', in C. Gordon (ed.), *Michel Foucault: Power/Knowledge,* The Harvester Press, Brighton, UK.

Foucault, M. (1986), 'Space, knowledge and power', in P. Rabinow (ed.), *The Foucault Reader,* Penguin, Harmondsworth.

Franck, K. (1985), 'Social construction of the physical environment: The case of gender', *Sociological Focus,* vol. 18, no. 2, pp. 143–60.

Gardner, G. (1978), *Social Surveys for Social Planners,* Holt, Rinehart & Winston, Sydney.

Gartner, A. (1986), 'Not feeling at home: Women and housing', in 'Forum on feminism and the built environment', *Urban Policy and Research,* vol. 4, no. 1, pp. 34–6.

Harman, E. (1988), 'Capitalism, patriarchy and the city', in C. Baldock & B. Cass (eds), *Women, Social Welfare and the State in Australia,* 2nd edn (1st edn, 1983), Allen & Unwin, Sydney.

Hayden, D. (1981a), 'What would a non-sexist city be like?', in E. Stimpson et al. (eds), *Women and the American City,* University of Chicago Press, Chicago.

Hayden, D. (1981b), *The Grand Domestic Revolution: A History of Feminist Designs for American Homes, Neighbourhoods and Cities,* Massachusetts Institute of Technology Press, Massachusetts.

Huxley, M. (1985), 'In search of "the good life"', *Urban Policy and Research,* vol. 3, no. 1, pp. 17–24.

Huxley, M. (1993) 'Feminisms/urbanisms: Women and cities in Australia', *Trames,* vol. 8, pp. 126–30.

Johnson, L. (1989), 'Making space for women: Feminist critiques and reformulations of the spatial disciplines', *Australian Feminist Studies*, vol. 9, Autumn, pp. 31–50.

Johnson, L. (1992), 'Housing desire: A feminist geography of suburban housing', *Refractory Girl*, vol. 42, pp. 40–6.

Kennedy, M. (1981), 'Toward a recovery of "feminine" principles in architecture and planning', *Women's Studies International Quarterly*, vol. 4, no. 1, pp. 75–81.

Kilmartin, L. & Thorns, D. (1978), *Cities Unlimited*, Allen & Unwin, Sydney.

Matrix (1984), *Making Space: Women and the Man-made Environment*, Pluto Press, London.

Pringle, R. (1988), 'Women and consumer capitalism', in C. Baldock & B. Cass (eds), *Women and the Welfare State in Australia*, Allen & Unwin, Sydney.

Reiger, K. (1985), *The Disenchantment of the Home: Modernizing the Australian Family, 1880–1940*, Oxford University Press, Melbourne.

Roberts, M. (1991), *Living in a Man-made World: Gender Assumptions in Modern Housing Design*, Routledge, London.

Saegert, S. (1981), 'Masculine cities and feminine suburbs: Polarised ideas, contradictory realities', in C. Stimpson et al. (eds), *Women and the American City*, University of Chicago Press, Chicago.

Saegert, S. (1985), 'The androgenous city: From critique to practice', *Sociological Focus*, vol. 18, no. 2, pp. 161–76.

Sarkissian, W. (1978), 'Planning as if women mattered: The story of Brown Hills', *Makara*, vol. 3, no. 3, pp. 9–12.

Shanks, M. & Tilley, C. (1987), *Social Theory and Archaeology*, Polity Press, Cambridge.

Smart, B. (1985), *Michel Foucault*, Routledge, London.

Stimpson, E. R. et al. (eds) (1981), *Women and the American City*, University of Chicago Press, Chicago.

Thompson, S. (1992), 'The home environment', *Refractory Girl*, vol. 42, pp. 27–9.

Transition: Discourse on Architecture (1988), Special issue on Women and Architecture, vol. 25, Winter.

Wajcman, J. (1991), *Feminism Confronts Technology*, Polity Press, Cambridge.

Watson, S. (1988), *Accommodating Inequality: Gender and Housing*, Allen & Unwin, Sydney.

Weedon, C. (1987), *Feminist Practice and Post-structuralist Theory*, Basil Blackwell, Oxford.

Wekerle, G., Petersen, R. & Morley, D. (1980), *New Space for Women*, Westview Press, Boulder, Colo.

White, D. et al. (1978), *Seeds for Change: Creatively Confronting the Energy Crisis*, Patchwork Press, Melbourne.

Chapter 13 | Abjection and architecture: The migrant house in multicultural Australia[1]

Mirjana Lozanovksa

This chapter will discuss the role that the migrant house and the migrant 'enclave' play in deconstructing a persistent and mythic, yet very problematic, hegemonic culture in Australia. It will be suggested that the strong negative reaction often associated with the migrant house can be understood by its similarity to *abjection*—an unconscious revulsion before our own bodies and an ambiguous but necesssary precondition for subjectivity. This argument is sited at the unsettling and blurred zones between spatiality and language— the spatiality of the body in the built environment and language as constitutive of the speaking social being.

The migration process entails leaving one place for another, and being inserted into a new language, a new symbolic order. In order to negotiate the new language the migrant must suppress the old language, so that both the motherland and the mother-tongue are disavowed. This process of separation and negotiation is marked by abjection.

While there has been little discussion about the relations between spatiality and languages within architecture and urban studies, my argument is that insights into the migrant house can be gleaned from exploring the relations between spatiality and language in the construction of the subject as a social and speaking being *and* as a (spatially) embodied being.

Zemja Nepoznata[2]

The *ideal city* and the *dream house* are key symbols in the grand narrative history of occidental architecture. As utopian spaces, the *ideal city* and *dream house* are abstract mathematical productions. The history of architecture has established a dialectical relation between this *ideal-dream* and the 'real' inscriptions on the ground—the REAL city and the REAL suburb. These spaces are constituted as maps, they are cartographic markings where land is divided and governed as well as owned (Lefebvre 1991). My argument is that a discourse based on the dialectic between the utopian and the real overlooks *other* spaces that are not only more difficult to know about, but that would actually destabilise the above dialectic. These *other* spaces are perhaps unmappable and ungeometric; in a strictly structural analysis they would be seen to be the spaces in the crevices, in the interstices between architecture, yet perhaps are better described as the spaces of contradiction and ambiguity, the spaces of limit in which the unlimited unfolds. They are spaces that are repressed in the geometry of the ideal-dream.

I have set up this general formulation—Utopia-Real-Other—as a gesture towards one possible context for tracing specific spaces of migration. The city is a significant vision for the becoming of a (male) migrant. Late capitalist forces structure his desires for the city differently from that of the bourgeois subject of the First World. John Berger's descriptions in *A Seventh Man* contest typical oppressive representations of the (male) migrant:

> Every day he hears about the metropolis. The name of the city changes. It is all cities, overlaying one another and becoming a city that exists no-where but which continually transmits promises. Envisaged, the future about to begin is a wall, not a space: a wall not unlike the wall of an ancient city, except that its surface is not time-honoured and hand cut but time-defying and like the surface of a television screen behind which random images appear, yet which, when empty, is an opaque cloud that nothing can penetrate. (Berger & Mohr 1989, pp. 23, 60)

These descriptions suggest ways of structuring the drive to become a migrant. Notions of utopia (the *ideal city* and the *dream house*, the *ideal-dream*) are constructed through stories, through fabrications by those that return, through a strange mixture of the experience of journey in space and its narra-tion in language. Western cities are reinterpreted, translated and sublimated in the language of the migrant. This distinction between a wall and a space will recur in my chapter as one way of exploring the relation between archi-tecture and subjectivity.

In the second part of her seminal paper 'Can the subaltern speak?', Gayatri Chakravorty Spivak (1988) makes reference to Derrida's schema, self-other-*tout-autre*, as a possible generative point for approaching the socially subordinated for two reasons: firstly, he locates the tendency to constitute the Other-as-marginal as a European problem. It is a problem that is enclosed in the 'blank part of the text' in which the denial of representation renders the Other invisible. Secondly, his inscription of the *tout-autre* (the 'quite-other' as opposed to the 'self-consolidating other'), of 'rendering *delirious* that interior voice that is the voice of the other in us' (Derrida, quoted in Spivak 1988, p. 294) is an inclusion that prevents the Other from disappearing within the transparency of the (European) subject. For Spivak, Derrida's schema is useful because it writes the *blank* part of the text, which though blank is still *in the text*. In acknowledging a possible internal dialogue within the decentred (European) subject, it is a schema in which the impossibility of other more radical external dialogues is kept alive. Utopia-Real-Other is formulated with a special interest in spatiality and thus may turn out to have effects that are quite different from Derrida's schema.

Context

Spivak's statement 'to ignore the subaltern today is, willy-nilly, to continue the imperialist project' (Spivak 1988, p. 298) is a critique of the claim that 'the oppressed can speak for themselves'. She argues that a First World intellectual masquerading as an absent non-representor may disguise in this transparency a complicity with the investigating subject, and thus reconstitute the mechanics of the coloniser. In writing about the migrant in multicultural Australia these parameters of the (European) sovereign subject and the subaltern are differently constructed. Australia has a complicated relation to contemporary post-colonial studies. Its historical narratives as a colony of the British empire *and* as an industrially advanced nation that put into practice extensive migration policies, have conflicting and contradictory effects. Unlike Canada which is the most similar as a colony, Australia's monolingual institutional discourse, English, combined with labouring migrants from Europe, has constructed a division between England and Europe as the possible origin for culture in Australia. Frequently, to say you are a migrant from Europe, 'a European', is to identify with a marginal group. Whilst there is a complex network of forces, the hegemonic culture in Australia is mediated firstly by England, and only as a second level of colonisation by Europe. The southern European migrant ('invited' into Australia in 1965, after the White Australia Policy) is a particular subaltern within the diaspora which constitutes Australia, and it is his/her specificity that I will be attempting to speak to in this chapter.

While to ignore the subaltern continues the imperialist project, to not ignore the subaltern entails its own problems about theorising difference and ethnicity. The problematic of representation is taken up in a conversation between Gayatri Chakravorty Spivak and Sneja Gunew, two leading theorists of the margins:

> SG: I think that one forgets when one speaks within very obviously privileged academic contexts about, say, immigrant groups within Australia, that one is very much in danger of homogenizing, and of misrepresenting ...
>
> GCS: I don't think, really, that we will solve the problem today ... I think it has to be kept alive as a problem. It is not a solution, the idea of the disenfranchised speaking for themselves ... (Gunew & Spivak 1990, p. 63)

In another text Gunew distinguishes the 'homogenisation which is imposed upon them by those who position themselves outside multiculturalism' (Gunew 1992a, p. 43). Referring to the term 'migrant writing', used in the Penguin *New Literary History of Australia*, Gunew explains that the only acceptable mode in which the subaltern can speak is as an enforced unified voice. A homogeneity is always already implied in the construction, so the only possible subaltern speaking position is as a unified 'authentic' migrant voice. The term 'migrant' itself is a construction which perpetuates both a homogenisation and a negative marginal identity which can be made positive only through a collective position. Gunew speaks about the policy of multiculturalism advocated as 'cultural diversity' which eclipses both unequal power relations and the challenge to a homogeneous national culture (Gunew 1992a, 1992b).

The migrant house as an object of study entails two levels of theorising the margins. The one introduced above is within discourse on culture and subjectivity. The other is in relation to architecture—in which the only legitimate way of discussing the migrant house is as an individual house designed by a (non-migrant and non-female) architect. Although the mechanics of the constitution of the 'other' differ, both discourses—cultural and architectural—constitute the migrant and the migrant house as marginal. I use the term 'migrant house' to mean the house built by first-generation migrants of southern European descent who migrated in the 1960s (known as the Menzies era). This is typically the definitive implication of 'the migrant' and my task here is to explore the stereotypical in a way that opens up possibilities for an irruption of a *tout-autre*.

This chapter itself is just that—an interruption in the academic discourses about a stereotypical image of a migrant house.

Pečalbari   *Pustina*

Eagles and lions are mythical and masculine symbols of war and defence. The hegemonic culture recognises migrant houses by these mythical creatures which guard the gateways and sometimes the site perimeter of the migrant territory. The migrant houses are perceived as big and labelled 'Mediterranean palaces' by the hegemonic culture, although in actual size they are not half as big as the houses built by the elite in the southern and eastern parts of Melbourne. Eagles and lions adorn the gateways of the big migrant houses in a masculine gesture to fend off the enemy (Figure 13.1). But war against whom? Protecting what? What drives this extreme division between interior and exterior—this 'wall of war' architecture?

Migration is a movement from one symbolic order, one paternal language and law, to another. It entails the loss of the original symbolic.

In the gap between the language of the symbolic order that one enters and the father's language, the phallus as symbolic power is diminished. The migrant is already a decentred subject. The recovering of the subaltern as woman is frequently blocked by the construction of the migrant as 'man'. Referring to Spivak's paper, I would argue with the case of migration, the female as subaltern is kept mute, in behind the continuing construction of the neutral (male) subaltern. My task here is to explore the possible recovery of the subaltern woman through an exploration of architectural space. In relation to Spivak's question then, 'Can the subaltern speak?', my response is indirect, obtuse perhaps, and shifts the emphasis from boundaries of languages to physical walls, to architectural boundaries. In what ways do conditions of spatiality within the migrant house produce possibilities for the *becoming* of (female) subaltern subjectivities?

Figure 13.1   Eagles adorning the gateway to a 'Mediterranean palace'

Two moments of the *abject*, the cultural and the individual, are *nested* one within the other in a mode like Barthes's diagrammatic analysis of myths (Barthes 1986, p. 115). In Barthes's theory of myth, the signifier—or potent symbol—is both the final term in the linguistic system and the first term of the mythical system; it is the point of the sideways shift. This can be illustrated by way of the image of the lions and eagles that are constructed as the myth about migrants. Architecturally, the surface articulation or point of contact between the two levels of the *abject* is figured by the lions and the eagles on the site perimeter. But this point is the point of transfer from object to abject—the lions and eagles are no longer just ornamental objects, they become a sign—or representation—for the migrant as neither subject nor object. What do these figures signify—or mean—for the migrant, and what do they signify for the hegemonic culture? As sign, do they transfer signification between individual and culture? Irony is also at play—whilst for the migrant these figures are images of power and force, in the transfer into mythic signification they become figures of the marginal, they signify the migrant as non-citizen, as other. At the same time though, what meaning do they impose on their environs; as figures of war and defence they signify the environment as a hostile territory, they make visible mythic territorial divisions. They become figures of resistance. They become the sign for the *abject*, that is they are no longer objects within a subject/object bifurcation. The *abject* is the limit to games of war because it is a condition without the possibility of strategic positions.

In looking at the migrant house, it has been necessary to look at how the condition of the *abject* is articulated in psychoanalytic theories and in theories of culture. I will be using both Julia Kristeva's work on abjection and Mary Douglas's work on 'purity and danger' to explore the layered and nested levels of the abject that operate through the bodies and houses of migrants. I have selected two statements from Douglas and Kristeva, respectively, as points of contact between the individual subject and culture:

> That which is negated is not thereby removed. The rest of life, which does not tidily fit the accepted categories, is still there and demands attention. The body as we have tried to show, provides a basic schema for all symbolism. There is hardly any pollution which does not have some primary physiological reference. *As life is in the body it cannot be rejected outright.* (Douglas 1970, p. 193, italics added)

> Yet, facing the ab-ject and more specifically phobia and the splitting of the ego ... one might ask if those articulations of negativity germane to the unconscious (inherited by Freud from philosophy and psychology) have not become inoperative. The 'unconscious' contents remain here *excluded* but in a strange fashion: not radically enough to allow for a secure differentiation between subject and object, and yet clearly enough for a defensive *position* to be established—one that implies a refusal but also a sublimating elaboration. (Kristeva 1982, p. 7)

Kristeva's and Douglas's work is an exploration of the themes of personal revulsion and social taboos, associated with waste, which demonstrate a response in varying degrees of horror and fear to those unidentifiable 'matters' that transgress borders and boundaries: bodily fluids, faeces, spit, sperm, tears, menstrual blood, food, breast milk, urine, vomit, mucus, saliva, sexual fluids. Douglas constructs the body as a bounded system; she argues that the monitoring of its bodily orifices emphasises a 'danger' of the ambiguous matter that passes through in the same way as the monitoring of architectural exits and entries emphasises the threat of social disorder. The threat of disorder is constituted as a spatial confusion and a spatial ambiguity. Kristeva's work is a focus on the body as a necessary precondition for subjectivity. The very inability to either identify these fluids, products, traces, as part of the body—and therefore constituting the 'subject', or completely separate and distinct from the body, as 'objects'—articulates, in part, the condition of abjection. The abject is a pre-oedipal phase that is identified with the feminine and the maternal as a precondition for a self-contained and autonomous, speaking, social subject: a subject associated with the paternal and the phallus-governed symbolic. Thus, 'a "proper" subjectivity and sociality are founded on the (impossible) expulsion or exclusion of the improper, the unclean and the disorderly' (Grosz 1987, p. 108). Put simply, abjection is a confusion of the division between subject and object that functions around the configuration of the body. What abjection puts at stake, according to Kristeva's profound analysis, is the subject itself. But which subject?

Kýka   *Majka*

Through the metaphoric and metonymic inscription of the mother(land) on to the architecture of the house, the migrant house as the space of the abject becomes a precarious sort of 'projection' that is both sustained and maintained by the migrant, whilst at the same time engulfing her/him. Typical of the working-class migrant is the construction of big houses that might be seen as metaphoric substitutes for the loss of the motherland. The house gets bigger as her and his body diminishes.

The house as a mother-house figures frequently as the psycho-sexual space of the repressed in the (masculine) subject (see Bachelard 1964; Bal 1988). However, this fantasy, this repression, is put at risk through migrational movements. The signification of protection translates into one of struggle against internal and external forces: as the migrant builds his own version of home/mother/land in an alien and hostile territory, 'mother' must be protected in order to be protected by her. For the migrant (man and woman) mother is an architectural concept, the mother's body is the house. Yet this house is not able to be *objectified*, rather it creates an ambiguous space in which a strange blurred relationship is formed between the migrant's body and the architecture of the house. The migrant's own body is marked by an excess that renders it 'a fatigued body', 'body in need', the body of limits, whilst the house is presented as the clean and proper body, in which architectural order prevails—gateway, symmetry, front entry, facade, hard surfaces. It is this house which the eagles and walls defend.

What does the mother inscribed on to a defensive architecture signify? Feminine spaces such as the home have, at times, been transformed into major institutions of resistance. The home has been the site of political resistance in the form of meeting places, hiding places, bomb factories, escape hatches. From the signifier of passivity and peace, 'mother' becomes a signifier of resistance.

The image of territoriality of the *kýka* (migrant house) is a particular response in the hegemonic culture because it marks the limit to their homogeneity, it marks both the point of their (impossible) recognition of difference and, therefore, the instability of their 'host' subject position. Internally, their own disgust draws the subject into an abyss at the borders of the subject, into the space of the abject. And for the migrant, while 'fear cements his compound, conjoined to another world ... What he has swallowed up instead of maternal love is an emptiness, or rather a maternal hatred without ... words of the father' (Kristeva 1982, p. 6). The mother inscribed on to the architecture of the house is, therefore, an empty shell—there is no nurturing mother inside nor a father to give the word that will help the migrant resolve this abject mess.

In this situation, images of territoriality belie the ambiguity of boundaries, the space of the abject, the constant shuttling that it enforces between the body and the house, between space and language. The house, its perimeter boundary walls, its scale, its orderliness and presence, whilst having the image of territoriality, are effects of the instability of border lines between host and migrant. They speak of unstable identities of both, and they mark the site of the difficult relationship between spatiality and language.

While these examples are, after all, stereotypical, not every migrant house is actually of this architectural configuration. One peculiar example can dissolve such grandiose narratives. Thus, one migrant house, also distinct for having its backyard to the side of the house and therefore visible from the perimeter, contained, quietly and humbly, a whole menagerie of cement dogs, deer, giraffes and birds shaded under a tree just beyond the gateways of eagles and lions and the barred fence. Such playful parodies shatter any fixed notions of who can speak and of spatial territorialities; they take flight into the *smooth spaces* of possibility, of multiplicity and heterogeneity (Deleuze & Guattari 1987).

The image of territoriality may be most marked in the metaphoric inscriptions of the mother(land) on to the architecture of the *kyka* by the man migrant. The migrant house is characterised by a solidity and a form that has the effect of substitution for the mother(land). As metaphor it also signifies the desire to have access to the phallic symbolic of the *ideal-dream*.

Vnatre   *BHATPE*

Having constructed a defensive enclosure, the interior space might be thought to be a somewhat protected environment. The interior recreates *metonymic* versions of the motherland, the old culture irrupting as decorative clothing, as ornament. The interior is a space of femininities. Its context emphasises the relations between mothers and daughters and as such it is also the space that is almost totally unexplored in psychoanalytic theories. What does the mother(land) signify for the female subaltern, also a mother in/of the house? For the female subaltern who is always already a decentred subject before migration, the interiority of the migrant house may open different possibilities for the feminine. Gunew speculates that the old symbolic order is reattached to the maternal-feminine, 'to the female functions: customs, cooking, costumes and the old-tongues' (Gunew 1988, p. 37). Perhaps abjection is differently lived within the (impossible) female subject, perhaps it does not entail the same sort of sporadic rejections and separations because it is always close, perhaps it is less unfamiliar. Kristeva states that 'the abject is the violence of mourning for an "object" that has always already been lost' (Kristeva 1982, p. 15). While the defensive gesture of the exterior of the migrant house marked out a (delusive) territoriality between the symbolic order (of the hegemonic culture) and the space of the abject, the interiority of the migrant house provides a space in which the symbolic order has fewer territorial claims. The interior of the migrant house is a space without the law of the Father.

Within the interiority of the migrant house, a space that is signified by the feminine, metonymic irruptions of the mother(land) create a fertile space of *becoming*; surfaces of walls, floors and furnishings are veiled with a myriad of thin coatings—embroideries, lace, photographs, books, cloths, mirrors, ornaments—shiny technological objects are beside or underneath old immemorial belongings. The interior is the site for the secret language of the family, the space for the mother tongue. The architecture of the *kyka* is an enclosure, it encloses a space in which the unspeakable is uttered. The migrant house creates a space in which the subaltern can speak, though it is not a space in which (s)he can speak to the hegemonic culture, for the migrant is not born into a symbolic order in which the mother tongue is the Father's language.

Let us dwell though on the interiority of the migrant house as a space of *becoming* for the female subaltern, a space in which mother tongue and Father's language meet as an irruption of the abject. Within the house is the possibility of a double language, and the dangerous slippage from one to the other. It is the interiority of the migrant house that is contiguous with the unspeakable, and both of these are denoted as maternal-feminine. The mother tongue is not the Father's language, it is therefore a language which utters the *unspeakable* and *unsignifiable*. The architecture of the house thus inscribes a space for a secret language, a secret knowledge, a mother tongue which coexists with the Father's language coming from the outside. It is a space in which the Father's language only gains access as if it were territorialising a maternal, deterritorialised space. In relation to the Father's language then, the mother-tongue is constructed as the unspeakable language of guilt. It is a secret language and a secret power, it is a transgression of the language of the symbolic order, the new Father's language that the migrant subject was nonetheless not born into. The site of the *kyka* is therefore a transgressive space and from the position of the (instability) of the host culture it has to be rendered as corrupt or criminal in appearance.

The migrant house represents the site of the abject for the (unstable) subject position of the host culture. The abject is anterior to the subject/object bifurcation, abjection is above all ambiguity and it is this ambiguity which undoes the neat division between subject/object and host/migrant. The migrant house threatens the homogeneity and hegemony (which are only, in fact, arbitrary constructions); as the site of abjection, the migrant house is the limit to its (unstable cultural) subjectivity. The architecture of the migrant house constructs a reversal of the function of the tongue between the host culture and the migrant. The host culture responds to the migrant house in aesthetic terms: it is an architecture of 'bad taste'. Yet this mode of response renders the tongue into its function of 'tasting', of consuming. 'Bad taste' signifies consumption; it is a mild form of oral disgust. The host culture cannot speak about the migrant house, it can only (not) digest it through a term that refers to the tongue in its consumptive functions. The host culture is brought into a confrontation between itself and the *other* in the world in which the boundaries are blurred; it chokes on its own limits. The migrant house thus draws the host culture into the field of the abject, threatening it with an 'abyss that marks the place of its birth *and* obliteration, posing both an internal and an external threat to its stability' (Grosz 1987, p. 110). Thus there is a reversal of the function of the tongue: the host culture consumes (and spits out the food); the migrant speaks (utterances of the tongue).

But what of the mother in the interior, what of the mother's desire? What effects does the migrant house as a space for the mother tongue have on the mother's desire? A number of (female) theorists have recognised that signs of sexual difference, which in patriarchal culture are equivalent to signs of femininity, are collapsed into the question of *maternity*. In the interiority of the migrant house, a space signified by the feminine, what *fecundities* of femininity are possible? Is mother also a woman? Is mother as receptacle of the mother tongue the one that speaks? Is the presence of mothering inscribed on to the architecture of the house which means that the mother is not there to desire or to mother, or to protect her daughter? In her work is she displaced? In order to trace the (im)possible mother's desire I have borrowed the following sentence from Jean Hess:

> When I entered these homes I always felt embraced by a room, just as I was often embraced by the woman who had invited me inside. (Hess 1981, p. 30)

Hess is describing her entry into domestic interiors of Northern Mexico, and yet it is one among many displacements describing the relationship between white women and the female subaltern. The house as maternal space which welcomes *back* the white woman in its embrace articulates the inscriptions of the mother's body on to its architecture. These displacements engulf the mother in the lace of her own making, in her own metonymic versions of mother(land).

But what about the mother? In the following descriptions of 'mother' Gunew suggests a different figure:

> ... suddenly small and worn out, and remember nostalgically the energy, the stream of inventiveness which adjusted our balance to the alien fog pressing against the window. Recall too the sudden mysterious raging eruptions. *The mother's thwarted desire* ... She always worked; her salary on which the family survived was seen as supplementary. I do not recall the mother tongue other than in that first father's language she gave me, laboriously. No wonder that for me it remained a secret reserve. (Gunew 1985, p. 107)

For the female migrant the motherland signifies the loss of the mother. Metonymic practices within the migrant house produce a space/place of mourning. The house becomes tomb or museum, but only as a place of cleansing and mourning. It is, however, a tomb space without a body. For the mother, separation from the motherland might appear as the most fragile and archaic form of abjection, a primal repression. For the female subaltern there cannot be only one division, one separation: 'Why? Perhaps because of maternal anguish, unable to be satiated within the encompassing symbolic' (Kristeva 1982, p. 12). Cleansing and dressing the interior which is also metonymically the motherland, which is also signifier of the mother, means that the mother can mourn, but that mourning is rejected. The maternal anguish of the female subaltern? Rage, loss, abjection.

Separate rooms and a passage constitute a division within the migrant house. Outbuildings constitute a division of the external space as well as an architecture of difference. These spaces create the possibility of *becoming differently*. They are spaces of production, of making and remaking oneself. For the daughter within the space of the migrant house in which the mother tongue is the first father's language, the mother(land) signifies an 'untouchable, impossible, absent body of the mother' (Kristeva 1982, p. 6) the loss of the mother is lived closely, intimately, abjectly. Only in 'a room of her own', a study, can the daughter remake herself, and she can only remake herself *heterogeneously* through the experience of abjection. Only in naming the abject in its layered, woven, ambivalent conflictual flux can she mark out a territory, a territory of signs, objects and words that establish a distance, a space to keep at bay the dangers of absorption it poses.

Mala Majka   Majka Makedonija

Kristeva writes of the translation of subjectivity from questions of being to questions of place: 'Where am I?' instead of 'Who am I?' inherent in the process of exile. If migration entails the space of abjection as a spatial configuration constructed within the migrant house, it is understood that the building of the house is an ongoing process. It can never attain a solid (stable) subjectivity; 'for the space that engrosses the deject, the excluded, is never *one*, nor *homogeneous*, nor *totalizable*, but essentially divizible, foldable, and catastrophic' (Kristeva 1982, p. 8). Migrants are productive bodies—they build houses. Migrant enclaves are the result of bodies *wanting/desiring* space. Within these enclaves are explorations of the possibilities of speaking *differently*, the possibilities of the weaving, the braiding, the layering of different mother tongues with the Father's language. Migrants can speak amongst one another.

The bigger picture is seen to be quite monstrous from the perspective of the Anglo-Celtic mono-culture in Australia (Figure 13.2).

Aah yuk! Is the response, sometimes unspoken, to images of so-called 'Mediterranean palaces' in Australia. It is an initial response from the self-named host culture, that positions itself outside multiculturalism in (non-Aboriginal) Australia. But what lurks behind this response—that on the surface seems just to be a typical white middle-class response about aesthetics and good-taste, that seems to be an over-determined signifier of class, race and ethnicity? What is unspoken in this response that so much academic and political effort goes into defending the good taste of white middle-class Anglo-Celtic culture in Australia? What are the anxieties of the hegemonic culture?

Figure 13.2   Lion-taming territory

Kristeva suggests that oral disgust—aah yuk— signifies the abject. As a refusal of the limits of the self it would indicate, in this case, the refusal of the limit of the host culture and the limit of the individual subject. Kristeva identifies oral disgust as the most archaic form of abjection and one would extrapolate that 'aah yuk' as a distinctly non-verbal response signifies that the body has already begun to transgress the boundaries between inside and outside, into the space of self-repugnance: abjection.

I want to recount, briefly, a description by Sneja Gunew of the film, *No Strangers Here*, produced by the Department of Immigration of Australia in the 1950s. It is set in 'Littletown', and narrated by the editor of the town's newspaper. The story begins when he receives several anonymous letters, signed 'a true Australian', basically saying that foreigners are not wanted here.

As the editor strolls through town he notices the arrival of a foreign family; although their country of origin is carefully not specified, they are uncannily blonde and good-looking. The family rather quickly finds their niche in the town—the father works in the brickworks, the son goes to school, the daughter is an aide in the local hospital, and the mother remains at home where the editor decides to pay her a visit. He enters her home with the immortal words: 'Please tell me the story of your life'. On the brink of answering the mother rushes over to the oven where something more urgent is calling for attention. She offers the editor a slice of home-made cake and he in turn requests the recipe, which is published in the local paper under the heading 'Easy to mix'. The mother offers food instead of words. Food, as we know in Australia, is a more digestible way to accept the face of multiculturalism (Gunew 1992b, p. 30).

Food rather than fluency is what is expected. Words and houses provoke anxieties because they are reminders of the unstable status of the host culture. Architectural productivity, migrants building houses, function as a mode of resistance, a counter-power against the forces of the hegemonic culture. These houses demonstrate the arbitrariness of the host–migrant dynamic, which makes evident the arbitrariness of power operating in linear and dichotomous centre–margin structures. Thus it is evident that power cannot so easily be pinned down, that it operates as a network which flows in many directions and across many nodal points, with potential areas of contradictions: counter-powers. In building their own houses, migrants also attest to the complexities in the relations between architecture and power, that architecture can be a mode of resistance. To the extent that ideologies do not produce space but rather are in space, the particular ideology of the *dream house*, translated through home ownership in Australia, results in a quite different effect with respect to the migrant house—that of threatening the homogeneity and the national culture. While the anxiety seems to be one of aesthetics, anxieties which are lurking in the shadows strike at the constitution of culture itself, of knowledge, of language and the construction of space.

While Australia is always a construct that is mediated by somewhere else, the image of the migrant enclave is a reminder that somewhere else is not inevitably the image of England or Ireland. Within Australia other motherlands irrupt as spaces of abjection (Gunew 1988).

Abjection in the context of the migrant enclave opens possibilities for irruptions of mother tongues, of utterances which pay due to the muteness of *maternal spaces*, the muteness which is a result of the disavowal of the debt the individual and society owe to maternity. At a second level of abjection, the migrant enclave signifies this 'muteness' and this 'debt' (owed to) the maternal space for the 'host' culture. The horror in which the 'host' culture responds to the migrant enclave signifies the abject as some sort of return of the mother, but she returns as the devouring mother. Words, utterances from mother tongues, threaten the Father language. English can be swallowed up in those most 'improper' appropriations. The mother returns to devour her offspring. Most threatening are those that can slip from one, from the Father's language, to the other, the mother tongue.

In warding off these (non)unsightly spaces, the hegemonic culture wards off the unnameable: the mother tongues are suppressed within the majka-houses, within the migrant enclaves. However, as Kristeva notes, what is excluded can never be fully obliterated, but its remains hover at the borders of our existence. The migrant as abject is neither a subject nor an object; (s)he is ambiguous. Majka-houses disturb identity, system and order, respecting no definite positions, rules, boundaries or limits of culture or language. They can threaten the apparent unity of the host subjectivities with disruption and dissolution. And also as a second level of abjection the migrant enclaves represent the limit to the unity of the hegemonic culture. Abjection is what the symbolic order must reject, cover over or contain. The abject in turn beckons the host culture ever closer to its edge.

Notes

1 I would like to thank Louise Johnson for her thoughtful editing of this chapter.
2 The words in Macedonian are a gesture about the *difference* between languages; they are 'indigestible elements' (Gunew & Yeatman 1993) that cannot be reduced to translatability.

References

Bachelard, G. (1964), *The Poetics of Space*, Beacon Press, Boston.
Bal, M. (1988), *Death and Dissymmetry: The Politics of Coherence in the Book of Judges*, University of Chicago Press, Chicago.
Barthes, R. (1986), *Mythologies*, Paladin, London.
Berger, J. & Mohr, J. (1989), *A Seventh Man*, Granta Books, Cambridge.
Deleuze, G. & Guattari, F. (1987), '1227: Treatise on nomadology: The war machine', in *A Thousand Plateaus: Capitalism and Schizophrenia*, University of Minneapolis Press, Minneapolis.
Douglas, M. (1970), *Purity and Danger: An Analysis of Concepts of Pollution and Taboo*, Pelican, Harmondsworth.
Grosz, E. (1987), 'Language and the limits of the body', in E. Grosz & T. Threadgold (eds), *Futur* Fall: Excursions into Post-Modernity*, Pathfinder Press & Power Institute, Sydney.
Grosz, E. (1989), *Sexual Subversions: Three French Feminists*, Allen & Unwin, Sydney.
Gunew, S. (1985), 'The mother tongue and migration', *Australian Feminist Studies*, vol. 1, no. 1, pp. 105–8.
Gunew, S. (1988), 'Home and away: Nostalgia in Australian (migrant) writing', in P. Foss (ed.), *Island in the Stream*, Pluto Press, Sydney.

Gunew, S. (1992a), 'PMT (Post Modernist Tension): Reading for (multi) cultural difference', in S. Gunew & K. O'Longley (eds), *Striking Chords: Multicultural Literary Interpretations*, Allen & Unwin, Sydney.

Gunew, S. (1992b), 'Against multiculturalism: Rhetorical images', *Typereader, Journal of the Centre for Studies in Literary Education*, vol. 7, Autumn, pp. 28–41.

Gunew, S. & Spivak, G. C. (1990), 'Questions of multiculturalism', in S. Harasym (ed.), *The Post-Colonial Critic: Interviews, Strategies, Dialogues*, Routledge, New York.

Gunew, S. & Yeatman, A. (eds) (1993), *Feminism and the Politics of Difference*, Allen & Unwin, Sydney.

Hess, J. (1981), 'Domestic interiors in Northern Mexico', *Heresies 11*, vol. 3, no. 3, pp. 30–3.

Kristeva, J. (1982), *Powers of Horror: An Essay on Abjection*, Columbia University Press, New York.

Lefebvre, H. (1991), *Production of Space*, Blackwell, Oxford.

Spivak, G. C. (1988), 'Can the subaltern speak?', in C. Nelson & L. Grossberg (eds), *Marxism and the Interpretation of Culture*, Macmillan Education, London.

Notes on the contributors

Associate Professor **Nick Beattie** has qualifications in architecture and town planning and has spent some time in the architecture profession before entering academia. Head of the School of Architecture and Building at Deakin University, his research has been predominantly in the area of environmental quality and the relationship between behavioural science and design theory.

Michael Berry is Professor of Urban Studies and Planning at Royal Melbourne Institute of Technology and Acting Executive Director of the Australian Housing and Urban Research Institute. He has researched and written extensively in the fields of urban social theory, housing policy, urban politics and environmental economics.

Frances Devlin Glass is a Senior Lecturer in the School of Literature and Journalism, Deakin University. She has published in the areas of Australian and Irish literature and women's studies, and is one of the editors of Joseph Furphy's *Such is Life*.

Graeme Davison is Professor of History at Monash University. He is author of *The Rise and Fall of Marvellous Melbourne* and *The Unforgiving Minute: How Australia Learned to Tell the Time* and is currently working on a history of postwar Melbourne.

Lionel Frost teaches economic history at La Trobe University. He has a special interest in urban history and the ways in which the Australian experience was particular and differed from elsewhere. Lionel is the author of *Australian Cities in Comparative View* and *The New Urban Frontier: Urbanisation and City Building in Australasia and the American West*.

Roy Hay teaches economic and social history in the School of Australian and International Studies, Deakin University. His main research areas are the history of social policy, industrial history and, most recently, the social history of soccer in Australia. Publications include *The Origins of the Liberal Welfare Reforms, 1906–14* and 'British football, wogball or the world game: Towards a social history of Victorian soccer', in J.O'Hara (ed.), *Ethnicity and Soccer in Australia*.

Renate Howe is Associate Professor in Australian Studies at Deakin University. Her research interests are in the areas of urban history, with a policy focus, and women's history. Her books include *New Houses for Old. 50 Years of Public Housing in Victoria, 1938–1988* and, with Shirley Swain, *The Challenge of the City. Centenary History of Melbourne Central Mission*.

Margo Huxley is Associate Professor in Urban Policy at Royal Melbourne Institute of Technology, teaching graduate courses in urban policy and planning. Her research interests and publications are in the fields of feminist urban studies, large-scale property investment projects and gender-aspects of community activism, urban policy analysis, local government practice and planning theory and education.

Louise C. Johnson is a geographer who teaches Australian studies at Deakin University. She has worked in urban history, producing *Gaslight Sydney* in 1984, and is currently researching and publishing in the areas of feminist theory, industrial restructuring and the gendering of city spaces.

Mirjana Lozanovska teaches design in the School of Architecture at Deakin University. She is currently completing her doctoral thesis on the relations between (sexual) difference and architecture.

Guenter Lehmann teaches at Deakin University's School of Architecture, lecturing on the city and on architectural design and theory. His experience includes several teaching appointments in the United States and extensive travels and studies of urban architecture and urban life worldwide. He is also an editor of *Exedra*.

Brian McLoughlin, Professor of Town and Regional Planning at Melbourne University, has researched and published in urban history, sociology and theory as well as in planning practice. He has most recently explored the latter in his book *Shaping Melbourne's Future? Town Planning, the State and Civil Society*.

The essay Brian wrote for this collection was to be his last. He died in Los Angeles on 18 May 1994 and will be greatly missed by all in urban studies.

Lyn Richards teaches sociology and computer-based qualitative research methods at La Trobe University. She has carried out extensive research on women as mothers and in suburbia. In her book, *Nobody's Home. Dreams and Realities in a New Suburb*, Lyn has used intensive interviews to piece together a detailed view of life in an outer-Melbourne suburb.

Peter Spearritt is Director of the National Centre for Australian Studies at Monash University. He shops in Italian supermarkets in the Melbourne suburbs of Clifton Hill and Fairfield and is a habitué of second-hand bookshops and fading antique establishments.

Acknowledgments

The publisher thanks the following for permission to reprint from copyright works:

Chapter 1
Cornell University Press for the visual 'Percentage of population dwelling in cities at the latest census' (originally published 1899), from *The Growth of Cities in the Nineteenth Century: A Study in Statistics*, by A. F. Weber, 1967, Cornell University Press, Ithaca, New York.

Chapter 3
Allen & Unwin for extracts from 'The Australian city in history' by M. Berry in *Urban Political Economy*, by L. Sandercock & M. Berry, 1983, Allen & Unwin Australia, St Leonards, NSW.

Chapter 4
National Capital Planning Authority for the visual 'MFP aims' from *MFP An Urban Development Concept. A Report to the Department of Industry Technology and Commerce*, 1990, National Capital Planning Authority, Canberra.

Chapter 6
Cambridge University Press for extracts from *Shaping Melbourne's Future. Town Planning, the State and Civil Society*, by J. B. McLoughlin, 1992, Cambridge University Press, Oakleigh, Victoria.

Chapter 8
Oxford University Press for extracts from *Nobody's Home. Dreams and Realities in a New Suburb*, by L. Richards, 1990, Oxford University Press, Melbourne.

Chapter 10
University of Chicago for the visual 'The growth of the city' from *The City*, edited by R. E. Park, E. W. Burgess & R. D. McKenzie, 1967, University of Chicago Press, Chicago. Introduction © 1967 by The University of Chicago. All rights reserved. Published 1925. Sixth impression 1970.

Chapter 11
Pan Macmillan for the 'Sketch of Sandy Stone (1957)' by B. Humphries, from *The Life and Death of Sandy Stone*, by B. Humphries, 1990, Pan Macmillan, Sydney. Australian and New Zealand rights only.

Chapter 12
University of Chicago Press for the visual 'A, Suburban neighbourhood block plan; B, Proposed homes revitalization, same suburban block with new common space facilities' from 'Viewpoint', by D. Hayden in *Women and the American City*, edited by C. R. Stimpson, E. Dixter, M. J. Nelson & K. B. Yatrakis, 1981, University of Chicago Press, Chicago. © 1980, 1981 by The University of Chicago. All rights reserved. Published 1981.

Every attempt has been made to contact copyright holders. The publisher would be pleased to hear from any copyright holder whose work has not been acknowledged in this book.